# The Governors of North Carolina

The Executive Mansion in Raleigh, N.C., is a fine example of the Queen Anne cottage style and was completed in December 1890. The first executive to occupy the mansion was Gov. Daniel Fowle. All images courtesy of the North Carolina State Archives, Office of Archives and History, Raleigh, unless otherwise indicated.

# The Governors of North Carolina

Edited by Michael Hill

Office of Archives and History
North Carolina Department of Cultural Resources
Raleigh
2007

Printed by Theo Davis Printing, Zebulon, N.C.

# Contents

# Introduction

S ome names are more familiar to us than others; likewise some stories are better known than others. Zebulon B. Vance took office as North Carolina's governor during the Civil War at age thirty-two, facing seemingly insurmountable challenges, in time becoming the most admired political figure in state history. The same cannot be said for William W. Holden, who carried to the office in 1865 and 1868 a well-deserved reputation as a spirited partisan and became the first chief executive in U.S. history to be impeached and removed. O. Max Gardner in 1931 restructured state government in an effort to stem the effects of the Great Depression. But only the most dedicated follower of North Carolina history will recall other stories. In 1711 a former governor, Thomas Cary, in a failed coup, launched cannonballs from offshore onto the house where his successor Edward Hyde was conferring. Thomas Burke endured two months of captivity in 1781 after his seizure by David Fanning and his band of Tories. J. C. B. Ehringhaus, under the stress that came with the office, told a crowd of farmers at Raleigh's Riddick Stadium in 1935 that he had had a "bellyful of politics." From the Roanoke colonies (1584-1587) to the dawn of the twenty-first century, the story of the governors is a prism through which to view Tar Heel history.

The Office of Archives and History (then the Department) in 1958 first issued a biographical guide to governors, with revised editions in 1968 and 1974. The book was titled *North Carolina Governors* with inclusive dates. The author was Beth Crabtree, a staff member with the agency from 1942 to 1975. Miss Crabtree spent most of her career as an editor with the Historical Publications Section of Archives and History. Her objective, and indeed the larger aim of that section, was to publish books and pamphlets intended for a popular audience and for use in schools. The biographical guide to governors, a ready reference tool, found its audience, but regrettably long has been out of print.

In the intervening years the University of North Carolina Press has issued the six-volume series edited by William S. Powell entitled the *Dictionary of North Carolina Biography*. The biographical sketches contained therein were of considerable assistance in the preparation of this book. An additional source that has been consulted is Robert Sobel and John Raimo, eds.,

*Biographical Directory of the Governors of the United States, 1789-1978.* Beyond these reference books my collaborators and I have consulted a host of other works, primary and secondary, all of these cited, in shortened form, at the close of each sketch. We have indicated where the major manuscript collections pertaining to the governors may be found as well.

The objective has been to outline the ninety-nine governors' lives in about six hundred words with particular emphasis on achievements while in office. Exceptions have been made, and longer sketches prepared, for selected chief executives, notably William Tryon, Zebulon B. Vance, William W. Holden, James B. Hunt Jr., James G. Martin, and Michael F. Easley. The reasoning here has been that the first three served during times of trial, respectively, the War of the Regulation, the Civil War, and Reconstruction. The three modern governors each were elected to two or more four-year terms, giving them the opportunity to leave a deeper imprint on the state's history.

Former governors Luther Hodges (*center*) and Terry Sanford (*right*) visit with Gov. Dan Moore in 1967.

This directory is a group effort. The book, long in the making, is a product of the Research Branch of the Office of Archives and History. In 1986 Jeffrey J. Crow, then administrator of the Historical Publications Section, proposed to Jerry C. Cashion, then supervisor of the branch, that his staff take on the revision of the Crabtree volume. He agreed, but over the course of time, other projects took priority. In the late 1990s work commenced in earnest on the sketches.

Dennis F. Daniels, who worked with the branch from 2001 to 2003, wrote about the Roanoke colonies and proprietary governors. Ansley H. Wegner, who since 2000 has been a research historian with the branch, covered the royal governors. Wilson Angley, who retired in 1999, took on preparation of the essays on governors from 1776 through 1835. Jerry L. Cross, who retired in 2000, covered the period up to 1900, while I worked on the twentieth-century governors. The sketch on Gov. Michael F. Easley was written after consultation with his Press Office in February 2006, during his second term with three years remaining. Lisa K. Keenum, former administrative assistant in the branch, assisted with preparing the manuscript. In the summer of 2002, Tom Vincent, then a public history intern, conducted an initial survey of photographs in the State Archives. Susan Trimble furthered the photo research and designed and typeset the work. Donna Kelly, administrator of the Publications office, guided the book through the editing process and prepared the detailed index.

The earlier editions included a set of appendixes, giving the birthplace, pre-office occupation, military experience, education, place of death, and other facts about the Tar Heel governors. Our decision was to forego these added pages in favor of a useable index. Most of those details may be found in the respective sketches.

In lieu of any existing known portrait, each governor's signature has been placed at the head of each sketch, if extant. Each twentieth-century entry contains an official "head shot," or one more formal, and one "action shot." All images are from the North Carolina State Archives, Office of Archives and History, Raleigh, unless otherwise indicated. Contact the iconographic archivist for the details of specific photographs.

Another distinct difference sets this edition apart from the Crabtree volumes. The editors in the Historical Publications Section suggested that the essays be arranged alphabetically rather

A photo of all living governors is highly unusual. (*Left to right.*) James Martin, James Hunt, James Holshouser, Robert Scott, and Terry Sanford pose on the lawn of the Executive Mansion during the events surrounding the opening of the new North Carolina Museum of History in April 1994.

than chronologically. The advantages of such an arrangement are several. The least remembered of the chief executives, the proprietary governors, are interfiled with the recent figures, Eastchurch alongside Easley. Fathers and sons, the Spaights and the Scotts, share the same pages. The three governors Martin, covering three disparate eras, are neighbors. The greatest benefit is the least expected, the opportunity to randomly dip into the life stories of North Carolina leaders over the course of 420 years.

Michael Hill
Research Branch Supervisor

# Abbreviated Citations Used in References and Primary Sources

*ANB*     John A. Garraty and Mark C. Carnes, eds. *American National Biography*. 24 vols. New York: Oxford University Press, 1999.

*BDC*     *Biographical Directory of the United States Congress, 1774-1989.* Bicentennial Edition. Washington, D.C.: U.S. Government Printing Office, 1989.

*DAB*     Allen Johnson and Dumas Malone, eds. *Dictionary of American Biography*. 20 vols. New York: Charles Scribner's Sons, 1928-1936.

*DNB*     Leslie Stephen and Sidney Lee, eds. *Dictionary of National Biography*. 63 vols. New York: MacMillan, 1885-1900.

*DNCB*    William S. Powell, ed. *Dictionary of North Carolina Biography*. 6 vols. Chapel Hill: University of North Carolina Press, 1979-1996.

ECU       East Carolina University, Special Collections Department, Joyner Library, Greenville.

NCSA      North Carolina State Archives, Raleigh.

SHC       Southern Historical Collection, Manuscripts Department, Wilson Library, University of North Carolina at Chapel Hill.

SS        Secretary of State's Office Records. North Carolina State Archives, Office of Archives and History, Raleigh.

UNC       University of North Carolina

U.S.      United States

# Chronological List of Governors

Ralph Lane . . . . . . . . . . . . . . . . . . . . . . . . . . 1585-1586
John White . . . . . . . . . . . . . . . . . . . . . . . . . . 1587-1590
Samuel Stephens . . . . . . . . . . . . . . . . . . . . . . . 1662-1664
William Drummond . . . . . . . . . . . . . . . . . . . . . . 1665-1667
Samuel Stephens . . . . . . . . . . . . . . . . . . . . . . . 1667-1670
Peter Carteret . . . . . . . . . . . . . . . . . . . . . . . . 1670-1672
John Jenkins . . . . . . . . . . . . . . . . . . . . . . . . . 1672-1675
Thomas Eastchurch . . . . . . . . . . . . . . . . . . . . . . 1675-1676
John Jenkins . . . . . . . . . . . . . . . . . . . . . . . . . 1676-1677
Thomas Miller . . . . . . . . . . . . . . . . . . . . . . . . . 1677
Seth Sothel . . . . . . . . . . . . . . . . . . . . . . . . . . 1678
John Jenkins . . . . . . . . . . . . . . . . . . . . . . . . . 1678-1679
John Harvey . . . . . . . . . . . . . . . . . . . . . . . . . . 1679
Henry Wilkinson . . . . . . . . . . . . . . . . . . . . . . . . 1680
John Jenkins . . . . . . . . . . . . . . . . . . . . . . . . . 1680-1681
Seth Sothel . . . . . . . . . . . . . . . . . . . . . . . . . . 1682-1683
John Archdale . . . . . . . . . . . . . . . . . . . . . . . . . 1683-1686
Seth Sothel . . . . . . . . . . . . . . . . . . . . . . . . . . 1686-1689
John Gibbs . . . . . . . . . . . . . . . . . . . . . . . . . . 1689-1690
Philip Ludwell . . . . . . . . . . . . . . . . . . . . . . . . 1689-1691
Thomas Jarvis . . . . . . . . . . . . . . . . . . . . . . . . . 1691-1694
John Archdale . . . . . . . . . . . . . . . . . . . . . . . . . 1694-1696
Thomas Harvey . . . . . . . . . . . . . . . . . . . . . . . . 1694-1699
Henderson Walker . . . . . . . . . . . . . . . . . . . . . . . 1699-1703
Robert Daniel . . . . . . . . . . . . . . . . . . . . . . . . . 1703-1705
Thomas Cary . . . . . . . . . . . . . . . . . . . . . . . . . 1705-1706
William Glover . . . . . . . . . . . . . . . . . . . . . . . . 1706-1708
Thomas Cary . . . . . . . . . . . . . . . . . . . . . . . . . 1708-1711
Edward Hyde . . . . . . . . . . . . . . . . . . . . . . . . . 1711-1712
Thomas Pollock . . . . . . . . . . . . . . . . . . . . . . . . 1712-1714
Charles Eden . . . . . . . . . . . . . . . . . . . . . . . . . 1714-1722
Thomas Pollock . . . . . . . . . . . . . . . . . . . . . . . . 1722
William Reed . . . . . . . . . . . . . . . . . . . . . . . . . 1722-1724
George Burrington . . . . . . . . . . . . . . . . . . . . . . . 1724-1725
Sir Richard Everard . . . . . . . . . . . . . . . . . . . . . . 1725-1731
George Burrington . . . . . . . . . . . . . . . . . . . . . . . 1731-1734
Nathaniel Rice . . . . . . . . . . . . . . . . . . . . . . . . . 1734
Gabriel Johnston . . . . . . . . . . . . . . . . . . . . . . . 1734-1752
Nathaniel Rice . . . . . . . . . . . . . . . . . . . . . . . . . 1752-1753
Matthew Rowan . . . . . . . . . . . . . . . . . . . . . . . . 1753-1754
Arthur Dobbs . . . . . . . . . . . . . . . . . . . . . . . . . 1754-1765
William Tryon . . . . . . . . . . . . . . . . . . . . . . . . . 1765-1771
James Hasell . . . . . . . . . . . . . . . . . . . . . . . . . . 1771

Thomas Jordan Jarvis. . . . . . . . . . . . . . . . . . . . 1879-1885
Alfred Moore Scales . . . . . . . . . . . . . . . . . . . 1885-1889
Daniel Gould Fowle . . . . . . . . . . . . . . . . . . . 1889-1891
Thomas Michael Holt . . . . . . . . . . . . . . . . . . 1891-1893
Elias Carr. . . . . . . . . . . . . . . . . . . . . . . . . 1893-1897
Daniel Lindsay Russell Jr. . . . . . . . . . . . . . . . . 1897-1901
Charles Brantley Aycock . . . . . . . . . . . . . . . . . 1901-1905
Robert Brodnax Glenn . . . . . . . . . . . . . . . . . . 1905-1909
William Walton Kitchin. . . . . . . . . . . . . . . . . . 1909-1913
Locke Craig . . . . . . . . . . . . . . . . . . . . . . . . 1913-1917
Thomas Walter Bickett . . . . . . . . . . . . . . . . . . 1917-1921
Cameron Morrison. . . . . . . . . . . . . . . . . . . . . 1921-1925
Angus Wilton McLean . . . . . . . . . . . . . . . . . . . 1925-1929
Oliver Maxwell Gardner . . . . . . . . . . . . . . . . . . 1929-1933
John Christoph Blucher Ehringhaus . . . . . . . . . . . . 1933-1937
Clyde Roark Hoey . . . . . . . . . . . . . . . . . . . . . 1937-1941
Joseph Melville Broughton . . . . . . . . . . . . . . . . 1941-1945
Robert Gregg Cherry. . . . . . . . . . . . . . . . . . . . 1945-1949
William Kerr Scott . . . . . . . . . . . . . . . . . . . . 1949-1953
William Bradley Umstead. . . . . . . . . . . . . . . . . . 1953-1954
Luther Hartwell Hodges . . . . . . . . . . . . . . . . . . 1954-1961
Terry Sanford . . . . . . . . . . . . . . . . . . . . . . . 1961-1965
Daniel Killian Moore . . . . . . . . . . . . . . . . . . . 1965-1969
Robert Walter Scott . . . . . . . . . . . . . . . . . . . . 1969-1973
James Eubert Holshouser Jr. . . . . . . . . . . . . . . . . 1973-1977
James Baxter Hunt Jr. . . . . . . . . . . . . . . . . . . . 1977-1985
James Grubbs Martin. . . . . . . . . . . . . . . . . . . . 1985-1993
James Baxter Hunt Jr. . . . . . . . . . . . . . . . . . . . 1993-2001
Michael Francis Easley . . . . . . . . . . . . . . . . . . 2001-

## NATHANIEL ALEXANDER
## 1805-1807

*N*athaniel Alexander (1756-1808), who served as a surgeon in the American Revolution, lived near Harrisburg in a house on the present site of Lowes (Charlotte) Motor Speedway. Born on March 5, 1756, in present-day Mecklenburg (then Anson) County, he was the eldest of six children born to Moses Alexander and the former Sarah Taylor. Little is known of his early youth or preparatory education, but in 1776 he graduated from the College of New Jersey (now Princeton University) with a degree in medicine. Two years after graduation, he was commissioned a surgeon in the North Carolina Continental Line, where he served until the close of the Revolution. In the field he labored with great difficulty, given the scarcity of supplies. Alexander married Margaret Polk, daughter of Col. Thomas Polk of Charlotte. They had no children.

Nathaniel Alexander practiced medicine for several years in South Carolina following the Revolution but then returned to his native Mecklenburg County. He was active in Charlotte in establishing a local Masonic lodge. He represented the county in the lower house of the North Carolina General Assembly in 1797 and in the upper house in 1801 and 1802, affiliating himself in the legislature with the ascendant Jeffersonian Republicans. He was then elected to the U.S. House of Representatives, where he served from 1803 to 1805. He resigned from Congress in November of 1805, having been elected by the state legislature to replace James Turner as governor. Reelected without opposition in 1806, he served as chief executive for just over two years.

Although a Republican, Alexander enjoyed considerable Federalist support as well. The Raleigh *Minerva*, a Federalist newspaper, freely acknowledged that he was "an ornament to the predominant party," and like few of them, a "scholar and a true patriot." As governor, Alexander attempted to settle the lingering border dispute with Georgia and was an early advocate of education and internal improvements. Historians have acclaimed him as the forerunner of the prominent line of politicians with a grasp of the importance of education.

It was during Alexander's governorship that the Court Act of 1806 brought significant reform to the state's judicial system, creating a separate superior court in each county. The legislation had been generally supported by Republicans, but opposed by Federalists. Alexander himself feared that the additional courts would place undue demands on both judges and eligible jurors. Ironically, it was almost certainly his call for repeal of this legislation in 1807 that cost him a third term as governor. Because many of his Republican supporters deserted him in the election of that year, he was defeated by Federalist Benjamin Williams on the third ballot. He died in Salisbury on March 6, 1808, less than a year after leaving office, and was buried in the cemetery of the First Presbyterian Church in Charlotte.

REFERENCES: *DNCB*, vol. 1; Gilpatrick, *Jeffersonian Democracy in N.C.*; Johnson, *Ante-Bellum N.C.*; Sobel and Raimo, *Bio. Dir. of Governors*, vol. 3.

◇ ◇ ◇

*John Archdale*

# JOHN ARCHDALE
## 1683-1686; 1694-1696

*J*ohn Archdale (1642-1717) served as Albemarle County's acting governor between 1683 and 1686 and as Carolina's provincial governor from 1694 to 1696. He was born in Buckinghamshire, England, to Thomas and Mary Nevill Archdale ca. May 5, 1642. His grandfather Richard Archdale was a London merchant who established the family among the English gentry. In 1664 the Gorges family (Archdale's sister Mary married Ferdinando Gorges) sent Archdale to Maine as a commissioner to help reestablish their claim to that colony. Archdale married Ann Dodson Cary, a widow with two children, in December 1673 and fathered four children. Archdale converted to Quakerism, apparently between 1673 and 1681.

In 1681 Archdale purchased John Berkeley's Carolina proprietorship and worked with proprietor William Craven to improve the Lords Proprietors' investment. In 1683 he arrived in Albemarle as Carolina's collector of quitrents. Being the resident proprietor, he filled in as governor when Seth Sothel was out of the colony. As acting governor, Archdale worked to prevent war with the Indians. During his tenure the number of Quakers increased, and Archdale protected them from prosecution. He was back in England by 1686.

In August 1694 the proprietors appointed Archdale as Carolina's provincial governor. Archdale reached North Carolina in June 1695 and remained for six weeks helping to restore order and invigorating the Quakers. He retained Thomas Harvey as deputy governor. Archdale arrived in Charles Town in August 1695. His tenure lasted about a year. He focused his attention on South Carolina and allowed Harvey to implement his reforms in North Carolina.

Archdale appointed his nephew John Blake as South Carolina's deputy governor. Trying to maintain balance, he placed both Quakers and Anglicans on his council. The assembly enacted legislation referred to as "Archdale's Laws" that remained the basis for South Carolina's legal system for two decades. Archdale improved relations with the Indians and the Spanish and built better roads and fortifications. Conscientious objectors were provided with an exemption from military service. He attempted to rectify the problems between French Huguenots and English settlers. Archdale also pursued a course of religious tolerance. The North Carolina and South Carolina assemblies passed messages of gratitude to Archdale for his efforts.

John Archdale was no longer a proprietor when Thomas Archdale sold the proprietorship to his cousin Joseph Blake. John Archdale won a seat in the House of Commons in 1698, but was never sworn. In 1705 Archdale bought William Berkeley's proprietorship. As a proprietor Archdale worked to overturn laws that hurt non-Anglican religious groups. In 1707 Archdale published a pamphlet entitled, *A New Description of the Fertile and Pleasant Province of Carolina with a Brief Account of Its Discovery and Settling and the Government thereof to the Time, with Several Remarkable Passages of Divine Providence during my Time.* In 1708 he gave his proprietorship to his daughter Mary and her husband John Danson. He spent the remainder of his life at his manor and died ca. July 4, 1717.

REFERENCES: *ANB*, vol. 1; *DAB*, vol. 1; *DNCB*, vol. 1; Hood, *Public Career of John Archdale*; Jones, *Quakers in American Colonies*; Monroe, "Religious Toleration"; Raimo, *Bio. Dir. of Governors of U.S.*; Salley, *Narratives of Early Carolina*; Sirmans, *Colonial N.C.*; Weeks, *Southern Quakers and Slavery.*

◈ ◈ ◈

## SAMUEL ASHE
## 1795-1798

*S*amuel Ashe (1725-1813), prominent leader for the Patriot cause, was born near Bath to parents of considerable wealth, social status, and political influence. His mother, the former Elizabeth Swann, was the daughter of Samuel Swann, eminent planter and longtime member of the colony's Executive Council. Ashe's father, John Baptista Ashe, was a prominent planter and Speaker of the North Carolina House of Commons. Orphaned soon after his family's removal to the Lower Cape Fear region, young Ashe was reared to maturity in the elegant plantation home of his maternal uncle, Samuel Swann, himself Speaker of the North Carolina assembly for nearly two decades. There he benefited from the best in educational opportunities and from cultured and cosmopolitan surroundings. Ashe was first married to a cousin, Mary Porter, by whom he had three sons. His second marriage was to Elizabeth Merrick.

After entering the practice of law, Ashe gained prominence as an assistant attorney for the Crown. Despite this background, however, he became actively involved in the Stamp Act resistance and played a leading role in the radical Sons of Liberty organization. When Gov. Josiah Martin refused to convene the legislature in 1774, Ashe was one of eight prominent Patriots to organize the revolutionary provincial council at Johnston Courthouse. During that same year he became active in the North Carolina Council of Safety, serving briefly as president in 1776. As a leading delegate to the provincial congress, Ashe was appointed to the committee that drafted the state's original constitution at Halifax in 1776. In April of the following year, he served as Speaker of the state senate during the first meeting of the

General Assembly under that document. Still later, he was appointed by the assembly to a superior court judgeship, a position that he occupied with distinction for nearly twenty years. In 1787 he was one of three judges to decide the landmark case of *Bayard v. Singleton*, which asserted the constitutional doctrine of legislative review.

On November 11, 1795, the seventy-year-old Ashe resigned his judgeship in order to accept his election as governor. Reelected on two subsequent occasions, he served the constitutional maximum of three consecutive years. Although earlier a Federalist, Ashe had since become an ardent Republican and a supporter of states' rights. It was therefore only with difficulty that he weathered the storm of pro-Federalist, anti-French feelings that arose along the coast and swept through maritime and commercial circles in 1797-1798. The feelings were brought about by repeated French violations of America's neutrality, the seizure of her ships, and the mistreatment of her seamen. Indeed, a Wilmington brawl involving crewmen from a French privateer resulted in the death of one American seaman and a sense of outrage throughout the state.

It was during the last year of Ashe's administration that information began to surface regarding massive land frauds in that portion of North Carolina that had become Tennessee. Ashe cooperated fully with the early phases of the investigation of those frauds, and helped to prevent the destruction of crucial evidence. Ashe died at "The Neck," his plantation, on February 3, 1813, and was interred there on the grounds.

REFERENCES: *DAB*, vol. 1; *DNCB*, vol. 1; Gilpatrick, *Jeffersonian Democracy in N.C.*; Sobel and Raimo, *Bio. Dir. of Governors*, vol. 3; Sprunt, *Chronicles of the Cape Fear River*.

# CHARLES BRANTLEY AYCOCK
## 1901-1905

*N*o North Carolina governor, with the possible exception of Zebulon B. Vance, has been as venerated and memorialized as Charles Brantley Aycock (1859-1912), with whose term in 1901 the Democratic Party inaugurated a seventy-two-year hold on the state's highest elected position. The "Education Governor" was born near Nahunta (present-day Fremont) in Wayne County on November 11, 1859, on the farmstead of his parents, Benjamin and Serena Hooks Aycock (the restored birthplace is now a state historic site). The elder Aycock served in the state senate from 1862 to 1866. Charles, the youngest of ten, attended private academies in Fremont, Wilson, and Kinston. At sixteen he taught for a term in a public school in Fremont. At UNC, where he enrolled in 1877 and graduated three years later, Aycock honed his debating skills. In 1879 he delivered in Durham County his first public address, appropriately on the value of education. In 1881 Aycock married Varina Woodward; they had three children. In 1891, two years after Varina's death, he married her sister Cora; they had seven children.

Charles B. Aycock was licensed to practice law in 1881 and soon set up practice in Goldsboro with Frank A. Daniels. Aycock, who had edited a small weekly, the *Ledger*, in Chapel Hill, in 1885 co-founded the *Daily Argus* in Goldsboro, but it was politics that consumed his energies. In 1890 he sought but failed to gain the Democratic nomination to the U.S. House from the Third District. Aycock distrusted the Republican Party, and, reacting to what he viewed as abuses of the political system during Reconstruction, endorsed the idea that politics should be reserved for the white race. "Aycock believed in the right of the white man to rule as profoundly as he believed in God," according to a 1912 biography.

As he sought to build a political reputation, Aycock worked tirelessly on behalf of the public schools. His experience with the local school board

Gov. Charles B. Aycock, a lawyer by trade, championed the need for universal education and believed that it would lead to higher literacy rates and universal suffrage.

in Wayne County convinced him that education was the key to wise and purposeful social change. From 1893 to 1897 he was U.S. attorney for the eastern district of the state. His stock as a stump speaker rose in this period, and in 1898 he pressed his views on race and education in a statewide series of debates with Populist Cyrus Thompson. In 1899 Aycock worked closely with legislators to disfranchise black voters by means of literacy tests, poll taxes, and the "grandfather clause." A groundswell of support led to his nomination for governor by the Democrats in 1900. He was elected over Republican Spencer B. Adams by 60,000 votes, the largest margin for any candidate in state history to that date.

As governor, Aycock, touting the "Dawn of a New Day," continued to press for educational progress.

His views on white supremacy notwithstanding, he opposed attempts within the legislature to fund white schools from the white tax base and black schools from the black base. He believed that universal education would lead to higher literacy rates and in time to universal suffrage. Aycock opposed but was unable to stop lynchings during his term. He advocated reforms of child labor and temperance laws but met mixed success with the legislature. Aycock supported increased corporate taxes and devised a compromise for more equitable tax assessment on railroad property.

After his term as governor, Aycock returned to the practice of law, first in Goldsboro and after 1909 in Raleigh with Robert W. Winston. He received honorary degrees from the University of Maine in 1905 and UNC in 1907. In 1911 he declared his candidacy for the U.S. Senate. Those plans were cut short on April 4, 1912, by his death on a speaker's platform in Birmingham, Alabama, where he was addressing an educational organization. Aycock, a Baptist, is buried in Oakwood Cemetery in Raleigh.

REFERENCES: Alderman, "Charles Brantley Aycock"; *ANB*, vol. 1; Ashe et al., *Biographical History*, vol. 1; Connor and Poe, *Charles Brantley Aycock*; Daniels, "Charles Brantley Aycock"; *DNCB*, vol. 1; Orr, *Charles Brantley Aycock*; Sobel and Raimo, *Bio. Dir. of Governors*, vol. 3. PRIMARY SOURCES: Aycock Collection, NCSA.

# THOMAS WALTER BICKETT
## 1917-1921

*T*o Thomas W. Bickett (1869-1921), the first North Carolina governor to reach the office by way of a statewide party primary, fell the task of leading the state through World War I. The "War Governor" (one of several Tar Heel chief executives to share that nickname) was born on February 28, 1869, in Monroe to druggist Thomas Winchester Bickett and his wife, the former Mary Covington. His father died when young Bickett was thirteen years old. Educated in the public schools of Monroe and at Wake Forest College, where he graduated in 1890, Bickett himself taught in public schools in Marion and Winston-Salem before studying law at UNC in 1892. The following year he was admitted to the

Gov. Thomas Walter Bickett, pictured here in 1917 with Belvin Maynard, was a gifted orator who used his talent to lead North Carolina's efforts during World War I by giving speeches to lift spirits and sell war bonds.

bar, and in 1895, after working briefly in Monroe and Danbury, he moved to Louisburg, where he joined an already successful practice. In 1898 he married Fannie Yarborough of Louisburg; only one of their three children survived infancy.

In 1906 Bickett was elected to represent Franklin County in the state House. In his single term he made his mark as the sponsor of the "Bickett Bill," which set aside a half-million dollars to fund land purchases and building construction to facilitate care for the mentally handicapped. At the Democratic convention in Charlotte in 1908 Bickett drew acclaim for his speech nominating Ashley Horne for governor and was himself nominated for attorney general. In his two four-year terms in that office, Bickett successfully defended the state's

interests in almost four hundred cases before the state supreme court and five cases before the U.S. Supreme Court, including a boundary dispute with Tennessee. In the 1916 Democratic primary for governor, the first held since the enactment of the primary law the previous year, Bickett defeated Elijah L. Daughtridge and in the fall defeated Republican Frank A. Linney.

Three months after Bickett's inauguration the United States entered World War I. An exceptional orator, the governor delivered speeches to lift spirits, sell Liberty bonds, and lead the war effort in North Carolina. In Ashe County in 1918 he took a direct role in solving a problem with local desertions. In his farewell address Bickett noted that 2,338 North Carolinians died in the war and stated that all of his

8

achievements paled in comparison to the contribution of the 80,000 Tar Heels who had taken part in the conflict.

In his inaugural address in 1917 Bickett laid out a program of recommendations with attention given to moving farmers from tenancy to land ownership, the importance of agricultural education, the need for telephones in all rural homes, an increase of the school term from four to six months, the need for increased spending on public health, and prison and hospital reform. Bickett's initiatives met remarkable success, as the legislature adopted forty of forty-eight proposals during his term.

The parole system was overhauled, and the legislature, with the governor's endorsement, approved a $3 million bond program to permit expansion at state colleges and universities and increased funds for charitable institutions. Tax reform measures modernized the state's revenue structure. Though not committed to an extensive program of road building, Governor Bickett laid the groundwork for his successors by enlarging the duties of the State Highway Commission.

At the conclusion of his term in office, Bickett set up a law practice in Raleigh with Attorney General James S. Manning. On December 27, 1921, three weeks after he had attended the reception for Allied commander Marshal Ferdinand Foch in Monroe, the ex-governor suffered a stroke at his home in Raleigh and died the following day. His body lay in state in the Capitol before the funeral in Raleigh's Christ Church and burial in Louisburg.

REFERENCES: Connor et al., *History of N.C.*, vol. 4; *DNCB*, vol. 1; Horton thesis, "Thomas Walter Bickett"; Martin and House, *Bickett Papers*; *News and Observer*, December 29, 1921; *Proceedings of the Bar Association* (1922); Sobel and Raimo, *Bio. Dir. of Governors*, vol. 3. PRIMARY SOURCES: Mrs. Bickett Papers, NCSA.

◇ ◇ ◇

# THOMAS BRAGG
## 1855-1859

Thomas Bragg (1810-1872) was a member of the prominent Bragg family of Warren County; Confederate general Braxton Bragg was his brother. Born on November 8, 1810, in Warrenton, he was one of the six sons of Thomas Bragg, a carpenter, and his wife Margaret. Thomas Bragg read law with John Hall of Warrenton and set up practice in Northampton County in 1833. He was appointed county attorney and became entranced with politics. But he was a Democrat in a Whig stronghold; consequently, his early political career was less successful than his law practice. He served one term in the state House in 1842-1843. He married Isabelle Cathbert in October 1837; they would have seven children.

Through his work at the national Democratic conventions in 1844, 1848, and 1852, Bragg rose to a party leadership position in the state. Pitted against Whig Alfred Dockery in the 1854 gubernatorial election, he eked out a victory by just over 1,400 votes out of more than 94,700. Two years later, with the Whig Party in rapid decline, Bragg easily defeated John A. Gilmer in the first state election to see more than 100,000 votes cast.

His two-term administration reflected a blending of old Whig and Democratic programs. The law eliminating the freehold requirement to vote for state senators was finally passed; Bragg continued support for internal improvements, particularly the North Carolina Railroad; and he pushed for an improved banking system to help stabilize the economy. Yet, the threat of secession hung over his entire tenure. Bragg was a strong states' rights Democrat who vocally objected to encroachments by the federal government, but he urged moderation in resistance and did not favor secession. He was elected to the U.S. Senate in 1859 and served until March 1861. He made few public statements about the looming crisis; yet he privately lamented to his friends that he saw no future success in leaving the Union even though it might seem justified. Despite his concerns for the South, Bragg would not abandon North Carolina in the event of secession, stating "I will stand by the old State, and if the worst shall ultimately come, as I very much fear, I will go down with her, and when all is over I will do what I can to save what is left of her."

He returned to Raleigh after leaving the Senate only to be called a few months later by President Jefferson Davis to replace Judah P. Benjamin as attorney general of the Confederacy. Bragg began his duties in November 1861, but the Davis administration was fraught with political bickering, and Bragg resigned on March 18, 1862. He spent the last years of the war in Raleigh.

The war virtually bankrupted Thomas Bragg; however, he reestablished his law practice, earning a reputation as a strong defender of constitutional law and personal liberty. Feeling that those rights had been violated by Gov. William W. Holden in his struggles with the Ku Klux Klan, Bragg joined the team of prosecutors in the impeachment and removal of the governor from office. Thomas Bragg died at his Raleigh home on January 21, 1872, and was buried in Oakwood Cemetery.

REFERENCES: *Cyclopedia of Eminent and Representative Men*, vol. 2; *DNCB*, vol. 1; Montgomery, *Sketches of Old Warrenton*; Peele, *Lives of Distinguished North Carolinians*. PRIMARY SOURCES: Bragg Papers, NCSA; Bragg Papers, SHC.

## JOHN BRANCH
### 1817-1820

*J*ohn Branch (1782-1863), in addition to serving as governor of North Carolina, was governor of the Florida Territory, secretary of the navy, and U.S. senator.

Born on November 4, 1782, in the town of Halifax, he was the son of John Branch Sr., and his first wife, Rebecca Bradford. Because of his father's considerable wealth and local prominence, young Branch benefited from educational advantages and from a comfortable and cultured upbringing. Later, as an adult and public figure, he would be known for his refined tastes and generous hospitality. Branch was twice married. His first wife, Elizabeth Foort, was the mother of his nine children. His second wife was Mary Eliza Jordan Bond.

After attending UNC and reading law under Judge John Haywood, Branch entered a long and varied career in politics. In 1811 he began the first of seven terms as a representative of Halifax County in the state senate, the last term (1822) following his governorship. For two years (1815-1817) he was Speaker of that body. Branch was elected governor on December 3, 1817, and began the first of three consecutive terms allowable under the existing constitution.

Significantly, his governorship came at a time when North Carolina was conspicuous in the nation for its provincialism and inertia. As chief executive, he lent his moral and political support to the ambitious reform measures of Archibald D. Murphey. He therefore took significant steps to promote public education, initiate internal improvements, liberalize the penal code, and stem the exodus of North Carolinians to areas of the country regarded as more promising. It was during his governorship that the North Carolina Supreme Court came into being as a separate and independent body.

In 1822 Branch entered national politics with his election to the U.S. Senate. Subsequently he was appointed secretary of the navy by President Andrew Jackson. As a staunch advocate of states' rights, Branch opposed internal improvements on the national level and was generally Jacksonian in his view of the federal government. He fell out of favor with Jackson, however, during the "Eaton Affair" and, as a result, resigned from the cabinet. In 1832 he sought unsuccessfully to purge vice-presidential candidate Martin Van Buren from the Democratic ticket, and came to be publicly identified with John C. Calhoun and the doctrine of nullification.

After his return to North Carolina, following one term in the federal House of Representatives, Branch's personal and political opposition to Jackson contributed significantly to the formation and ascendancy of the Whig Party in the state. In the state Constitutional Convention of 1835, Branch argued for the removal of religious qualifications for office and against the disfranchisement of free blacks. In 1838 he was defeated in his bid for a fourth term as governor by Edward B. Dudley, the office having become elective as a result of the progressive reforms three years earlier.

Branch later moved with his family to Florida, and in 1843 was appointed governor of that territory by President John Tyler. Indeed, it was during his term in office that Florida became a state. Branch again returned to North Carolina in 1851 where he remained until his death on January 4, 1863. His burial was in Enfield, in his native Halifax County.

REFERENCES: *ANB*, vol. 3; *DAB*, vol. 2; *DNCB*, vol. 1; Hoffmann, "John Branch and Origins of the Whig Party"; Sobel and Raimo, *Bio. Dir. of Governors*, vol. 3. PRIMARY SOURCES: Branch Family Papers, Duke; Branch Family Papers, SHC; Branch Papers, NCSA.

# CURTIS HOOKS BROGDEN
## 1874-1877

*C*urtis Hooks Brogden (1816-1901) was elevated to the governor's office upon the death of Tod R. Caldwell and, over the course of his administration, faced strong opposition from a heavily Democratic legislature. The son of Pierce and Amy Bread Brogden, he was born on November 6, 1816, into the yeoman farmer class of Wayne County society. He attended the local field schools when possible, but essentially was self-educated. Reaching his impressionable teen years during the height of Andrew Jackson's popularity in North Carolina, he became an advocate of Old Hickory's brand of democracy. Just shy of his twenty-second birthday, he entered the race in 1838 for the legislature as the representative from Wayne County. He was elected and became the youngest member of that session of the House of Commons. Thus commenced a career of public service that spanned half a century and included seven terms in the lower house, three in the state senate, a decade as state comptroller, a year and a half as lieutenant governor, two and a half years as governor, and two years as a congressman.

As the nature of the Democratic Party changed in the last decade of the antebellum period, Brogden allied himself to the philosophy and policies espoused by William W. Holden in the *North Carolina Standard*. He admired and supported the editor and the two formed a lifelong friendship. The 1857 General Assembly elected Brogden state comptroller, a position he held through the Civil War and its immediate aftermath. In 1862 Brogden broke with the Democrats and voted for Zebulon B. Vance in the gubernatorial election. He quietly supported Holden during the war and afterwards followed him into the Republican Party. A large black population in Wayne County helped return him to the state senate in 1868 and reelected him two years later. He favored the Reconstruction Acts and military rule, and he wrote a number of letters justifying Governor Holden's actions in regard to the Ku Klux Klan uprising. As a state senator, he voted for Holden's acquittal in the impeachment trial.

Brogden's Republican loyalty and service to the party were rewarded in 1872 when he was nominated to run as lieutenant governor on the ticket with incumbent Tod R. Caldwell. A year and a half later, on July 11, 1874, Caldwell died in office, and Brogden became governor. In that post,

Brogden faced a hostile Democratic legislature (fewer than one-third of its members were Republicans) but won some support because he was less aggressive than his predecessor and more willing to compromise. He called for consolidation of the state's railroad holdings; an adjustment in, but not repudiation of, the state debt; and a higher caliber of education, placing emphasis on the need for a state-supported black college. During his term of office UNC reopened in September 1875.

Governor Brogden chose not to seek re-election in 1876, preferring to stand as a candidate for Congress. Elected in the Republican primary over incumbent John A. Hyman, the first black congressman from North Carolina, Brodgen represented the Second District for one term. There he worked to gain for his district and for North Carolina internal improvements. Brodgen was not renominated for the post, and Democrat William W. Kitchin took the seat.

For the next eight years, the former governor encountered frustration in his attempts at elected office. His last victory came in 1886 when he represented Wayne County in the state House for one term. Brogden, who never married, retired to his home in Goldsboro where he died on January 5, 1901, at age eighty-four. He was buried in that city's Willowdale Cemetery.

REFERENCES: *BDC*; *Cyclopedia of Eminent and Representative Men*, vol. 2; *DNCB*, vol. 1; Hamilton et al., *Graham Papers*.

## JOSEPH MELVILLE BROUGHTON
### 1941-1945

*J*. Melville Broughton (1888-1949), the only native of Wake County to serve as governor of North Carolina, led the state through most of the World War II era. Born in Raleigh on November 17, 1888, the "War Governor" was the son and namesake of Joseph Melville Broughton and the former Sallie Harris. His father, a real estate developer and insurance salesman, and uncle, Needham Broughton, helped organize Tabernacle Baptist Church in Raleigh, where the future governor for many years served as Sunday School superintendent and, for most of his adult life, taught the men's Bible class. In Raleigh young Broughton attended the public schools and Hugh Morson Academy. From there he moved on to Wake Forest College, where he played football and graduated in 1910.

Subsequently he served as principal of Bunn High School in Franklin County from 1910 to 1912 and, for a few months, as a reporter for the *Winston-Salem Journal.* Broughton studied law at Wake Forest and at Harvard and in 1914 began practicing in Raleigh. In 1916 he married Alice Willson; they had four children.

In Raleigh Broughton took an active role in civic and political affairs, serving on the school board from 1922 to 1929 and as city attorney for several years. In 1926 and 1928 voters elected him to the state senate, where he advanced workmen's compensation and secret ballot legislation. After two terms Broughton returned to his law practice, preferring civil practice to criminal litigation. He was a respected legal scholar penning articles on trusts and the legal status of women. Broughton served as a trustee for his alma mater, Wake Forest College, as well as Shaw University and, in later years, UNC. In 1936, a year in which he served as president of the state bar association, he delivered the keynote speech of the Democratic state convention. In 1940 Broughton led a field of seven candidates for the Democratic nomination after the first primary. Wilkins P. Horton, who placed second, declined to call for a runoff, and in the fall Broughton defeated Republican Robert H. McNeill. Mounting concern over the war in Europe overshadowed the campaign.

As governor Broughton, who as a legislator had failed in his attempts to extend the school term to eight months, endorsed and saw the legislature extend the term to nine months and add a twelfth grade to public schools. A retirement plan was instituted for state employees, and, for the first time, the state provided aid to public libraries, the Art Society, and the Symphony Society. Governing boards for state hospitals and charitable institutions were consolidated. Broughton appointed a board of inquiry to investigate poor conditions in the mental hospital at Morganton. The governor launched an ambitious "Good Health Program" to extend medical care and hospital construction across the state. As part of that program the Medical Care Commission was established. The legislature, on the governor's recommendation, removed the sales tax on all food items intended for home consumption. Like his predecessors Ehringhaus and Hoey, Broughton opposed the transfer of authority from the states to Washington and warned against increased federal power.

The Japanese attack on Pearl Harbor and U.S. entry into World War II took place eleven months into Broughton's term. As chief executive in the state where more men were trained for service than any other, Broughton took charge of extensive civil defense and preparedness exercises. On April 9, 1941, he attended the commissioning of the USS *North Carolina* in New York. In 1944 he was nominated as a "favorite son" candidate for vice-president.

In 1948 J. Melville Broughton defeated William B. Umstead who had been appointed to fill the unexpired term of Josiah Bailey in the U.S. Senate. Broughton took office on December 31, 1948, but died just over two months later, on March 6, 1949. He is buried in Montlawn Memorial Park in Raleigh.

REFERENCES: *BDC*; Corbitt, *Broughton Papers*, *DNCB*, vol. 1; Henderson and others, *North Carolina*, vol. 3; Lemmon, *N.C.'s Role in WWII*; *News and Observer*, March 7, 1949; Sobel and Raimo, *Bio. Dir. of Governors*, vol. 3. PRIMARY SOURCES: Broughton Papers, NCSA.

Gov. J. Melville Broughton accepts an apple via Air Express, November 1, 1944.

## THOMAS BURKE
## 1781-1782

Thomas Burke (ca. 1744-1783), skilled in the literary as well as the political arts, was taken prisoner by Loyalists shortly after taking office as governor. He was born in County Galway, Ireland, the son of Ulick Burke and the former Letitia Ould. Little is known of his early youth or domestic circumstances, but he apparently was reared by a maternal uncle and accorded the advantages of a university education. Following family quarrels, Burke emigrated to Virginia and took up residence in Norfolk. There he established himself initially as a physician but later turned to the practice of law. It was while in Virginia that the multifaceted Burke began to write poetry. He married Mary ("Polly") Freeman in 1770; their union produced one child, a daughter named Mary.

In 1772 Burke moved to Hillsborough where he acquired a small plantation and resumed the practice of law. Rising quickly to prominence, he represented Orange County in all but the first of the Provincial Congresses where he was an outspoken advocate for independence. In 1777 and briefly in 1778, Burke represented Orange County in the House of Commons. On three occasions he won election to the Continental Congress, where the form of government for the new nation was slowly taking shape. As a delegate to the Continental Congress,

Burke emerged as a strong advocate of states' rights and limited central government. He also earned a reputation for his brashness and irascibility, several times becoming the center of controversy.

On June 25, 1781, Burke was chosen by the General Assembly to serve as North Carolina's third governor under the constitution of 1776. The state, however, was ravaged by war and on the brink of anarchy. The recent departures of Greene's and Cornwallis's armies had left in their wakes roving bands of Loyalist and Patriot guerrillas, subject to no civil or military authority. Government on both the state and county levels had almost completely broken down. In his inaugural address to the General Assembly, Burke acknowledged that the former rule of law had "changed into a licentious contempt of authority," yet stubbornly resolved to bring order out of chaos. Governor Burke took extraordinary measures to reform the militia, increase essential revenues, banish intractable Loyalists, and defend against renewed British attack from both Virginia and South Carolina. Acting on his own authority, he established special courts and assumed for himself veto power over legislative acts.

Less than three months after assuming office, Burke's frantic efforts came to an end at Hillsborough when he, along with several other state officials and officers of the Continental Line, was taken prisoner by the Loyalist leader David Fanning. Transported southward to Wilmington and then to Charlestown, Burke was released on parole after an ordeal of two months. Fearing that his life was in danger, however, Burke escaped from his very loose confinement and returned to North Carolina and the governorship, thereby violating both his parole and the code of honor in the eyes of many contemporaries.

When the embittered Burke convened the General Assembly in April of 1782, his rather ambiguous offer to retire from public office was accepted almost without remark. Having served only ten months as governor, two of those as a prisoner, he returned to Hillsborough a ruined and deeply disillusioned man. He died less than two years later, on December 2, 1783, and was interred on the grounds of his plantation, Tyaquin.

REFERENCES: *DAB*, vol. 3; *DNCB*, vol. 1; Douglass, "Thomas Burke"; Watterson, "The Ordeal of Governor Burke." PRIMARY SOURCES: Burke Papers, NCSA; Burke Papers, SHC.

◈ ◈ ◈

## GEORGE BURRINGTON
## 1724-1725; 1731-1734

*G*eorge Burrington (ca. 1682-1759) served North Carolina both as a proprietary governor and as the first royal governor, with the distinction of being removed from office both times. He was born in Devonshire, England, and historians believe that he was the son of one of several

Gilbert Burringtons alive at the time. Regardless of his parentage, George Burrington was from a prominent family with powerful connections, including the duke of Newcastle. It was Newcastle who secured Burrington's initial military commission and, later, his royal governorship. He likely influenced the proprietary appointment as well. Burrington was probably married, but no records have been found to prove this. There is merely a secondhand account of the governor mentioning his "big [bellied] wife" in Virginia. He had a son, George, who was born in 1738.

George Burrington was sworn in as proprietary governor on January 15, 1724, and immediately began to antagonize North Carolina's political set. Insults, threats, and even occasional physical violence were directed toward prominent figures. After a particularly violent episode at Christopher Gale's house on August 23, 1724, Gale, the chief justice, went to England with the support of seven of the councillors to convince the Lords Proprietors to dismiss Burrington. In the summer of 1725, Gale returned to North Carolina, successful in his goal. Burrington likely remained in North Carolina until hearing that his home colony was to come under royal authority. In 1729 Burrington traveled to England to secure the royal governorship.

Burrington was sworn into office as the first royal governor on February 25, 1731. Although he met with initial enthusiasm, he soon managed to alienate even some of his former allies on the council. In May Chief

Justice William Smith resigned and traveled to England seeking Burrington's dismissal. Smith remained there until Newcastle, in the spring of 1733, decided to replace Burrington. His successor, Gabriel Johnston, would not arrive in North Carolina until November 1734.

In his term of almost four years, one fraught with controversy, Burrington nevertheless was able to do some good in North Carolina. He was quite interested in fostering internal improvements, and frequently journeyed through the colony inspecting roads and bridges and helping to plan new roads that would prompt immigration and make travel easier. Burrington was also a key figure in the exploration and development of the Lower Cape Fear region. His legacy remains, however, not in the good things that he accomplished, but rather in the conflicts and confrontations. Mystery surrounds several key events in his governorship, including an alleged attempt to murder him, for which no revealing contemporary records exist. Burrington was killed during an apparent robbery attempt on February 22, 1759, in St. James Park, London. In his late seventies, George Burrington struggled with the assailant, but was overpowered and thrown into a canal.

REFERENCES: *ANB*, vol. 4; *DNCB*, vol. 1; Ekirch, *"Poor Carolina"*; Lee, *Lower Cape Fear*; Price, "A Strange Incident"; Saunders, *Colonial Records of N.C.*, vols. 3 and 4.

## HUTCHINS GORDON BURTON
### 1824-1827

Despite some uncertainty as to place, Hutchins Gordon Burton (1774-1836) appears to have been born in Mecklenburg County, Virginia, the son of John Burton and the former Mary Gordon. Orphaned as a small boy, Burton was reared by his uncle, Col. Robert Burton, in what is now Vance (then Granville) County. He attended UNC from 1795 to 1798, studied law under Judge Leonard Henderson, and in 1806 began the practice of law in Charlotte. Burton married the former Sarah Wales Jones, daughter of Revolutionary Patriot Willie Jones of Halifax.

Burton was elected from Mecklenburg County to the lower house of the General Assembly in 1809 and 1810, and from the latter year until 1816 served as the state's attorney general. He then returned to the House of Commons representing the town of Halifax, his wife's hometown. In 1819 he was elected to the U.S. House of Representatives, where he served for the next five years. In his committee assignments, he focused largely on the workings of the U.S. Post Office, military and judicial affairs, and the improvement of transportation. In 1824 he supported the unsuccessful candidacy of William H. Crawford for president of the United States.

It was in 1824, as well, that Burton resigned his seat in Congress to begin his first term as governor of North Carolina, having been elected after six ballots over Montfort Stokes and Alfred Moore. Two successive terms would follow, comprising the maximum three terms permitted under the existing constitution.

As governor Burton repeatedly emphasized the need for public education, especially on the primary level. Sadly, he observed, it was arguably more difficult to obtain "the common rudiments of education" than when the state constitution was adopted half a century earlier. Though he also stressed the need for internal improvements, he considered education to be of even greater importance. In 1825 a significant milestone was achieved with the creation of the Literary Fund to provide support for common schools. As governor, Burton was president of the board charged with the fund's management. However, unfortunately, the available monies proved woefully inadequate for their intended purpose. Frustrated by the shortage of funds, Burton supported several lotteries with educational objectives, including the preparation of a state history.

In 1825 Burton presided over the festivities associated with the visit of General Lafayette of Revolutionary War fame. Two years later he hosted the visit of future president, Martin Van Buren. Following his third term as governor, Burton returned to Halifax and later made plans to move to Texas. It was while en route to examine property there that he died near Lincolnton on April 21, 1836. He was interred at Beatty's Ford in the Unity Church cemetery.

REFERENCES: Coon, *Beginnings of Public Education*; *DAB*, vol. 3; *DNCB*, vol. 1; Sobel and Raimo, *Bio. Dir. of Governors*, vol. 3. PRIMARY SOURCES: Burton Papers, SHC.

## TOD ROBINSON CALDWELL
### 1871-1874

Tod Robinson Caldwell (1818-1874), the first lieutenant governor in North Carolina history, succeeded his predecessor William Woods Holden as chief executive when the latter was brought to trial on impeachment charges. Caldwell was born on February 19, 1818, in Morganton and was the son of Irish immigrant merchant John Caldwell and his wife, the former Hannah Robinson. He attended a local school before traveling to Hillsborough to study under prominent educator William J. Bingham. A member of the class of 1840 at UNC, he received high honors upon graduation. David L. Swain, president of the university, personally tutored the promising Burke County student in law. Tod Caldwell married Minerva Ruffin Cain in 1840; they would have three daughters and two sons.

In 1841 Caldwell began a law practice in Morganton and shortly afterwards became county prosecuting attorney. A keen mind and strong oratorical ability earned him a reputation as one of the best criminal lawyers in the state. Eager for the political arena, he sought and won election to the House of Commons in 1842 at age twenty-four, beginning a series of five legislative terms (four in the House and one in the state senate) before the Civil War. Caldwell greatly admired Henry Clay and eagerly adopted the principles of the Whig Party. He was an ardent nationalist and bitterly denounced all talk of secession. He broke the pattern of most North Carolina Whigs, however, by not abandoning his Union loyalty after the state had joined the Confederacy. He refused to take any part in the war and suffered doubly when his only surviving son was killed fighting for the South at Gettysburg.

With the war's end, Caldwell served briefly as president of the Western North Carolina Railroad before reentering politics. He attended the Convention of 1865, but when the provisional government gave way to the Conservatives led by Jonathan Worth, Caldwell joined forces with W. W. Holden to form the Republican Party in the state. Radical Reconstruction paved the way for a revised constitution in 1868 that called for the position of a lieutenant governor. Caldwell's Union allegiance and service to the Republican Party were rewarded with the candidacy for the lieutenant governorship on the ticket with Holden. Two and a half years into the term, he took over the executive duties when Holden was suspended from office pending his trial on impeachment charges. Caldwell became governor on March 22, 1871, with the conviction and removal of Holden.

As governor, Caldwell called for a methodical resolution of the state debt; tried to pump new life into the school system; proposed new laws to restore order in the society, particularly in regard to the newly established rights of black citizens; and asked for a vigorous prosecution of bond fraud leaders George W. Swepson and Milton S. Littlefield. A Conservative legislature, hostile to the Republican regime, nullified virtually all of his efforts except for prosecution of the bond frauds. Caldwell maintained a conciliatory tone and sense of moderation during his tenure. His efforts to reinvigorate the public school system met with opposition in the General Assembly, and he evinced little interest in reopening UNC. Caldwell did enjoy a measure of success in education with the appointment of Alexander D. McIver as superintendent of public instruction.

In the 1872 gubernatorial election, Caldwell narrowly defeated Conservative candidate Augustus S. Merrimon. Two years later, on July 10, 1874, while attending a meeting of the directors of the North Carolina Railroad in Hillsborough, Governor Caldwell was stricken with a gall bladder attack and died the next day. His body was returned to Morganton for burial.

REFERENCES: *Burke County Heritage*; Cheney, *N.C. Government*; *Cyclopedia of Eminent and Representative Men*, vol. 2; *DNCB*, vol. 1; Hamilton et al., *Graham Papers*, vol. 8; Phifer, *Burke Co. History*. PRIMARY SOURCES: Caldwell Papers, SHC.

# ELIAS CARR
## 1893-1897

*E*lias Carr (1839-1900), leader of the statewide Farmers' Alliance and the broader agrarian movement, exemplified the fading tradition of the planter-governor. The son of Jonas and Elizabeth Hilliard Carr, he was born on February 25, 1839, at Bracebridge Hall, the 2,000-acre family plantation in Edgecombe County. Orphaned by the age of four, young Carr grew up in the home of his aunt and uncle in Warren County.

There he attended a local school before leaving for the Bingham School in Orange County. He completed his education at UNC (1855-1857) and the University of Virginia. In 1859 he married Eleanor Kearny; they would have six children.

Carr bought his brother's interest in Bracebridge Hall and prepared for the life of a planter, but the Civil War interrupted his plans. He enlisted in the Forty-first Regiment (Third Cavalry) in 1861. Nine months later he received a planter's exemption and returned home. There Carr applied progressive farming techniques and sound business practices. Consequently, he suffered fewer losses than most of his contemporaries during the war. He was community-oriented and civic-minded, as shown by service on the Edgecombe County Board of Commissioners, Sparta Township school commission, and as first president of the North Carolina Society of the Sons of the Revolution. Yet, he lacked political ambition and, prior to 1892, never sought a high elective office. He was most comfortable in his agricultural work.

Carr served as the first president of the Farmer's Institute of Edgecombe County. In 1887 Gov. Alfred M. Scales commissioned him to attend the National Farmers' Conference, and the following year he was elected the first president of the North Carolina Farmers' Association. He served on the first board of trustees of the North Carolina College of Agriculture and Mechanical Arts (present-day North Carolina State University). Nonetheless, the Farmers' Alliance was the vehicle that cast the spotlight on Carr. Organized in North Carolina in 1887, the Alliance soon absorbed the Farmers' Association. Two years later Carr was elected president of the state Farmers' Alliance and was re-elected in 1890. He led the group's effort to secure legislation increasing the tax to improve rural schools. Ever increasing political activity by farmers forced Carr into an arena he had long avoided.

A growing disenchantment within the Democratic Party between supporters of agricultural interests and those favoring business and industry threatened to split the party in 1892. Carr, a steadfast Democrat, but with strong ties to the farmers' movement, seemed the most likely gubernatorial candidate to hold the sparring factions together to prevent a Republican upset. Though a splinter group did run a third-party candidate, the Farmers' Alliance supported Carr and, with the conservative Democratic vote, provided a comfortable margin of victory.

Considering his lack of political experience and the polarized factions surrounding his administration, Carr had a successful governorship. He recommended legislation to improve the notoriously bad road system; enthusiastically supported the geological survey; and campaigned for better rural schools. In calling for the latter, Carr urged the passage of a compulsory attendance law and advocated a tax increase during a period of depression to fund school improvements. The governor preferred to see things firsthand so he made occasional, unannounced visits to the state's educational, charitable, and penal institutions before making recommendations. Carr's ninety-nine-year lease of the North Carolina Railroad to the Southern Railway in 1895 engendered massive criticism, much from his own party. That and the Fusionist-controlled legislature (a loose coalition of Republicans and Populists) virtually handicapped him for the last two years of his term. Carr retired to the peaceful farm life at Bracebridge Hall after his service as governor. He died on July 22, 1900, and was buried in the family cemetery on the grounds.

REFERENCES: *DAB*, vol. 3; *DNCB*, vol. 1; Henderson and others, *North Carolina*, vol. 3; Steelman, "Role of Elias Carr in N.C.'s Farmers' Alliance"; Turner and Bridgers, *Edgecombe Co. History*. PRIMARY SOURCES: Carr Papers, ECU; Williams Papers, ECU.

◇ ◇ ◇

## PETER CARTERET
## 1670-1672

*P*eter Carteret (b. 1641) inherited a suffering and divided Albemarle County and the duty to implement the Fundamental Constitutions. He was born on the British Island of Jersey, the son of Helier de Carteret and Rachel La Cloche Carteret. Proprietor George Carteret was his fourth cousin. Carteret arrived in Albemarle County in February 1665 with several government appointments. In 1668 Gov. Samuel Stephens made Carteret lieutenant colonel of the militia.

Following Stephens's death, the Albemarle Council chose Carteret as

acting governor on March 10, 1670. The Lords Proprietors later confirmed his appointment. When Carteret assumed control, Albemarle was suffering because economic disasters and disease had brought the colonists to the brink of poverty and starvation. Adding to Albemarle's problems, the Lords Proprietors expected Carteret to implement the Fundamental Constitutions. The new plan of government increased tensions between the anti-proprietary faction consisting of pre-1663 charter settlers and the proprietary faction made up of post-1663 charter settlers. The anti-proprietary faction apparently feared that the new government's feudal structure might force them to give up such status as they had achieved. The Fundamental Constitutions also rendered land titles given by the Virginia Council or purchased from Indians invalid, which, if enforced, would result in the loss of land for the anti-proprietary faction. Furthermore, quitrents were to rise, and a new complicated land division system was to be enacted. The Fundamental Constitutions, however, provided the proprietary faction with the opportunity to take control of the government.

Carteret, a supporter of neither faction, was troubled about the future of the Albemarle region. In May 1671 the council sent a letter to the proprietors expressing opposition to parts of the Fundamental Constitutions. The council did not receive a response. Consequently, the council in April 1672 sent Carteret and John Harvey to London to present their grievances to the Lords Proprietors and to obtain aid from them. Only Carteret made the trip to London.

Before Carteret left for London, the temporary plan of government as instructed by the Fundamental Constitutions was instituted. The assembly also reviewed all the laws as instructed by the proprietors and re-enacted ones that it considered proper for the colony. Carteret was assigned to present the laws to the Lords Proprietors for review.

Carteret's trip to London turned out to be a disaster. He learned that the Lords Proprietors planned to dispose of their interest in Albemarle to fellow proprietor and Virginia governor William Berkeley. The proprietors were unsympathetic to Carteret because they expected to be free of Albemarle. However, even after years of nego- tiations, their plan never came into realization.

Aside from his governmental duties, Carteret ran a plantation at Colington Island owned by four proprietors. The plantation was unsuccessful because of scarce labor and supplies and natural disasters. Because of insufficient financing, Carteret often paid the expenses of running the plantation using his own money. He had hoped to go back to the Albemarle region in some capacity other than governor; however, he never returned. By 1680, the Lords Proprietors were blaming Carteret for the problems that led to Culpeper's Rebellion. Carteret's death date is unknown.

REFERENCES: Butler, "The Governors of Albemarle County"; *DNCB*, vol. 1; Parker et al., *Colonial Records*; Raimo, *Bio. Dir. of Col. and Rev. Governors*; Rankin, *Upheaval in Albemarle*.

## THOMAS CARY
### 1705-1706; 1708-1711

*T*homas Cary (d. ca. 1718) is best known for the uprising (Cary's Rebellion) that bears his name. As governor he knew how to adjust his sails in changing political winds. Cary was the son of Walter Cary and Ann Dobson and was born in Buckinghamshire, England. Cary's mother later married governor and Lords Proprietor John Archdale. Cary became a successful merchant and shipowner in South Carolina. When Archdale became provisional governor, Cary served as provincial secretary and council member.

In 1705 provisional governor Nathaniel Johnson chose Cary to succeed Robert Daniel as the deputy governor. Upon arrival, Cary supported the Anglicans and required an oath of allegiance to hold public office as required by law. By enforcing the law, Cary kept the Quakers out of government, since their faith kept them from making an oath. In response, the dissenters and unhappy Anglicans sent John Porter to England in October 1706 to persuade the Lords Proprietors to remove Cary.

In 1707 Cary served as representative to the South Carolina Assembly where he became Speaker of the House. While Cary was out of North Carolina, William Glover presided as acting deputy governor. Following the return of Porter, who obtained Cary's ouster, in October 1707 Glover was elected as president of the council allowing him to continue as acting governor. Cary, who returned in November 1707, saw an opportunity to regain the governorship by seeking support from dissenters, the group he removed from public offices. He also built a support base with Bath County residents weary of Albemarle County's dominance.

In October 1708, Cary and his supporters regained control of the government. Glover fled to Virginia claiming that Cary "threatened and avowed . . . to take away my life." As acting governor, Cary voided laws enacted under Glover and replaced suspected disloyal officials with dissenters. He also lowered the quitrents for Bath County and reformed land grant policy to encourage immigration. Cary remained in power until early 1711 when he transferred power to Edward Hyde.

Cary left for Bath County but did not retire quietly. In March 1711, the assembly enacted laws aimed at dissenters and voided laws under Cary. Hyde sought the arrest of Cary. In May 1711 Hyde and around 150 men went after Cary and his followers in Bath County. Cary made his house into a fortress "with five pieces of Cannon" and about forty men. Hyde evidently tried to come to terms with Cary, but he was unsuccessful. Deciding against attacking a fortified position, Hyde retreated. Virginia's governor Alexander Spotswood offered to mediate the dispute, but Cary refused. Cary decided to move against Hyde and overthrow the government. Cary with his supporters sailed for Thomas Pollock's plantation where Hyde and about sixty supporters had established a fortress. Cary attacked Hyde's position with cannon from the ship and tried to land some of his men, but the attack was repulsed. After a request from Hyde and the council, Governor Spotswood sent a British ship and marines to aid Hyde. With the arrival of the professional military, Cary and his chief lieutenants dispersed. Cary and five followers were captured in Virginia, and Governor Spotswood had them sent to London for trial in 1711. After a year, the men were released without any punishment, likely from a lack of clear evidence. Cary returned to North Carolina in 1713 and spent his remaining years in Bath County. He was dead by July 1718.

REFERENCES: *ANB*, vol. 4; Booth, *Seeds of Anger*; *DNCB*, vol. 1; Edgar and Bailey, *Bio. Dir. of S.C. House*, vol. 2; Lefler, "Anglican Church in N.C."; Parker et al., *Colonial Records*, vols. 4, 5, and 10; Saunders, *Colonial Records of N.C.*, vols. 1 and 2.

## RICHARD CASWELL
## 1776-1780; 1784-1787

Richard Caswell (1729-1789) was the first governor of the independent state of North Carolina under the Constitution of 1776. He was born on August 3, 1729, in Joppa, Maryland, one of the eleven children of Richard Caswell and the former Christian Dallam. Educated in the local parish school, he was obliged from an early age to assist in the management of his father's farm and mercantile business. Because of the family's declining fortunes in Maryland, young Caswell came to the New Bern area in 1745 in search of job opportunities and desirable land. He established permanent residence in the present-day Kinston vicinity and acquired a homesite for his parents and younger siblings. As a surveyor, he also developed a lifelong interest in land speculation. Caswell was first married to Mary Mackilwean, who died after five years. His second marriage was to Sarah Heritage, who survived him.

In addition to his surveying work, Caswell served as a clerk of court in Orange and Johnston Counties, gaining experience in courtroom procedure and practical juris-prudence. Eager for wealth and advancement, he became a student of the law and was admitted to the bar in 1759. From 1754 through 1775, he sat continuously as a member of the colonial assembly, first as a representative from Johnston County and later from Dobbs County and the town of New Bern. In 1771 he attained the Speakership of that body. During that same year he led the right wing of Gov. William Tryon's army in its crushing defeat of the Regulators at the Battle of Alamance.

With the approach of the Revolution, Caswell assumed a position of leadership, serving on the committee of correspondence, as a member in all five provincial congresses, and as a delegate to the first and second Continental Congresses. Following his return from Philadelphia, Caswell's defiance of royal rule and his assertions of legislative supremacy grew increasingly bold. By late summer of 1775 he had become, in Gov. Josiah Martin's words, "the most active tool of sedition" in the colony. Caswell was appointed treasurer of the rebellious colony's southern district and was made commander of militiamen from the New Bern area. Early the following year he led the brigade in the decisive victory over Loyalist forces at Moores Creek Bridge.

When the Fifth Provincial Congress convened at Halifax in late 1776, Caswell served as its presiding officer and as chairman of the committee to draft the state's constitution. Moreover, this same provincial body elected Caswell to serve as interim governor of the newborn state until the first meeting of the General Assembly. When the assembly convened in April of the following year, Caswell was elected to the first of three successive one-year terms allowable under the state constitution. In time, Caswell would become convinced that the constitutional powers of the governorship were too tightly constrained. As governor, Caswell exerted every effort to raise and supply troops for the war effort on both the state and national levels. He also was forced to contend with continual friction between Indians and settlers on the western frontier, with sporadic British raids along the coast, and with Tory hostilities throughout the state.

When his third regular term as governor expired in April 1780, Caswell left office exhausted and in poor health. Immediately, however, he was pressed into duty as overall commander of the state militia. Four months later he shared with Gen. Horatio Gates the ignominy of defeat at the Battle of Camden. Despite the poor showing of his troops at Camden, Caswell was elected from Dobbs County to the state senate in 1780. There he served for the next four years, two of those as Speaker. Concurrently, he also served as state comptroller general and was responsible for management of public funds.

In November 1784 Caswell was returned to the governorship by the assemblymen. Reelected during each of the next two years, he again served the maximum three consecutive terms permitted under the constitution. Though independence had been won, Caswell's second period in office was nevertheless fraught with major difficulties, as both the state and nation struggled to come of age. Prominent among these difficulties were the breakaway "State of Franklin," continuing unrest among the Cherokee in the mountains, and the troubled constitutional relationship with the federal government.

Caswell was elected to the federal Constitutional Convention in Philadelphia in 1787 but was unable to attend because of poor health. During the following year he won a controversial election to the state constitutional convention in Hillsborough but was not actually seated. He further won election to the state senate in 1789 and to the Fayetteville constitutional convention that same year. He was to die, however, before the historic Fayetteville meeting, and was thus denied the opportunity to vote for ratification. The last few years of Caswell's life brought the loss of several members of his immediate family and a further and progressive deterioration of his health. He died in Fayetteville on November 8, 1789, having suffered a stroke in the Senate chamber. His burial took place near Kinston at his Red House Plantation.

REFERENCES: Alexander, "Training of Richard Caswell"; *DAB*, vol. 3; *DNCB*, vol. 1. PRIMARY SOURCES: Caswell Papers, NCSA; Caswell Papers, SHC .

## ROBERT GREGG CHERRY
### 1945-1949

*R*.Gregg Cherry (1891-1957), a veteran of World War I, led the state through the closing months of World War II and the years of readjustment to a postwar economy, a period of general prosperity. The "Iron Major" was born near Rock Hill, South Carolina, on October 17, 1891. His mother, the former Hattie Davis, died when he was an infant. His father, a farmer and Confederate veteran, Chancellor Lafayette Cherry, died when he was seven. Young Cherry was raised by his uncle, Henry M. Lineberger, of Gastonia. In 1912 Cherry graduated from Trinity College (forerunner of Duke University), where he was captain of the basketball team. Two years later he completed a law degree at Trinity and returned to Gastonia to practice.

In 1917, with the entry of the United States into World War I, Gregg Cherry organized men from the Gastonia area into a unit that became Company A of the 115th Machine Gun Battalion, part of the Thirtieth Division. The outfit saw service in France and Belgium and was part of the force that cracked the Hindenberg Line. After the war Major Cherry was active in the National Guard. In 1921 Cherry married Mildred Stafford; they had no children.

While abroad Cherry had his name placed into contention for mayor of Gastonia. Shortly after his return he was elected to the post and then reelected in 1921. The voters of Gaston County sent him to the state House for five consecutive terms beginning in 1931. Initially opposed to a sales tax, Cherry changed his position, and his support was instrumental in its approval in 1933. He served as Speaker of the House for the 1937 session, during which time he earned his nickname "Iron Major" for the firm guiding hand offered to his colleagues. In 1941 and 1943 he was elected to the North Carolina Senate. In 1944 Cherry defeated liberal Ralph McDonald in a bitterly fought Democratic gubernatorial primary and Republican Frank C. Patton in the fall. Cherry had the support of the political organization of O. Max Gardner and is often identified with the "Shelby Dynasty," although he was from a neighboring county.

As governor Cherry expanded mental health services by increasing hospital facilities and personnel. The state acquired Camp Butner, used by

Gov. R. Gregg Cherry chats with Alice Vivian White, Miss North Carolina of 1947.

the military during the war, for construction of a mental hospital. During his term the state committed to creating a four-year medical school at Chapel Hill. The compulsory age for attendance in the public schools was raised from fourteen to sixteen. Governor Cherry successfully advocated increased teacher salaries and laid the groundwork for the road-building program initiated by his successor Kerr Scott. Philosophically, Gregg Cherry was a conservative and, like his predecessor J. Melville Broughton, advocated conserving money to cushion the shock of postwar adjustment.

Personally, Gregg Cherry was roughhewn, plainspoken, and at times profane, with a fondness for whiskey and chewing tobacco. In 1946 he personally intervened and settled the Erwin Mills strike in Durham. When a white mob in Northampton County attempted to lynch a black man in 1947, the governor reacted swiftly to bring the parties responsible to justice. In 1948 he hosted President Harry S. Truman, with whom he had much in common, in Raleigh on the occasion of the dedication of the memorial at the Capitol honoring the three presidents from North Carolina. That same year Cherry bucked the pressure of other southern governors to support the Dixiecrat presidential bid of South Carolina governor Strom Thurmond and remained loyal to the Democratic Party. After his term as governor Cherry returned to the practice of law in Gastonia.

R. Gregg Cherry, a Methodist, was a trustee of Duke University and UNC. He died on June 25, 1957, and is buried in Gaston Memorial Park in Gastonia.

REFERENCES: Abrams, *Conservative Constraints*; Corbitt, *Cherry Papers*; *DNCB*, vol. 1; Henderson and others, *North Carolina*, vol. 4; Lemmon, *N.C.'s Role in WWII*; *News and Observer*, June 26, 1957; Sobel and Raimo, *Bio. Dir. of Governors*, vol. 3. PRIMARY SOURCES: Cherry Papers, Duke; Cherry Papers, NCSA.

## HENRY TOOLE CLARK
## 1861-1862

*H*enry Toole Clark (1808-1874) was the second of three chief executives to serve North Carolina during the Civil War. The son of Maj. James W. and Arabella Toole Clark, he was born on February 7, 1808, on his father's Walnut Creek plantation in Edgecombe County. He studied first in the school of George Phillips in Tarboro and then attended school in Louisburg before entering UNC from which he was graduated in 1826. Although he studied law and passed the bar, he never practiced the profession. Instead, he returned home to manage his father's plantation and business interests that extended as far as Alabama and Tennessee. In 1850 Clark married a cousin, the widow Mary Weeks Hargrave, daughter of Theophilus Parker of Tarboro; they would have five children.

After brief service as the Edgecombe County clerk of court, Clark was elected by his fellow citizens to the state senate in 1850. He was returned in every election through 1860. A Democrat and member of the planter aristocracy, he nevertheless promoted internal improvements, seeking and acquiring an appropriation to build a plank road from Tarboro to Jamesville. His high character and strong moral values commanded the respect of both parties; thus, he was elected president of the senate in 1858 and 1860. When Gov. John Ellis became seriously ill in June of 1861, it fell upon Clark, as president of the senate, to assume the duties of the chief executive. The position was made official by the death of Ellis on July 7.

The war dominated Clark's administration. He had been a secessionist, and in his first message to the legislature on August 16, he declared the cause of the Confederacy to be just, offering a plan of preparedness for defense of the state, particularly the long, exposed coastline. His suggestions, however, were overridden by the Confederate authorities in Richmond who had assumed control of all military affairs and turned a deaf ear to the governor's request for assistance. With Union occupation of eastern North Carolina, the citizens unfairly blamed Clark for their problems. A man of modest political talent and lacking personal charisma, the governor was unable to boost morale or rally the people to the Confederate cause. He did not run for a full term in 1862.

Clark held some local offices in Edgecombe County after the war but ventured back into the state arena for only one term in the senate in 1866-1867. He retired to his plantation where he died in 1874. He was buried in the cemetery of Calvary Episcopal Church in Tarboro.

REFERENCES: Barrett, *Civil War in N.C.*; *DNCB*, vol. 1; Johnston and Mobley, *Vance Papers*, vol. 1; Turner and Bridgers, *Edgecombe Co. History*; PRIMARY SOURCES: Van Noppen Papers, Duke.

## LOCKE CRAIG
## 1913-1917

*B*ertie County native and Buncombe County resident Locke Craig (1860-1924), the first governor from the mountain region since Zebulon B. Vance, made transportation improvements and conservation efforts the hallmarks of his administration. The "Little Giant of the West" was born in the east on August 16, 1860, in Bertie County to Baptist minister Andrew Murdock Craig, who was of Scottish ancestry, and the former Clarissa Gilliam. Young Craig attended local schools and the Horner School in Henderson. Shortly after the Civil War his father died. His widowed mother moved with him to Chapel Hill where he enrolled in UNC at age fifteen. Upon graduation in 1880 he taught chemistry there for one year. Teaching, he found, was not his calling, and, after study of the law, he was admitted to the bar in 1882. The following year he established a practice in Asheville, where he would live the rest of his life with the exception of his term in the governor's office. In 1891 he married Annie Burgin of McDowell County; they had four sons.

In 1892 and 1896 Locke Craig served as a presidential elector for William Jennings Bryan, which whetted his appetite for politics. The experience led to his election to the state House for two terms in the eventful 1899-1900 and 1901 sessions. An acquaintance of Charles B. Aycock from their student days in Chapel Hill, Craig took a leading role in the white supremacy campaign, both on the stump and in the well of the House. Craig lost the Democratic nomination for the U.S. Senate in 1902 to Lee Overman and, in a three-way race with W. W. Kitchin and Ashley Horne, lost his party's nomination for governor in 1908. The latter race was very close, extending to sixty-one ballots at the convention in Charlotte, and four

Gov. Locke Craig, a lawyer by trade, spurred economic growth in the state by pushing for an adjustment in the railroad freight rate structure. Governor Craig sits on a bench at the State Capitol in the early 1920s.

years later Craig by acclamation was his party's nominee. In the fall of 1912 he defeated Republican Thomas Settle and Progressive Iredell Meares.

In his inaugural address Craig issued his "Pledge of Progress," promising to carry forward the education reforms of his predecessors. In the course of the speech, he denounced the railroad freight rate structure as discriminatory to North Carolina business. That system allowed railroad companies to charge higher rates within the state than those paid by shippers in neighboring states. The readjustment of those rates in 1915, negotiations in which the governor took a personal role, spurred economic development and was the signal achievement of his administration.

During his term a framework was established for the extension of the road system with the creation of the State Highway Commission in 1915. The number of miles in the system increased from 5,000 in 1913 to 15,000 four years later. The Central Highway (later known as the Old Hickory Highway) was completed across most of the state, including the section up the mountain at Old Fort built with convict labor. The State Fisheries Commission was created in 1915. Governor Craig took an interest in the welfare of victims of the July 1916 floods in western North Carolina and coordinated relief efforts. In 1916 the governor mobilized the National Guard for service along the U.S. border with Mexico. He worked to have Cuba withdraw its claim for payment of Reconstruction bonds.

Governor Craig served as president of the Appalachian Park Association and took a leading role in the development of Pisgah National Forest. In 1915, at his urging, the state purchased six hundred acres at the summit of Mount Mitchell for the creation of the first state park.

At the conclusion of his gubernatorial term, Craig returned to his law practice and his home on the Swannanoa River in Asheville. He died on June 9, 1924, and is buried in that city's Riverside Cemetery.

REFERENCES: Ashe et al., *Biographical History*, vol. 6; *DNCB*, vol. 1; Jones, *Craig Memoirs*; Jones, *Craig Papers*; *News and Observer*, June 10, 1924; *Proceedings of the Bar Association* (1925); Sobel and Raimo, *Bio. Dir. of Governors*, vol. 3. PRIMARY SOURCES: Craig Papers, Duke.

# ROBERT DANIEL
## 1703-1705

*T*he brief tenure of Robert Daniel (1646-1718) as North Carolina governor was marked with tension between Anglicans and non-Anglicans and between Indians and colonists. The tensions eventually erupted into religious rebellion and open warfare with Indians following Daniel's governorship. Daniel lived in Barbados and in 1677 came to South Carolina where he had acquired land and settled in 1679. He married twice and was the father of five children. As a landgrave (a member of the Carolina nobility), Daniel acquired over 31,000 acres of land, but sold most of it. By his death, he owned 1,519 acres in North and South Carolina and five town lots.

Daniel was active in the political affairs of South Carolina, being a leader in the faction called the "Goose Creek Men." He supported Seth Sothel, who removed Gov. James Colleton from office, and created problems for Gov. Phillip Ludwell. In 1697 the Lords Proprietors had Daniel's assistance in London in drafting a revised version of the Fundamental Constitutions. He returned to South Carolina with the revised document and with an appointment from proprietor Lord William Craven as his representative. On the South Carolina Council, Daniel, a diehard Church of England supporter, mounted an effort to prevent a "dissenter" (non-Anglican) from being chosen as acting governor in 1700.

In 1703, provincial governor Nathaniel Johnson appointed Daniel as deputy governor of North Carolina. In that year, relations between colonists and Indians were becoming strained. Daniel received petitions from colonists telling about raids. The colonists sought "speedy Redres" and defense, so they did not have to "live in such dayly Jeapordy of our lives." To defuse growing tensions, some colonists of Bath County asked Daniel and his council to send an interpreter and to appoint envoys to negotiate with the Indians. Daniel called for raising a militia regiment to respond to threats, and tried to alleviate tensions by convening a meeting of the governor and council and "all the Indian Kings and Rulers in which they agreed upon a firm Peace." However, the peace proved to be elusive.

Daniel's greatest challenge came with his efforts to curb the power of religious dissenters (mainly Quakers) and bolster the Church of England in North Carolina. The governor placed Anglicans in the government and on his council. To get the Church of England established, Daniel had to remove dissenters from an assembly dominated by them. In 1704, Daniel received the instrument he needed to remove dissenters from the assembly, a requirement that public officials swear an oath of allegiance to Queen Anne. Since the Quakers' faith forbade them from taking an oath, they were effectively barred from public office. A simple affirmation, as Quakers earlier expounded to hold office, was not allowed. With no Quakers, the assembly soon after enacted a law that required support of the Church of England.

After leaving the governorship, Daniel remained active in North Carolina but, by 1709, had made South Carolina his permanent home after giving his North Carolina property to his wife Martha. In the spring of 1716, Daniel was appointed deputy governor of South Carolina, but he was out of office by the fall of 1717 after a tumultuous tenure. He died in May 1718.

REFERENCES: *DNCB*, vol. 2; Edgar and Bailey, *Bio. Dir. of S.C. House*, vol. 2; Lawson, *New Voyage*; Parker et al., *Colonial Records*, vols. 4 and 7; Parramore, "The Tuscarora Ascendancy"; Raimo, *Bio. Dir. of Col. and Rev. Governors*; Salley, *Commissions and Instructions*; Salley, *Narratives of Early Carolina*; Saunders, *Colonial Records of N.C.*, vols. 1 and 2; Todd, *Graffenried's Account of the Founding of New Bern*.

# WILLIAM RICHARDSON DAVIE
## 1798-1799

*W*illiam Richardson Davie (1756-1820), who had a distinguished record in the Revolution, guided the creation of UNC and is known as the "Father of the University." Born on June 22, 1756, in County Cumberland, England, he was the son of Archibald Davie and the former Mary Richardson, recently resettled from Scotland. In 1764 Davie moved with his family to the Waxhaw region near Lancaster, South Carolina, where his maternal uncle was minister of the Old Waxhaw Presbyterian Meeting House. Davie's wife was the former Sarah Jones of Halifax, niece of the leading Anti-Federalist Willie Jones. They were the parents of six children.

Graduating from the College of New Jersey (now Princeton University) in 1776, Davie returned home to fight for the Patriot cause. Seriously wounded in 1779, he retired for a time from military activity to read law under Judge Spruce Macay in Salisbury. Returning to battle with the approach of Cornwallis's army, Davie served as commissary general under Nathanael Greene during the last stages of the Revolution. After the war, Davie moved to Halifax to practice law. In 1784-1785 he represented nearby Northampton County in the state House; from 1786 through 1798 he served as a representative for the town of Halifax. As a member of the House, he associated himself with progressive legislation and assumed a leadership position in the Federalist Party.

Elected by the General Assembly to the Constitutional Convention of 1787, Davie supported the Great Compromise regarding congressional representation, but left before the meeting was concluded and the Constitution was signed. During the next two years he worked for its approval in North Carolina, and as a delegate to the state constitutional conventions of 1788 and 1789. Indeed, it was his motion during the latter meeting that resulted in ratification.

Only three weeks later, Davie introduced and secured passage in the General Assembly of a bill to establish UNC. Thereafter, he further fostered the institution by marshalling financial support, launching initial construction, and recruiting faculty. On December 4, 1798, Davie was elected governor by the General Assembly on a wave of Federalist support. During his single term, Davie focused on the fixing of common boundaries with Georgia, South Carolina, and Tennessee; monitoring investigations into the Tennessee land frauds; and increasing the state's overall military preparedness. Indeed, he himself was appointed a brigadier general in the army being prepared nationally to repel an anticipated French invasion.

Davie left the governorship to accept President John Adams's appointment as one of three peace envoys to France. During the following year, the trio of prominent Federalists negotiated a final settlement, thus bringing to an end the undeclared war that had subsisted between the two countries since the XYZ affair. When Davie returned to North Carolina, the political landscape had changed. Thomas Jefferson was president, and the Republican Party was in the ascendancy. In 1803, in the last of his many campaigns, he was unsuccessful in his bid for a seat in Congress.

Disillusioned and enervated, he withdrew to Trivoli, his Lancaster County, South Carolina, plantation. There he immersed himself in the life of a country squire, tending crops, raising horses, and enjoying the company of books and friends. He died on November 5, 1820, and was buried in the Waxhaw Presbyterian Church cemetery.

REFERENCES: *DAB*, vol. 5; *DNCB*, vol. 2; Robinson, *William R. Davie*; Sobel and Raimo, *Bio. Dir. of Governors*, vol. 3. PRIMARY SOURCES: Davie Papers, NCSA; Davie Papers, SHC.

## ARTHUR DOBBS
### 1754-1765

*A*rthur Dobbs (1689-1765) arrived at his post as royal governor with the colonies on the brink of war and brought with him the instructions, money, and supplies to get North Carolina involved in any conflict. He was born on April 2, 1689, in Ayrshire, Scotland, to Richard Dobbs and the former Mary Stewart. Only in Scotland temporarily, the family owned an estate near Carrickfergus, County Antrim, Ireland. At twenty-four, having served two years in the British army, young Dobbs returned to Ireland to oversee the estate. Dobbs married Anne Osburn Norbury in 1719, with whom he had three children, including Edward Brice who would accompany him to North Carolina. In 1762, he married fifteen-year-old Justina Davis, meeting with much ridicule.

Dobbs quickly rose to prominence, serving as high sheriff of the county, mayor of Carrickfergus, a member of the Irish Parliament, and in 1733, the engineer and surveyor general of Ireland. Dobbs showed early interest in the colonies, believing that proper development and increased trade would help to support British and Protestant domination. More than philosophically interested in the colonies, the scientific-minded Dobbs was active in attempts to locate a northwest passage and then later was involved in colonial land speculation. By the 1750s, he was responsible for about five hundred Protestant Northern Irish families immigrating to North Carolina.

He showed interest in a colonial governorship, expressing ideas for cultivating industry and advancing the British Empire. He was named governor of North Carolina in 1753 and arrived on its soil the following year, a vigorous sixty-six. Before reporting for duty, Dobbs met in Williamsburg with the governors of Virginia and Maryland about uniting forces against the French. He was warned about the weak and poorly equipped colonial militia, but brought money, arms, and the determination to alter their circumstances.

Dobbs was initially successful as governor, promoting unity, industry, military strength, and loyalty to the Crown and the Anglican Church. Always trying to avoid the conflict between northern and southern factions, he attempted to establish the capital near centrally located Kingston (present-day Kinston). Although the assembly appropriated money to purchase the land for that purpose from Dobbs, at cost, the British government disallowed the plan. He finally settled on moving to Brunswick in 1758, where he built a home and encouraged the building of St. Philip's Church.

The following year brought turmoil in the colony, because of the financial burdens of the French and Indian War and continued discord over the Granville Land District. Lord Granville was the only one of the original Lords Proprietors who refused to withdraw his claim to one-eighth of both Carolinas. The Granville Land District covered the northern half of North Carolina, and while not governed by the Earl Granville, the lands were granted by him and quitrents were due to him. Dobbs grew heavy-handed with the assembly of 1759 and dissolved the assembly of 1760 after they attempted to pass legislation creating paper currency for paying war debts. Losing popularity, Dobbs rekindled the north-south factionalism and sided with the southern politicians, who supported legislation for internal improvements.

After ten years' service, Dobbs received a desired leave of absence in 1764, but died on March 28, 1765, shortly before his scheduled departure for Ireland. He died in the arms of his wife Justina, whom he had wed in 1762. Dobbs was buried at St. Philip's Church in Brunswick, but no Anglican minister was in the province to lead the service.

REFERENCES: *ANB*, vol. 6; Clarke, *Arthur Dobbs*, *DNCB*, vol. 2; Robinson, *Five Royal Governors*.

# WILLIAM DRUMMOND
## 1665-1667

*W*illiam Drummond (ca. 1620-1677), first governor of Albemarle County, was given the responsibility by the Lords Proprietors to establish a government. He proved to be a capable leader whose efforts laid the foundation for representative government in North Carolina. Born and educated in Scotland, Drummond settled in Virginia as an indentured servant to Theodore Moye in 1637 and later to Stephen Webb in 1639. He was not a docile servant and he became involved in a plan with other indentured servants to run away; however, the plan was a failure. For his role, Drummond received a public flogging and an extension of his servitude by a year.

Drummond greatly improved his position in Virginia society by the 1650s. He became a large landholder, a prosperous attorney, and evidently a merchant. He also served as a justice of the peace and the high sheriff of James City County. In the early 1650s, Drummond married Sarah Prescott; they had at least five children. The Lords Proprietors commissioned Drummond as the first governor of Albemarle County in December 1664. Proprietor and Virginia governor William Berkeley apparently was influential in securing the position for Drummond because of their friendship.

The Lords Proprietors furnished Drummond with instructions to create a government composed of a council and an assembly that had authority over 1,600 square miles. Drummond wasted little time in establishing a functioning government. The first assembly convened by June 1665. Among its first actions was the issuance of a petition to the Lords Proprietors requesting a liberalization of the land policies.

The first governor of Albemarle County provided competent leadership for the developing colony. Drummond proposed new land policies to the Lords Proprietors because he felt the existing policies discouraged new settlers and forced current ones to leave. The proprietors, however, did not act upon his proposal. Drummond worked to settle the boundary problem between Albemarle and Virginia. Following attacks by Tuscarora Indians on Chowan River settlements in 1666, Drummond mobilized the colony for possible war. The troubles were settled before the fighting spread. He negotiated an intercolonial agreement with Virginia and Maryland to stop the planting of tobacco from February 1667 to February 1668. The hope was, that by stopping the planting of tobacco for a year, prices for the commodity would rise. However, Maryland pulled out of the plan causing it to fail. During his governorship, Drummond's friendship with Berkeley deteriorated. He openly accused Berkeley of trying to hurt the development of Carolina. The animosity between the two apparently started over a dispute regarding land leases in Virginia.

Drummond's term as governor ended in 1667. He returned to his Virginia plantation and remained active in business affairs. In 1676 Drummond joined with Nathaniel Bacon in the rebellion against the government of Governor Berkeley.

After the defeat of Bacon's followers, Berkeley's army captured Drummond on January 14, 1677. Six days later, he appeared before a court martial board charged with treason and rebellion against the king. Drummond was found guilty and was hanged that same day.

REFERENCES: Butler, "The Governors of Albemarle County"; *DNCB*, vol. 2; Parker et al., *Colonial Records*, vol. 2; Paschal dissertation, "Proprietary N.C."; Raimo, *Bio. Dir. of Col. and Rev. Governors*; Saunders, *Colonial Records of N.C.*, vol. 1; Wilcomb, "The Humble Petition of Sarah Drummond."

# EDWARD BISHOP DUDLEY
## 1836-1841

$E$dward Bishop Dudley (1789-1855) was the first governor of North Carolina elected by the vote of the people. He was born on December 15, 1789, a few miles north of Jacksonville in Onslow County.

His parents were Margaret and Christopher Dudley, a planter, merchant, and shipbuilder. By whatever method, young Edward received an education sufficient for a successful career in politics and business. In 1815, he married Elizabeth Haywood of the prominent Raleigh family; six children were born of the union. After Elizabeth's death, Dudley married Jane Cowan, widow of Gen. James Cowan.

In 1811 Dudley was elected to the first of two terms in the state House, and in 1814 he returned as a state senator. During the War of 1812, he served as colonel of the Onslow militia that was sent to protect Wilmington against a threatened invasion. Shortly after the war Dudley moved to Wilmington and quickly rose to political prominence. He was elected as a borough representative to the legislature in 1816, 1817, and again in 1834 and 1835. Since one political party dominated North Carolina politics between 1815 and 1832, Dudley was designated a Republican, but he disagreed with national leadership. Elected to fill the seat in Congress vacated by the death of Gabriel Holmes in 1829, he found his views incompatible with those of President Andrew Jackson and his followers. Dismayed by the tactics of the president and the compromising nature of the Congress, Dudley refused to run for a second term.

Dudley's return home coincided with a ground swell in the movement to awaken North Carolina from its "Rip Van Winkle" slumber. He assumed a pivotal role in the formation of the Whig Party, which challenged the Democratic leadership by supporting constitutional reform, stronger banks, railroad construction and other internal improvements, and education. In 1836 he hosted in his Wilmington home the committee that organized the Wilmington and Raleigh Railroad.

By 1835, the growing schism between residents of the western counties, who wanted fundamental changes in the nature and structure of state government, and those of the eastern counties, who wished to retain the status quo, had reached a critical point. A constitutional convention was called to work out the differences. The most notable change allowed the governor to be elected by popular vote, and the direct beneficiary was Edward Bishop Dudley. With the revival of the two-party system, Dudley became the choice of the Whigs in 1836 and defeated Richard Dobbs Spaight Jr. Two years later, he increased his margin of victory, defeating John Branch.

Dudley's administration initiated a period of progress. Perhaps most significant were internal improvements, with the completion of the Wilmington and Raleigh and the Raleigh and Gaston Railroads, and education, with the beginnings of the public school system and the openings of three colleges: Davidson, Greensboro Female, and Union Institute (later Trinity College, then Duke University). After his tenure as governor, Dudley returned to his position as president of the Wilmington and Raleigh Railroad. He retired to his home on the Cape Fear River, where he died on October 30, 1855.

He was buried in Oakdale Cemetery in Wilmington.

REFERENCES: *BDC*; Brown, *Onslow Co. History*; *DAB*, vol. 5; *DNCB*, vol. 2. PRIMARY SOURCES: Dudley Papers, NCSA.

## MICHAEL FRANCIS EASLEY
## 2001-

The first chief executive inaugurated in the twenty-first century was Michael Francis Easley (1950- ). Under his leadership, North Carolina transitioned its agricultural and manufacturing economy to one based on innovation and skill. Following the recession of 2000, Easley restored fiscal discipline to the state's finances by cutting state spending by over $1 billion while still increasing investments in education and infrastructure. Easley's goal as governor was to build "One North Carolina," where every citizen in every corner of every county had access to the educational opportunities they needed for success in the new economy.

Born on March 23, 1950, in Rocky Mount to Henry Alexander Easley Jr. and Huldah Marie Easley, Mike Easley was raised on a sixty-acre tobacco farm in Nash County. A Roman Catholic in an overwhelmingly Protestant region and state, Easley, the second of seven children, began his education in a parochial school before transferring to public schools in the ninth grade. He graduated from Rocky Mount Senior High School in 1968. For two years, he studied at Belmont Abbey College before transferring to UNC at Chapel Hill, where he graduated in 1972 with honors. He went on to attend the North Carolina Central University School of Law where he served as managing editor of the law review and graduated with honors.

After law school, Easley secured a post as an assistant prosecutor in the Thirteenth Judicial District for Brunswick, Columbus, and Bladen Counties. While working as an assistant prosecutor, Easley met Mary Pipines, an assistant prosecutor in neighboring New Hanover County. Easley and Pipines married in 1980, and, in 1985, they had one child, Michael Jr.

In 1982, Easley was elected district attorney for the Thirteenth Judicial District. In the late 1980s, *USA Today* named him among the nation's top "drug busters."

In 1992, North Carolina voters elected Easley to the first of two four-year terms as attorney general. As attorney general, he was a strong consumer advocate who targeted fraudulent telemarketers and unscrupulous lenders. Easley established a Citizens' Rights Division to combat hate crimes, child abuse, and elder abuse. He also worked to remove the state's prison cap to keep violent felons behind bars.

Negotiating with other attorneys general, Easley helped craft a settlement with the tobacco industry worth $206 billion over the course of twenty-five years. As a part of North Carolina's settlement, Easley created the Golden LEAF Foundation, which received one-half of the $5 billion coming to North Carolina from the national agreement. The Foundation is helping North Carolina make the transition from a tobacco-dependent economy.

Easley was elected governor in 2000. At his inauguration in January 2001, the new governor emphasized shared values and spoke of "one State, one people, one family, bound by a common concern for each other." In the weeks that followed, he instituted cuts and freezes to cope with a $2.5 billion state budget shortfall inherited from the previous administration. The governor closed numerous tax loopholes and called for a temporary half-cent sales tax increase to provide resources needed to fund education, including reducing class size and establishing a statewide academic pre-K program, "More at Four." Easley also launched an effort to reform the state's high schools and developed "Learn and Earn" early college high schools to give students across the state an opportunity to build their skills for the new global economy.

During his administration, Easley earned North Carolina a space in the top five in the country for net job growth, a number-one ranking for business expansions and locations, and a place among the top four states in the country for fiscal management. Easley implemented N.C. Senior Care, the state's first prescription drug assistance program for the elderly. He also negotiated the Clean Smokestacks bill that cut the state's coal-fired power plant emissions of multiple air pollutants that cause smog, haze, and health problems. The legislation won national awards and served as a national model for laws to protect clean air.

During this term, Easley also became the first governor in state history to issue a veto after voters approved the measure in a 1996 referendum. In November 2002, he vetoed Senate Bill 1283, which would have made dozens of unqualified appointments to boards and commissions and expanded the number of boards during a time of fiscal crisis. He has used his veto power five times since 2002, striking down legislation that would have taken authority away from the State Board of Education, increased fees from finance companies, charged local governments for removing billboards, illegally conveyed state property, and lowered teacher standards.

Easley sought and won a second term in 2004, setting a record for the most votes of any statewide elected candidate. In his second inaugural address in January 2005, Easley committed the state to a course where knowledge, talent, and skill would allow North Carolinians to compete

During Gov. Michael F. Easley's first term, North Carolina had to contend with several natural disasters. Here, the governor tours areas damaged by Tropical Depression Frances by helicopter on September 9, 2004. Photo courtesy of the Office of the Governor.

in a changing economy. "Opportunity must be afforded to all and responsibility required of all," he said. As the country was still under the shadow of war, Easley also took the opportunity to address patriotism in the state. "The fight for the protection of American values is not only the duty of the military," he said. "It is the patriotic duty of all of us."

In August 2005, Easley, a long-time advocate for a dedicated source of education funding, signed legislation to create the North Carolina Education Lottery. The more than $400 million in annual funds generated by the new lottery will be used for school construction for low-wealth schools, college scholarships for disadvantaged students, reduced class size, and the "More at Four" pre-K education program.

During his two terms in office, Easley successfully led North Carolina through its transition to become a major competitor in the new global economy. By investing in education, work force development, and infrastructure, Easley provided the tools needed to attract successful new industry and to grow existing businesses. These tools will help secure a strong, healthy economy for North Carolina years into the future.

REFERENCES: *Charlotte Observer*, October 29, 2000; *Greensboro News and Record*, October 15, 2000; *News and Observer*, April 14, 2001; *North Carolina Manual, 1997-1998* (1997); www.governor.state.nc.us.

◇ ◇ ◇

# THOMAS EASTCHURCH
## 1675-1676

*T*homas Eastchurch (d. ca. 1678) became Albemarle's governor with cunning and the aid of the proprietary faction. Little is known about his family background; however, the Lords Proprietors described Eastchurch "to be a gentleman of a very good family." By October 1669 Eastchurch was serving as surveyor general of Albemarle County. This was not the position coveted by Eastchurch. He wanted to be governor of Albemarle. Before his death in 1673, Lord High Treasurer Thomas Clifford, a relative of Eastchurch, recommended him to the Lords Proprietors for the governorship. Several proprietors promised the position to Eastchurch, but he did not obtain the post until he forcibly took power from Gov. John Jenkins.

In the fall of 1675 the proprietary faction won control of the assembly. Elected Speaker, Eastchurch had Jenkins, a leader in the anti-proprietary faction, arrested and imprisoned for what were "severall misdemeanors." Eastchurch assumed the chief executive powers, but maintained the title of Speaker. By spring 1676, Jenkins had escaped from prison with the aid of his supporters and reestablished himself as governor. Albemarle evidently functioned briefly with two chief executives. Eastchurch departed for London to appeal to the Lords Proprietors.

Eastchurch met with the Lords Proprietors in the fall of 1676. The proprietors viewed Eastchurch as a leader concerned about the "prosperity and wellfaire" of Albemarle. He convinced the proprietors that Albemarle's problems were the fault of the anti-proprietary faction. The proprietors commissioned Eastchurch as governor of Albemarle and "of all settlements as shall be made upon the rivers of the Pamplico and Newse." By adding the Pamlico and Neuse regions to Eastchurch's commission, the proprietors sanctioned the establish-ment of settlements to the south of Albemarle.

Eastchurch departed for Albemarle in the summer of 1677. During a stopover in the West Indies, Eastchurch met and married a wealthy woman (her name is not known). Deciding to extend his honeymoon, Eastchurch appointed his traveling companion and fellow proprietary

appointed official, Thomas Miller, as acting governor. Miller, a supporter of Eastchurch, arrived in Albemarle in July 1677 and claimed the governorship. By December of that year, Miller's misdeeds led to a revolt (Culpeper's Rebellion) by the colonists. The revolt led to Miller's imprisonment and subsequent trial.

Eastchurch arrived in Virginia in December 1677, but he did not proceed immediately to Albemarle because of the rebellion. He issued a proclamation calling for the disarming of the colonists, for the release of prisoners, for the restoration of Miller's government, and for the appointment of a delegation to visit Virginia to explain the causes of the revolt. The proclamation was ignored, but it did stop Miller's trial. The anti-proprietary leaders sent an armed force to northern Albemarle County to keep Eastchurch out of the colony. Eastchurch tried to gather a force in Virginia to invade Albemarle. He called on Virginia governor William Berkeley for troops, yet his plan never materialized. Eastchurch developed a fever and died in Virginia in early 1678.

REFERENCES: Booth, *Seeds of Anger*; Butler, "The Governors of Albemarle County"; *DNCB*, vol. 2; Parker, "Legal Aspects of Culpeper's Rebellion"; Parker et al., *Colonial Records*, vol. 2; Parramore, "The Tuscarora Ascendancy"; Paschal dissertation, "Proprietary N.C."; Powell, *Ye Countie of Albemarle*; Sainsbury, Fortescue, and Headlam, *Calendar of State Papers, Colonial Series*; Saunders, *Colonial Records of N.C.*, vol. 1; Smith thesis, "Culpeper's Rebellion."

## CHARLES EDEN
## 1714-1722

Charles Eden (1673-1722) was governor of North Carolina during a period of progressive change. Although there are but a few surviving records generated by Eden personally, most of those correspondence with the Society for the Propagation of the Gospel, he is generally credited with the improvements made during his administration. Eden's early life is even more of a mystery than his colonial career. There are no records of his activities, public or private, prior to his appointment in 1713 to become the next governor of North Carolina. Since the surviving part of his tombstone bears a portion of what was the Eden of Durham family crest, it can be assumed that he was from this notable family of County Durham, England.

An assembly that Eden called in 1715 passed far-reaching governmental reforms. The contemporary legal code was revised to include new laws intended to target behaviors that led to the widespread disturbances that occurred during previous administrations. Perhaps with the idea of enhancing trade, immigration, and communication, several transportation issues were addressed, including plans to improve roads, build new roads, and establish shipping channels. It was at that time that the Church of England was officially established in North Carolina, as well. Though a vestryman and devout Anglican, Eden was tolerant of religious diversity in the colony, and the laws reflected that. The governor sent troops to South Carolina in 1715 to fight alongside those colonists in their war with the Yemassee Indians. South Carolinians had been of military assistance during North Carolina's war with the Tuscarora.

Although extant records fail to fully document the relationship, Charles Eden is probably best remembered for his alleged association with the pirate Edward Teach, or Blackbeard. The primary document used to substantiate the link is a letter from Tobias Knight, Secretary of the Province, which was found among Teach's papers after his death. The letter indicates that Knight is expecting a visit from Eden shortly and that the governor would surely be "glad to see" Teach. While the statement is interesting, it is also both vague and conjecture. It seems that a great deal of what has been accepted as fact about Teach, his piracy, and his personal life has been drawn from ambiguous references and fictionalized sources.

Charles Eden married Penelope Golland, a widow with two children. He never had children of his own. In 1718 the Lords Proprietors made Eden a landgrave, the highest rank in the Carolina nobility, although it is unclear whether he ever took advantage of the land to which a landgrave was entitled. His was the last such appointment in the colony. Eden died at his beloved plantation, Eden House, on March 26, 1722, and was buried there. Shortly afterwards, the town nearest his home, known as "the Town on Queen Anne's Creek," was renamed Edenton in his honor. Charles and Penelope Eden's remains and gravestones were moved to St. Paul's Churchyard in Edenton in 1889.

REFERENCES: *ANB*, vol. 7; *DNCB*, vol. 2; Parker et al., *Colonial Records*, vol. 10; Rogozinski, *Pirates!*; Saunders, *Colonial Records of N.C.*, vol. 2; SS Records.

## JOHN CHRISTOPH BLUCHER EHRINGHAUS
### 1933-1937

*A* fiscal conservative, John Christoph Blucher Ehringhaus (1882-1949) balanced the state's budget during the worst economic crisis since Reconstruction, while offering nominal if unenthusiastic support for the initiatives of the New Deal. The "Depression Governor" was born in Elizabeth City on February 5, 1882. Proud of the Albemarle region's history and of his own German ancestry, Blucher Ehringhaus, as he was known, was the son of merchant Erskine Ehringhaus and the former Catherine Matthews. Educated in local schools, he was graduated from Atlantic Collegiate Institute in 1898 and from UNC in 1901. Two years later, Ehringhaus received his law degree in Chapel Hill and returned to his hometown to practice. In 1912 he married Matilda Haughton of Washington County; they would have three children.

From Pasquotank County in 1905, at age twenty-three, J. C. B. Ehringhaus was elected to the state house for the first of two consecutive terms. In the legislature, where he was the youngest member, he cosponsored the bill to establish East Carolina Teachers Training School (today East Carolina University) and supported a statewide system of high schools. In 1910 Ehringhaus was elected solicitor of the First Judicial District, a post he would hold for twelve years. In 1928 the Elizabeth City attorney canvassed the state on behalf of the Democratic ticket, Al Smith for president and O. Max Gardner for governor. Four years later Gardner backed Ehringhaus over his opponents in the Democratic primary, Lt. Gov. Richard T. Fountain and Revenue Commissioner Allen J. Maxwell. In his campaign in 1932 Ehringhaus called for a "program of progress" and for a balanced budget, goals that meshed with Gardner's policies. In the fall Ehringhaus easily

Gov. J. C. B. Ehringhaus sitting in the lobby of the Sir Walter Hotel in Raleigh listening to the radio in 1936.

defeated Republican Clifford C. Frazier. Ehringhaus balanced the budget through retrenchment, consolidation, and the introduction of a 3 percent sales tax on all items except food staples. That tax, tied to state assumption of school costs and reduction in local property taxes, ran counter to a campaign promise but, with the governor's backing, passed the 1933 legislature. The school year was extended from six to eight months. Ehringhaus cut the cost of state government by almost one-third through a reduction in employee salaries and drastic curtailment of spending, including a halt to all new highway construction for the 1933-1934 biennium. He endorsed penal reform and rural electrification and encouraged the consolidation of state offices, such as the highway and prison departments, and local governments.

In September 1933 Ehringhaus closed the tobacco markets in North Carolina and traveled to Washington, D.C., to lobby officials of the Agricultural Adjustment Administration for higher prices for the commodity. The move earned plaudits from Tar Heel farmers. Those same tobacco growers were unforgiving two years later when the governor refused to issue a call for a special session of the legislature to debate the proposed compact of tobacco-growing states. Ehringhaus appeared before a rally of six thousand farmers at Riddick Stadium in Raleigh on April 21, 1935, and, in a heated ninety-minute speech, held to his position that the compact would not benefit the state.

Ehringhaus offered his rhetorical support to President Franklin D. Roosevelt's New Deal programs but followed his own cautious path. He declined to provide state matching funds to the Emergency Relief Administration and delayed implementation of provisions of the Social Security Act, passed in 1935, until 1937. His popularity sank after 1935, and, in the speech at Riddick Stadium, he declared that he had had "a bellyfull of public office." He declined to run for the U.S. Senate and returned to the practice of law in Raleigh. An Episcopalian, Ehringhaus died on July 31, 1949, and was buried in Elizabeth City.

REFERENCES: Abrams, *Conservative Constraints*; Badger, *Prosperity Road*; Corbitt, *Ehringhaus Papers*; *DNCB*, vol. 2; *News and Observer*, April 22, 1936, and August 1, 1949; Puryear, *Democratic Party Dissension*; Sobel and Raimo, *Bio. Dir. of Governors*, vol. 3. PRIMARY SOURCES: Ehringhaus Papers, NCSA.

## JOHN WILLIS ELLIS
## 1859-1861

John Willis Ellis (1820-1861) led North Carolina out of the Union and into the Confederacy. The son of Anderson and Judith Bailey Ellis, he was born on November 23, 1820, in eastern Rowan County (later Davidson County). He attended Randolph Macon College for one year before entering UNC from which he graduated in 1841. Ellis then studied law under Judge Richmond M. Pearson and set up his practice in Salisbury in 1842. He was twice married, first to Mary White, who died only two months after their 1844 marriage. On August 11, 1858, six days after his election as governor, Ellis married Mary McKinley Daves, daughter of John Daves of New Bern. They had two daughters.

A Democrat, Ellis was elected a member of the House of Commons in 1844. In 1848, Dorothea L. Dix selected Ellis as liaison to champion her call for the establishment of an insane asylum. Ellis was twenty-eight when the General Assembly elected him a judge of the superior court, an office he held until 1858 when he won his party's nomination for governor. Ellis handily defeated his opponent, Duncan K. McRae.

As governor, Ellis pushed for faster movement of railroad freights, better plank roads and turnpikes, improvements in education, and completion of delayed river navigation projects. Hanging over his accomplishments, however, was the growing cloud of secession and sectional crisis. Running for reelection in 1860, Ellis denounced the abolitionists but steered clear of advocating dissolution of the Union. He used the constitutional question and southern rights to overshadow the issue of ad valorem taxation, which was the trump card of his Whig opponent, John Pool. Even so, Ellis won by a much smaller margin than he had two years earlier.

On November 20, 1860, Ellis outlined a three-part strategy: participation in a conference of southern states to discuss the situation in the country, a state convention of the people to establish North Carolina's position, and reorganization of the militia including creation of a corps of volunteers. In his inaugural address on January 1, 1861, he continued to urge moderation, but a group from the Wilmington area decided to seize Forts Caswell and Johnston despite the governor's objection. He immediately ordered them to return control to the Union.

By early March deteriorating relationships had convinced Ellis that the state soon would have no choice but to join the Confederacy. When President Lincoln called for troops in April to put down the insurrection, the governor placed the state's sympathies with the South. After answering the president, "You shall get no troops from North Carolina," Ellis ordered state troops to seize all Federal forts and the Fayetteville arsenal, closing with a telegram to Confederate president Jefferson Davis, indicating that the state would support the Confederacy fully. All that was left was to make secession official at the May 20 convention.

Years of riding the circuit as a judge had weakened John Ellis's health. Battling consumption, he tried to govern from a sick bed, relying upon a committee to help in decision making. He forced himself to make public appearances to maintain the morale of the people but finally gave in and, in a futile effort at recovery, journeyed to Red Sulphur Springs, Virginia. He died there on July 7, 1861, at age forty-one. Governor Ellis's first burial took place in the family cemetery in Davidson County, but his remains later were removed to the Old English Cemetery in Salisbury.

REFERENCES: Brawley, *Rowan Co. History*; *Cyclopedia of Eminent and Representative Men*, vol. 2; *DNCB*, vol. 2; Haywood, *Builders of the Old North State*; Tolbert, *Ellis Papers*, vols. 1 and 2. PRIMARY SOURCES: Ellis Papers, SHC.

## SIR RICHARD EVERARD
## 1725-1731

Sir Richard Everard (1683-1733) served as the last governor of North Carolina under the proprietary government. Born at Langleys, in what is now Great Waltham, to Sir Hugh Everard and the former Mary Browne, young Everard assumed the baronetcy at his father's death in 1706. He then resigned his commission in Queen Anne's army and sold the family property at Langleys in order to pay debts, later purchasing property at Broomfield Green. On June 13, 1706, Everard married Susannah Kidder, daughter of the Right Reverend Richard Kidder, who was the bishop of Bath and Wells. Together they produced four children, Richard, Hugh, Susannah, and Anne.

Chief Justice Christopher Gale personally delivered the North Carolina council's complaints about Gov. George Burrington to the Lords Proprietors, and in January 1725, Burrington was dismissed. A letter from Everard, seeking appointment as Burrington's successor, was then read to the proprietors and approved. Everard took the oath of office in Edenton on July 17, 1725, at which time Burrington learned of his dismissal. Although he was undoubtedly aware that the proprietors were inclined to transfer North Carolina back to the royal government, Everard diligently followed his instructions and suspended the granting of lands. The move was unpopular, especially among those pursuing the settlement of the Cape Fear region. Because of his actions, Everard lost supporters, many of whom returned their favor to Burrington who had disregarded the proprietors' policies on land grants.

By 1728 it was evident that Burrington likely would be restored to the governorship after the transfer to the king, and Everard resumed granting lands, collecting the fees associated with the grants. In an effort to increase the incoming fees, Everard signed countless "blank patents," duly signed grants on which the location of the land and acreage were left to be filled in by the purchaser. Many of the grants were never recorded, allowing the "owners" to avoid payment of quitrents. Modern estimates are that as many as 400,000 acres of prime Cape Fear area land were transferred by means of the questionable documents. As expected, Burrington was appointed as the first royal governor of North Carolina effective January 1730. However, Everard remained in North Carolina as governor until Burrington's arrival in February of the following year. Following his replacement's installation, Everard and his family returned to England.

Sir Richard Everard died at his home in London on February 17, 1733, and was buried in Great Waltham. Both of his sons, Richard and Hugh, died without issue, and the baronetcy became extinct. Only his daughter Susannah remained in the colonies, having married David Meade of Virginia. After the death of her husband, she lived in Halifax.

REFERENCES: *DNCB*, vol. 2; Ekirch, *"Poor Carolina"*; Paschal dissertation, "Proprietary N.C."; Sainsbury, Fortescue, and Headlam, *Calendar of State Papers, Colonial Series*, vols. 34-39; Saunders, *Colonial Records of N.C.*, vols. 2 and 3. PRIMARY SOURCES: Moore Papers, NCSA.

# DANIEL GOULD FOWLE
## 1889-1891

*T*he first governor to occupy the new Executive Mansion, Daniel Gould Fowle (1831-1891) died just over two years into his term of office. The fourth child of Samuel Richardson and Martha Marsh Fowle, he was born in the Beaufort County town of Washington. Young Daniel, who loved the outdoors, attended Washington Academy until the age of fourteen and then traveled to Orange County to study at the Bingham School. After graduation from Princeton in 1851, Fowle entered the law school of Judge Richmond M.

Pearson. In 1854 he established a law practice in Raleigh. On April 15, 1856, Fowle married Ellen Brent Pearson, daughter of Judge Pearson. She died in 1862, leaving him two daughters. Fowle remarried in 1867; with his new bride, the former Mary E. Haywood of Raleigh, he had four more children. She did not live long enough to move into the mansion.

Fowle strongly opposed secession as the sectional crisis deepened, yielding only when it became an accomplished fact. Volunteering initially for the "Raleigh Rifles," Fowle served as an officer in several regiments before being captured at Roanoke Island in February 1862. He was paroled on the condition that he not engage in further hostilities against the United States government.

In October 1862 Wake County voters elected Democrat Fowle to the state house. Gov. Zebulon B. Vance appointed him state adjutant general with the rank of major general on March 14, 1863, but he resigned that post four months later. He won election to a second term in the legislature in 1864, and three months after the completion of the session in 1865, provisional governor William W. Holden appointed him judge of the superior court. The General Assembly that convened in the fall of 1865 elected Fowle to the permanent position of superior court judge; he resigned in December 1867 rather than rubber stamp decisions of the military commander during Reconstruction.

Fowle returned to his law practice and in 1880 lost to Thomas Jarvis in his bid for the governorship; in 1884 he lost a race for a seat in Congress.

A split in the Democratic Party over favoritism to business and industry gave him an opportunity at the governor's seat in 1888. Supported by the "Liberal Democrats," he was elected on a platform that promised regulation of the railroad industry. Heavy rain forced his inauguration indoors, and on January 17, 1889, Daniel G. Fowle took the oath of office in Stronach's Warehouse a short distance from the Capitol.

Fowle's tenure as governor suffered a temporary setback when the 1889 General Assembly reversed promises of railroad reform by refusing to pass the railroad commission bill. Fowle found himself in the middle of a power struggle between industry interests that wanted protection from unfavorable legislation and a growing populist movement that demanded changes in the system. He could do little but try to smooth ruffled feathers. The "farmers" legislature of 1891 did establish a railroad commission over which the governor was to preside, but Fowle did not live to exercise his influence.

In educational endeavors, Fowle was more successful. He recommended a tax levy in counties unable to sustain the public schools for the required four months and proposed a state university for women. The legislature chartered the State Normal and Industrial School for Women (present UNC at Greensboro) in February 1891.

Daniel G. Fowle achieved another distinction as governor when he moved into the as yet unfinished Executive Mansion in January 1891. His oldest daughter, Helen, assumed the role of hostess. Fowle enjoyed the new residence three months before his death on April 8, 1891. He was buried in Oakwood Cemetery a few blocks northeast of the governor's house.

REFERENCES: Bushong, *N.C.'s Executive Mansion*; *Cyclopedia of Eminent and Representative Men*, vol. 2; *DNCB*, vol. 2; Dowd, *Sketches*. PRIMARY SOURCES: Fowle Papers, NCSA.

◇ ◇ ◇

# JESSE FRANKLIN
## 1820-1821

*J*esse Franklin (1760-1823) of Surry County, veteran of the Revolution, came to the governor's office at the age of sixty; his most noteworthy achievement during his term was reform of the penal code. Born in Orange County, Virginia, on March 24, 1760, he was the son of Bernard and Mary Cleveland Franklin. Soon after the outbreak of the American Revolution, the family removed to Surry County. Young Franklin enlisted in the regiment of his maternal uncle, Col. Benjamin Cleveland, and fought in the crucial battles of King's Mountain and Guilford Courthouse. By war's end he had risen to the rank of major. Franklin's wife was the former Meeky Perkins of Rockbridge County, Virginia. Together they had three sons and five daughters.

Following the Revolution, Franklin settled in Wilkes County, which he represented in the House of Commons from 1784 to 1787 and from 1790 to 1792. In December of 1789 he was appointed to the Council of State under Gov. Alexander Martin. After returning to Surry County in 1792, Franklin represented that county in the House of Commons in 1793-1795 and 1797-1798, with a single term in the U.S. House of Representatives during the intervening period.

In 1798 Franklin returned to Congress as a senator, having been chosen by the General Assembly over former and future governors, Alexander Martin and Benjamin Smith. Following a brief return to the state legislature as a senator from Surry in 1805, he was again sent to the U.S. Senate, where he served from 1806 to 1813. Concurrently, his younger brother Meshack sat in the House of Representatives. In 1814 and 1815 Franklin was defeated in his Senate bids by Francis Locke and Nathaniel Macon respectively. In 1816 he was one of three men chosen to negotiate settlements with the Cherokee and Chickasaw Indians, his fellow commissioners being David Meriwether and Andrew Jackson, hero of the War of 1812 and future U.S. president.

On the state level, Franklin continued to represent Surry County in the upper house of the General Assembly, and for four successive terms he again served on the Council of State, under governors William Miller and John Branch. On December 5, 1820, he was elected governor. By that time Franklin was sixty years old, overweight, and in declining health. Despite these factors, however, he carried out his duties conscientiously and with his characteristic simplicity and practicality. Although a fiscal conservative and an advocate of limited government, Franklin contributed at least modestly to the nascent reform movement led by Archibald D. Murphey. His most notable contributions came in connection with the state's penal code, which under his urgings was rendered less severe and punitive. He also advocated reform of the state militia and settlement of remaining border disputes with neighboring states. He returned to Surry County at the end of his first term, declining to stand for reelection. Franklin died at his Surry County home August 31, 1823, following a long illness. In 1906 his body was moved to the Guilford Courthouse National Military Park near Greensboro.

REFERENCES: *DAB*, vol. 6; *DNCB*, vol. 2; Sobel and Raimo, *Bio. Dir. of Governors*, vol. 3. PRIMARY SOURCES: Jesse Franklin Indian Treaty Papers, SHC.

## OLIVER MAXWELL GARDNER
### 1929-1933

*O*. Max Gardner (1882-1947), whose political organization dominated state politics for a generation, took office only months before the stock market crash of 1929 and responded to the economic crisis with retrenchment and centralization of governmental functions. Like his brother-in-law Clyde R. Hoey, part of the "Shelby Dynasty" (a term Gardner disliked), the future governor was born on March 22, 1882, in the Cleveland County town. His father, Oliver Perry Gardner, was a physician, legislator, and Confederate veteran. His mother, the former Margaret Young, died when Max, the youngest of twelve, was ten years old so he was raised by his sisters. In 1900 Max Gardner enrolled at the North Carolina College of Agriculture and Mechanical Arts (present-day North Carolina State University), and in 1906 he studied law at UNC. At both schools he captained the football team. In 1907, the year he returned home to practice law, he married Fay Lamar Webb, daughter of Judge James L. Webb and niece of Congressman E. Yates Webb. O. Max and Fay Gardner had four children.

In 1910 Gardner was elected to the state senate and four years later was returned for a second term, during which he served as president pro tem. In 1916, the year Thomas W. Bickett was elected governor, Gardner was elected lieutenant governor. In 1920 Gardner entered the race to be Bickett's successor. In the first primary Robert N. Page was eliminated, but in the second one, Cameron Morrison, with the backing of the political machine of Sen. Furnifold Simmons, defeated Gardner. The Shelby attorney returned to his law practice and to his farm. With partner O. M. Mull he founded Cleveland Cloth Mill. Gardner remained active in party politics and in 1928 was unopposed for the Democratic nomination. He defeated Republican Herbert F. Seawell handily in the fall.

For eight years, under the administrations of Morrison and McLean, the state had witnessed relative prosperity. The onset of the Depression presented Governor Gardner with unforeseen challenges. In 1930 he authorized a study of state government by the Brookings Institution, which recommended a massive shift of power from county courthouses to Raleigh with the state taking responsibility for all secondary road maintenance and public school costs. Other reforms included

Gov. O. Max Gardner, a graduate of the North Carolina College of Agriculture and Mechanical Arts and Shelby attorney, oversaw the state through the early years of the Depression. Governor Gardner at his desk, January 4, 1930.

reduction of property taxes, limits on local bond issues, and the creation of a central purchasing agency. With the governor's support the legislature approved workmen's compensation, the secret ballot, and abolition of the chain gang system. Gardner counted as his proudest achievement the consolidation of UNC, the College of Agriculture and Mechanical Arts in Raleigh, and the North Carolina College for Women in Greensboro. In each of these efforts his moves were opposed by special interests and required all the governor's leadership abilities. Gardner promoted his "Live-at-Home" program to encourage the planting of crops for subsistence. While deriving favorable attention, the program failed to stimulate the state's economy. During Gardner's term labor strikes took place in Gastonia and Marion leading him to call out the National Guard.

By 1933 Gardner had in place a political organization to rival that of Senator Simmons, who had been defeated in 1930. The next four governors came to office with Gardner's backing. In 1933 Gardner moved his law practice to Washington, D.C. Gardner financially supported Boiling Springs Junior College, which in 1942 changed its name to Gardner-Webb in his honor. During World War II Gardner served on the board of the Office of War Mobilization and Reconversion, and in 1946 he was appointed Undersecretary of the Treasury by President Truman. The following year he was named Ambassador to Great Britain but died on February 6, 1947, only hours before he was to sail for London. A Baptist, he is buried in Shelby's Sunset Cemetery.

REFERENCES: Abrams, *Conservative Constraints*; Albright, "O. Max Gardner";

Bell, *Hard Times*, *DNCB*, vol. 2; Gill and Corbitt, *Gardner Papers*; Morrison, *Governor O. Max Gardner*; *News and Observer*, February 1947; *Proceedings of the Bar Association* (1947); Puryear, *Democratic Party Dissension*; Sobel and Raimo, *Bio. Dir. of Governors*, vol. 3; Weathers, *Cleveland Co. History*. PRIMARY SOURCES: Gardner Papers, SHC.

◇ ◇ ◇

# JOHN GIBBS
## 1689-1690

John Gibbs became chief executive when Gov. Seth Sothel was banished from the Albemarle region. When Philip Ludwell arrived with his governor's commission, Gibbs did not give up the governorship and caused an uprising. Gibbs's birth date and parents are unknown. The Gibbs family from Devonshire, England, was active in colonization. Gibbs was related to Lords Proprietor Christopher Monck. His wife was apparently named Mary; they had a son and a daughter. After being nominated by Monck, Gibbs received the rank of cacique in October 1682, making him a member of the Carolina nobility based upon the Fundamental Constitutions. In 1683 the proprietors authorized officials in the southern colony (now South Carolina) to provide Gibbs with 3,000 acres of rent-free land, but he evidently did nothing with the land.

Prior to becoming governor, Gibbs was residing in Virginia.

With Sothel's banishment in the fall of 1689, Gibbs was the Carolina nobility's highest-ranking member, which entitled him to claim Albemarle's governorship. Gibbs was unable to enjoy the chief executive's office for long because Philip Ludwell arrived in the spring of 1690 with a governor's commission from the proprietors. Ludwell set up his government, but Gibbs was determined not to leave the governorship. On June 2, 1690, Gibbs issued a declaration claiming his right to the governorship based on the Fundamental Constitutions and called on the people to obey him. Gibbs referred to Ludwell as a "rascal, impostor, and usurper" and stated his readiness to fight anyone to keep Ludwell from the governor's office.

On July 6, 1690, Gibbs and about fifteen men entered the Pasquotank Precinct court and broke it up. He forbade the holding of a court without a commission from him. The force seized two magistrates and took them as prisoners to Gibbs's house. Next, Gibbs moved the prisoners to his Virginia plantation protected by a force of around eighty men. Upon news of Gibbs's action, the Albemarle Council sent the militia to stop this rebellion. However, the militia refused to enter Virginia without permission from that colony's government.

Ludwell sought assistance from Virginia's lieutenant governor, Francis Nicholson, in settling the situation. Nicholson secured the release of the prisoners and persuaded Ludwell and

Gibbs to go before the Lords Proprietors. Both men went to England and presented their views before the proprietors who upheld Ludwell's commission. By 1693 the Fundamental Constitutions were suspended removing Gibbs's right to claim the governorship. Yet, Gibbs was still asserting his right to the governorship in 1695. The Lords Proprietors again repudiated Gibbs by writing to Ludwell, "He is not a Governor nor can be, unless his power is derived from us."

It is not known if Gibbs ever returned to Albemarle. He designated attorney Edward Mayo to dispose of his concerns. From 1691 through 1694 Mayo made several appearances in court on Gibbs's behalf. By the late 1690s and early 1700s, Gibbs's deserted land was being redistributed to others. His date of death is unknown.

REFERENCES: *DNCB*, vols. 2 and 4; Parker et al., *Colonial Records*, vols. 2 and 7; Raimo, *Bio. Dir. of Col. and Rev. Governors*; Sainsbury, Fortescue, and Headlam, *Calendar of State Papers, Colonial Series*; Saunders, *Colonial Records of N.C.*, vol. 1.

# ROBERT BRODNAX GLENN
## 1905-1909

While a champion of educational progress and railroad regulation, Gov. Robert Brodnax Glenn (1854-1920) most effectively used the powers of his office to advance the cause of prohibition, approved by voters in 1908. The "Prohibition Governor" was born near Sauratown in Rockingham County on August 11, 1854, to tobacco farmer and attorney Chalmers Glenn and his wife, the former Annie Dodge. The elder Glenn, a captain in the Thirteenth North Carolina Regiment, was killed in fighting at South Mountain, Maryland, in 1862. In 1871 young Glenn enrolled at Davidson College from which he graduated in 1874. For one year he enrolled in a pre-law course at the University of Virginia, but in time followed his father's lead with study in Richmond Pearson's law school in neighboring Yadkin County. Glenn, admitted to the bar in 1877, practiced law initially in Rockingham County but soon moved to Stokes County. In 1878 Glenn married Nina Deaderick of Knoxville, Tennessee; they had two children.

From Stokes County Robert B. Glenn was elected to a single term in the state house in 1880. His political fortunes rose with his selection as a presidential elector for Grover Cleveland in 1884 and 1892. In 1885 Glenn moved his law practice to the larger town of Winston. From 1890 to 1893 he served in the Forsyth Rifles of the State Guard. From 1893 to 1897 Glenn was U.S. attorney for the western district of North Carolina, coinciding with Charles B. Aycock's service in the eastern district. Like Aycock, Glenn, who served a single term in the state senate in 1899-1900, spoke widely on behalf of white supremacy and supported the successful efforts in the legislature to disfranchise black voters.

In 1904 Glenn, campaigning as an "anti-organization" candidate, won the Democratic gubernatorial nomination over Charles M. Stedman, Wilfred Turner, and Theodore Davidson. In the fall he defeated Republican C. J. Harris by a wide margin. As governor Glenn continued

Gov. Robert Glenn (*in top hat*), who served in the Forsyth Rifles of the State Guard from 1890 to 1893, poses in front of the Civil War monument at the National Cemetery.

his predecessor's emphasis on public education by endorsing a minimum school term and compulsory attendance. Unlike Aycock, Glenn opposed the use of taxes paid by whites to educate blacks. He sought increased funding for hospitals, public health, and care of the insane.

Governor Glenn defended the state's right to regulate railway passenger rates. He made the arrangements to repay the state's Reconstruction bonds as ordered by the U.S. Supreme Court. Glenn's skills as an orator were tested by the campaign in 1908 to prohibit the sale or manufacture of liquor. During his legislative term Glenn had been among the leaders of the "drys." As governor he ridiculed the argument by opponents that whiskey helped business, and he worked to identify prohibition in the popular mind with education. In January 1908 the governor was the keynote speaker to the temperance convention in Raleigh. The legislature, at his urging, placed the issue before the voters, and on June 19, 1908, calling it the "proudest day of my life" and the "crowning act of my administration," Glenn signed the proclamation making North Carolina a prohibition state as of January 1, 1909.

After his term in office Glenn returned to the practice of law in Winston-Salem, representing clients such as Western Union and Southern Railway. He was a popular public speaker for the Presbyterian Church and the Lyceum Bureau and carried the fight for prohibition to other states. In 1915 President Woodrow Wilson, whom Glenn had known at Davidson College, appointed him to the International Boundary Commission, charged with negotiating matters between the United States and Canada. On a trip to Winnipeg, Glenn died on May 16, 1920. He is buried in Salem Cemetery in Winston-Salem.

REFERENCES: Chapman thesis, "Robert B. Glenn"; *DNCB*, vol. 2; *News and Observer*, May 1, 1920; Sobel and Raimo, *Bio. Dir. of Governors*, vol. 3; Whitener, *Prohibition in N.C.*

◇ ◇ ◇

## WILLIAM GLOVER
### 1706-1708

William Glover (d. prior to 1712), an attorney, had a long career as a public servant, culminating in his selection as acting deputy governor following the dismissal of Gov. Thomas Cary. Glover's tenure was marked with continuing tensions between Anglicans (supported by Glover) and dissenters (supported by Cary) that eventually led to Cary's Rebellion. Glover's parents and birthplace were never established.

In 1688 he was a resident of Henrico County, Virginia, where he served as a justice. He was evidently married to Mary Davis and possibly had three sons by her. Glover was also the guardian of John Davis of Henrico County, Virginia. By 1707 he was remarried to a woman named Catherine and had a daughter by the marriage.

Glover began his government career as a clerk for the courts, council, secretary, and the Crown. From 1700 to 1712, he participated on the Executive Council as a member or as president. While on the council, Glover had his share of foes not afraid to speak their opinion of him. In 1700, James Cole was accused of offering "sevrall abusive Indignities to the Honorable Wm. Glover Esqr." Six years later, James Norcome received "tenn Lashes on his bare Back" for saying "verry scandelous words and Expressions" against Glover and Christopher Gale. However, Glover's greatest challenge came from Thomas Cary and the uprising that he led.

While Cary was in South Carolina in 1706 and 1707, Glover served as acting governor since he was president of the council. In October of that year, John Porter, who had been sent to England to present grievances to the Lords Proprietors, returned with Cary's suspension and authority to choose new council members and a governor. With Glover still presiding, Porter convened the new councillors and had Glover elected as chief executive. Cary and Glover attempted but failed to resolve their dispute.

Glover, like previous governors, called for an oath of office, which kept Quakers out of public office since their faith did not allow for the swearing of oaths. By the summer of 1708, Porter called a meeting of current and former councillors and declared Glover's election illegal. Porter then decided to support Cary after the former governor changed his position about oaths. The events resulted in two men claiming the governorship, causing turmoil and violence for the colony. One contemporary account called the actions taken by both sides "liker the freaks of Madmen than the actions of men of reason." In October 1708, both sides tried to settle their differences in the assembly following elections that had rival delegates going to the assembly. Unfortunately for Glover, Cary's supporters controlled the assembly and elected him president. Glover went to Virginia claiming that Cary wanted "to take away my life."

Glover served on the council from 1711 to 1712 under Gov. Edward Hyde, who assumed the governorship from Cary. During Hyde's tenure, Cary led an armed uprising against the government, but Glover apparently was not an active participant in the suppression of it. He died sometime prior to October 1712.

REFERENCES: *DNCB*, vol. 2; Lefler and Powell, *Colonial N.C.*; Parker et al., *Colonial Records*, vols. 2, 3, 4, 5, and 7; Saunders, *Colonial Records of N.C.*, vols. 1 and 2; Todd, *Graffenried's Account of the Founding of New Bern*.

## WILLIAM ALEXANDER GRAHAM
### 1845-1849

*I*n addition to serving as governor, U.S. senator, and secretary of the navy, William Alexander Graham (1804-1875) was the Whig nominee for vice-president in 1852. The son of Gen. Joseph and Isabella Davidson Graham, he was born on September 5, 1804, at Vesuvius, the family home in Lincoln County. His father was a Revolutionary War soldier and a pioneer in the region's iron industry. Hillsborough Academy served as the forum for William's college preparation. He enrolled at UNC in 1820 and graduated with honors in 1824. He then studied law with Thomas Ruffin and opened a practice in Hillsborough in 1828. In 1836 he married Susannah Sarah Washington; the union produced ten children.

Attracted to the political arena, Graham endorsed Henry Clay's "American System," the basic platform of the emerging Whig Party. He served in the state House from 1833 to 1840. As Speaker from 1838 to 1840, he helped secure passage of the Public School Act of 1839. He left for the U.S. Senate in 1840 and held that office until March of 1843. Graham won the gubernatorial election of 1844 and took office on January 1, 1845. Three problems confronted him: foreclosure of state-held mortgages on the Raleigh and Gaston Railroad; collection of documents relating to the state's Revolutionary War history, a task imposed by the 1844 legislature; and execution of the earlier law establishing a school for the deaf and mute. Graham pushed the Whig agenda of internal improvements and education. He advocated a central railroad to connect with the existing Raleigh and Gaston and the Charlotte and Columbia then under construction. To help stabilize the fledgling school system, he proposed the appointment of a commissioner of education.

Graham returned to his law practice in Hillsborough in January 1849. He accepted the appointment as secretary of the navy extended by President Millard Fillmore in 1850. Achievements during his tenure included efficient reorganization of the coast survey and naval personnel, exploration of the Amazon, and the opening of foreign relations and trade with Japan. In 1852 the Whig Party nominated William A. Graham for vice-president on the ticket headed by

Gen. Winfield Scott. Defeated in the general election, Graham returned to Orange County where he was elected to the state senate in 1854.

Graham detested the idea of secession, equating it to southern self-destruction. He urged caution, patience, and compromise, earning him consideration as a presidential candidate by the Constitutional Union Party in 1860. In the 1861 State Convention, he tried to divert the issue of secession but acquiesced when no honorable alternative remained. As state senator from 1862 to 1864, his views frequently conflicted with those of the Confederate government; still, he sent five sons to fight for the South. Graham was elected to the Confederate Congress and took his Senate seat on May 2, 1864.

The General Assembly elected Graham to the U.S. Senate in December 1865, but Radical Republicans gained control of Congress and refused to seat the southern delegates. Officially retired, he took a leading role in the effort to overthrow Republican rule in North Carolina. Already in failing health, Graham accepted duties as an arbitrator on the Virginia-Maryland Boundary Commission. He died on August 11, 1875, at a meeting of that group in Saratoga Springs, New York. His body was returned to Hills-borough and interred in the cemetery adjacent to the Presbyterian Church.

REFERENCES: *ANB*, vol. 9; *BDC*; Clark, "William Alexander Graham"; *DAB*, vol. 7; *DNCB*, vol. 2; Hamilton et al., *Graham Papers*, vols. 1-8; Lefler and Wager, *Orange County*. PRIMARY SOURCES: Graham Papers, NCSA; Graham Papers, SHC.

# JOHN HARVEY
## 1679

*J*ohn Harvey (d. 1679) became governor in 1679 as the Lords Proprietors sought to restore Albemarle's legitimate government following Culpeper's Rebellion. Harvey, son of Thomas and Mary Harvey, was probably born in Warwickshire, England. His family immigrated to Virginia around 1640. In the 1650s, Harvey married Dorothy Took, daughter of James Took of Isle of Wight County, Virginia. By 1659, Harvey was living in the region that eventually became Albemarle County, making him one of the earliest permanent white settlers in North Carolina. In September 1663, Harvey received 850 acres of land situated between the Perquimans and Yeopim Rivers from Virginia governor William Berkeley for bringing seventeen settlers to Virginia. The peninsula became known as Harveys Neck. Harvey eventually sold 250 acres but maintained a 600-acre plantation to support his livestock.

Harvey began his political career in Albemarle County, as a member of Gov. Samuel Stephens's council and remained on the council until 1676 serving under governors Peter Carteret and John Jenkins. In April 1672, the council selected Harvey to accompany Carteret to London for a meeting with the proprietors to resolve problems in Albemarle. Harvey followed Carteret as far as New York, but events back home forced him to return to Albemarle.

During the 1670s, Albemarle was torn with dissension between the anti-proprietary and proprietary factions. The anti-proprietary faction included pre-charter settlers who feared and disliked the policies of the Lords Proprietors. Harvey served as a leader in the anti-proprietary faction. The tensions between the factions led to "Culpeper's Rebellion," which resulted in the anti-proprietary faction overthrowing the proprietary government of Thomas Miller. Harvey's participation in the rebellion was limited to the fact that he took Albemarle's Marshal General (High Sheriff) Edward Wade as a prisoner early in the uprising. He did not serve in the rebel government that controlled Albemarle for a year and a half.

The Lords Proprietors sought to re-establish the government in Albemarle. In 1678, the proprietors appointed Seth Sothel as governor. However, Sothel was captured and imprisoned by Algerian pirates while en route to Albemarle. In February 1679, the Lords Proprietors commissioned John Harvey to serve as acting governor until Sothel arrived in Albemarle. Because of the slow communication, Harvey did not receive his commission until July of that year. The proprietors evidently chose Harvey because he was not a major participant in the rebellion and was satisfactory to the rebel council. As an individual, Harvey was trusted and respected by most of the colonists.

The proprietors provided Harvey and the council with a temporary governing plan based upon the Fundamental Constitutions and with land policies more acceptable to the earliest settlers. In November 1679, the assembly enacted laws to bring order to the colony. In that same month, Harvey showed his continuing support for the anti-proprietary faction by presiding over the council as indictments were brought against Thomas Miller. By January 1680, Harvey was dead, and the colony was once again in need of a governor.

REFERENCES: Butler, "The Early Settlement of Carolina"; Butler, "The Governors of Albemarle County"; *DNCB*, vol. 3; Hathaway, "The Harvey Family"; Parker, "Legal Aspects of Culpeper's Rebellion"; Parker et al., *Colonial Records*, vols. 2 and 7; Powell, *Ye Countie of Albemarle*; Raimo, *Bio. Dir. of Col. and Rev. Governors*; Rankin, *Upheaval in Albemarle*; Sainsbury, Fortescue, and Headlam, *Calendar of State Papers, Colonial Series*; Saunders, *Colonial Records of N.C.*, vol. 1.

◇ ◈ ◇

# THOMAS HARVEY
## 1694-1699

*T*homas Harvey (d. 1699) was a longtime colonial official who became the second deputy governor of North Carolina following the death of Gov. Thomas Jarvis in 1694. He served on the colonial council from 1683 to 1695, serving as its president for his last four years. Harvey was the son of John and Mary Harvey of Snitterfield Parish in Warwickshire, England, and the cousin of John Harvey, governor of Albemarle County. Harvey was residing in Albemarle by 1670. In 1682, Harvey married Gov. John Jenkins's widow Johanna and, upon her death, married Sarah Laker. Harvey resided at Harveys Neck, a peninsula formed by the Perquimans and Yeopim Rivers.

Harvey evidently began his public service career in about March 1683 as a county court justice. By February 1684, he was serving as a member of Gov. Seth Sothel's council. Harvey was president of the council under governors Thomas Jarvis and Philip Ludwell. By the fall of 1694, Ludwell had left North Carolina leaving Harvey as acting chief executive. John Archdale, who became governor of the Carolina province in 1694, made Harvey the permanent deputy governor when he arrived in North Carolina in the summer of 1695.

As deputy governor, Harvey and his council faced challenges in governing. Issues involving land ownership had to be addressed. Harvey had to straighten out land titles that were in disorder because of Gov. Seth Sothel. Harvey and his council also had to enact the proprietors' liberal land policies. Completing government reorganization that was authorized by the proprietors in 1691 was another task. By the time of Harvey's death in 1699, many changes had been made to the government, including conversion of the unicameral assembly to a bicameral body, increased participation in legislative action by the elected members of the assembly, extension of the suffrage to include all freemen, and reorganization of the court system. As colonists settled beyond the original Albemarle County boundaries, the government found it necessary to create another county, Bath, in December 1696.

Unlike his predecessors, Harvey faced little discord from the colonists. External problems created the major challenges for the deputy governor. Harvey wrangled with the royal government on the issue of control over proprietary colonies. Virginia officials aided London in trying to gain control over Carolina. In addition, tension between North Carolina and Virginia increased because of a disputed boundary and other issues.

Harvey died on July 3, 1699, as a result of "continual sickness." The stress of performing his duties probably contributed to his death. In a July 1698 letter, Harvey complained to provincial governor John Archdale about how dealing with matters had strained his health, appealing for help in dealing with the situation. Harvey died leaving a widow with two young children ages six and four.

REFERENCES: *ANB*, vol. 1; *DNCB*, vol. 3; Fink, "Changing Philosophies and Practices in N.C. Orphanages"; Hathaway, "The Harvey Family"; Parker et al., *Colonial Records*, vols. 2 and 3; Raimo, *Bio. Dir. of Col. and Rev. Governors*; Saunders, *Colonial Records of N.C.*, vol. 1.

*Jas Hasell*

## JAMES HASELL
### 1771

James Hasell (d. 1785) was the acting governor in the summer of 1771 after William Tryon departed for his new post in New York and while Josiah Martin was delayed because of illness. He served as president of the council from 1760 to 1775, and in that capacity performed the duties of acting governor of North Carolina on several occasions. Son of merchant James Hasell, the younger Hasell was originally from Bristol, England. He immigrated to the American colonies where he lived briefly in Philadelphia before settling in New Hanover County, North Carolina, prior to 1735. Hasell married twice, first to Susannah ("Sarah") Sampson and second to Ann Sophia Von Blade Durlace. He and his first wife had a son, James.

Acquiring over two thousand acres and three Wilmington town lots by the 1740s, James Hasell was one of the largest landowners in New Hanover County. Having served as a justice of the peace since 1739 and having risen to social prominence, Hasell caught the attention of Gov. Gabriel Johnston. In 1747 Johnston nominated Hasell to the royal council; he was seated October 2, 1749, upon the death of Edward Moseley. As a longtime member of the Executive Council, Hasell held the distinction of having been present at more meetings than any other member, attending 368 meetings, just over 80 percent of the meetings for which he was responsible. In addition to his dependability, Hasell had a distinguished career on the council, serving several governors who relied upon him and commended him for his advice and unwavering loyalty to the Crown. Josiah Martin, in particular, found Hasell to be his most trusted confidant and tried to have him appointed lieutenant governor. Hasell was not timid in his leadership. As acting governor in January 1775, he terminated the assembly because of its perceived revolutionary spirit.

Although he had no formal legal education, James Hasell enjoyed a respectable career on North Carolina's higher courts. He served several times as chief justice of the General Court, as well as of the supreme and superior courts. He was named chief baron of the Exchequer Court in September 1753, and held that office until the American Revolution, resigning twice, temporarily, for terms as chief justice.

James Hasell's hobby was book collecting, and during his lifetime he accumulated one of the largest libraries in North Carolina. Many of his books are now in the North Carolina Collection at UNC at Chapel Hill. In his will, probated in 1785, Hasell left to his son James twenty pounds sterling with which to purchase mourning clothes, his own clothing, a gold watch, his riding horse, and the family "pictures." He left his stepdaughter Ann the same amount of money designated for mourning clothes. To his wife, Sophia, he left the rest of his estate, including over twelve thousand acres of land. The property was confiscated after his death but returned to the heirs in 1802.

REFERENCES: *DNCB*, vol. 3; Moore, *Rice, Hasell, Hawks, and Carruthers Families of N.C.*; Parker et al., *Colonial Records*, vol. 7. PRIMARY SOURCES: New Hanover Co. Wills.

## WILLIAM HAWKINS
## 1811-1814

*W*illiam Hawkins (1777-1819) was governor during the War of 1812. He was born in present-day Vance (then Granville) County on October 20, 1777, being one of twelve children of Philemon Hawkins III and the former Lucy Davis. He attended the College of New Jersey (now Princeton University) and later read law under Judge John Williams. Receiving his law license in 1797, he removed to Fort Hawkins, Georgia, where he worked for two years as assistant Indian agent under his uncle, former U.S. senator Benjamin Hawkins. In 1801, after returning to North Carolina, he was appointed by Gov. James Turner to negotiate a settlement with the remaining Tuscarora Indians of Bertie County. Hawkins's wife was Anne Swepson Boyd of Mecklenburg County, Virginia, whom he married in 1803. They were the parents of six children.

Hawkins represented Warren County in the lower house of the General Assembly in 1804 and 1805, and subsequently was a representative from Granville County in 1809, 1810, and 1811. During the last two of these legislative sessions he served as Speaker. On December 8, 1811, he was elected by his fellow assembly-men to the first of his three terms as governor, the maximum number permitted under the existing constitution.

Because his tenure as governor coincided so closely with the War of 1812, most of Hawkins's considerable energies and political skills were devoted to military affairs. Soon after taking office, he was called upon to provide seven thousand troops from the ranks of the state militia. Hawkins and the majority of North Carolinians supported the war; but Federalists in the legislature and throughout the state bitterly and persistently opposed it. Moreover, as the war progressed, serious disagreements arose between the state and federal governments with regard to their respective roles and obligations. It was widely felt that North Carolina was providing manpower to other states while its own coastline was virtually defenseless.

In July of 1813, British naval forces under Adm. George Cockburn entered state waters at Ocracoke Inlet and threatened an attack on New Bern. In the face of this emergency, militiamen hastened to the New Bern area from as far away as Raleigh. Hawkins himself conducted a survey of coastal defenses and reported to the legislature on his continuing efforts to secure military assistance from Washington. His third and last term as governor ended only weeks prior to the war's successful conclusion.

Hawkins returned to private life and to his Pleasant Hill plantation for a period of three years, but he returned to the House of Commons for a final time in 1817. He died in Georgia two years later, on May 17, 1819, and was buried there in the town of Sparta.

REFERENCES: *DNCB*, vol. 3; Gilpatrick, *Jeffersonian Democracy in N.C.*; Lemmon, *Frustrated Patriots*; Sobel and Raimo, *Bio. Dir. of Governors*, vol. 3. PRIMARY SOURCES: Hawkins Family Papers, SHC.

# LUTHER HARTWELL HODGES
## 1954-1961

*A*fter a career in business, Luther H. Hodges (1898-1974) made industrial development the hallmark of his administration and was instrumental in the establishment of the Research Triangle Park. The "Businessman Governor" was born in Pittsylvania County, Virginia, on March 9, 1898, to tenant farmer John James Hodges and the former Lovicia Gammons. Soon after his birth the family moved the short distance across the border to Spray (present-day Eden), North Carolina, where his father took a job in a textile mill. Luther Hodges served as a second lieutenant in World War I and in 1919 graduated from UNC. He returned to Spray, where at age twelve he had worked as an office boy in a

Gov. Luther Hodges, a career businessman before becoming governor, used the office to recruit new industry to the state. He is riding the "Tweetsie Railroad," which still operates near Boone. Hodges designated May 20, 1956, as "Tweetsie Homecoming Day."

mill, to take a position as secretary to the general manager of the Marshall Field and Company Mills. In 1922 he married Martha Blakeney of Union County; they would have three children. After her death in a house fire in 1969, he married Louise Finlayson in 1970.

Hodges remained with Marshall Field all of his business career, rising from personnel manager to general manager and, from 1943 until his retirement in 1950, vice-president. While residing in North Carolina, he served on the State Board of Education and the State Highway and Public Works Commission. In 1944, while living in New York, he served as chief of the textile division for the Office of Price Administration. In

1950 he headed the industry division of the Economic Cooperation Administration in West Germany, as part of the Marshall Plan, and in 1951 he was a consultant to the State Department regarding European industrial development.

In 1952 Hodges, with his wide administrative and management experience, launched a bid for lieutenant governor and, after a vigorous campaign to establish his name across the state, led a field of four Democratic aspirants. The second place finisher did not call for a runoff, and Hodges won in the fall. On November 7, 1954, Gov. William B. Umstead died, and Hodges became governor. In 1956, with only token opposition from within the party,

Hodges was the Democratic nominee and easily defeated Republican Kyle Hayes in the fall. Hodges served as governor for six years and two months, longer than any chief executive of North Carolina to that date.

Hodges's greatest challenge was one he inherited. With the advice of a panel appointed by Umstead and headed by Thomas Pearsall, the governor crafted a moderate stance toward integration of the public schools. The Pearsall Plan provided for payment for private schooling of any child assigned against the parents' wishes to an integrated public school and permitted local citizens by a majority vote to close schools. The plan lessened, but did not eliminate, public fears, and the state, unlike others in the South, moved slowly but peacefully toward integration. In 1959 Hodges did dispatch the National Guard to Henderson to halt textile strike violence.

Hodges's strong drive to recruit new industry, domestic and foreign, brought the state favorable national publicity. His greatest success was the Research Triangle, the business park founded in 1956, which he called the "heart and hope of North Carolina's industrial future." As governor Hodges sought to apply business management principles to state government, in part by creating the Department of Administration. He reorganized the State Highway Commission to lessen political influence and separated state prisons from that board.

Shortly after Hodges's term as governor ended, President John F. Kennedy selected him as secretary of commerce. He served in that post until December 1964. Thereafter his energies were directed largely to the Research Triangle Foundation, which he served as board chairman from 1965 to 1972, and Rotary International, which he served as president in 1967. Hodges retired to Chapel Hill and died on October 6, 1974. A Methodist, he is buried in Overlook Cemetery in Eden.

REFERENCES: *DNCB*, vol. 3; Hodges, *Businessman in the Statehouse*; Ivey, *Luther H. Hodges*; *News and Observer*, October 7, 1974; Patton, *Hodges Papers*; Sobel and Raimo, *Bio. Dir. of Governors*, vol. 3; Tanzer, *The Kennedy Circle*. PRIMARY SOURCES: Hodges Papers, SHC.

# CLYDE ROARK HOEY
## 1937-1941

*C*lyde R. Hoey (1877-1954) is remembered for his oratory, courtly manner, long white hair, and distinctive style of dress, replete with

Gov. Clyde Hoey, a journalist by trade, gave priority to a balanced state budget and exhibited little enthusiasm for federal New Deal programs. Hoey unveils a replica of the locomotive "Raleigh" on January 26, 1939.

swallowtail coat, striped pants, wing collar, high-topped shoes, and boutonniere. Like his predecessor J. C. B. Ehringhaus, the conservative Hoey gave priority to a balanced state budget and exhibited little enthusiasm for federal New Deal programs. Part of the "Shelby Dynasty," Clyde R. Hoey was born in the Cleveland County town on December 11, 1877, to Confederate veteran Samuel Hoey and the former Mary Roark. At age twelve Hoey left the public schools to work as a "printer's devil" in the office of the *Shelby Review* and later at the *Charlotte Observer*. At sixteen Hoey bought the Shelby newspaper and changed the name to the *Cleveland Star*. With a career established at an early age, Hoey had little time for further schooling but in

1899 studied law for one summer session at UNC. That same year he passed the bar; soon his active practice took him away from daily journalism. In 1900 Hoey, a Methodist, married Bess Gardner, sister of O. Max Gardner (governor, 1929-1933). To Clyde and Bess Hoey were born three children; he never remarried after her death in 1942.

In 1898, several weeks before his twenty-first birthday, Hoey was elected to the state House for the first of two terms. In 1903 he served a single term in the state senate. From 1913 to 1919 Hoey served as assistant U.S. attorney for the western district of North Carolina. In 1919, Hoey defeated Republican John Motley Morehead in a race for the U.S. House, but he declined to seek reelection two years later. Until his bid for governor in 1936 Hoey concentrated on his law practice and worked as a lobbyist for Duke Power Company and other companies. In the hotly contested race for the Democratic gubernatorial nomination in 1936, Hoey, with the assistance of his brother-in-law's political organization, defeated Ralph McDonald, A. H. Graham, and John McRae. Graham and McRae were eliminated in the first primary. The chief issue in the runoff was the sales tax, which McDonald denounced and Hoey was forced to defend but, in doing so, he argued for its eventual elimination. A leader of the "drys," Hoey campaigned for letting the people vote on the liquor issue. Hoey won over Republican candidate Gilliam Grissom in the fall.

During Hoey's administration as governor the state provided free textbooks for the elementary schools, increased teacher salaries, expanded the highway system, reformed child labor laws, instituted parole reforms, offered the first graduate courses at black colleges, and initiated the first advertising programs to attract tourists. The State Bureau of Investigation and the State Board of Alcoholic Beverage Control were created during his term.

In 1937 the state implemented provisions of the Social Security Act, but Hoey lent his support to few of the New Deal initiatives. In a speech to the governor's conference in 1937 Hoey cautioned against the loss of state authority with the increased use of federal funds. By the late 1930s the New Deal was no longer a major political force in North Carolina. Sen. Josiah Bailey led the opposition but in time was joined by Hoey and Gardner. Liberals such as Hoey's 1936 Democratic opponent Ralph McDonald were frustrated by the constraints within which the Roosevelt reforms were forced to operate.

In 1944 former governor Hoey defeated former governor Cameron Morrison in a race for the U.S. Senate. His election in the fall secured his place in the history books as only the second North Carolinian (after Jesse Franklin) to serve as governor and in both houses of the legislature and both houses of Congress. On May 12, 1954, the political veteran died in his Senate office in Washington; he is buried in Sunset Cemetery in Shelby.

REFERENCES: Abrams, *Conservative Constraints*; *BDC*; *Charlotte Observer*, May 13, 1954; Connor et al., *History of N.C.*, vol. 6; Corbitt, *Hoey Papers*; *DNCB*, vol. 3; Puryear, *Democratic Party Dissension*; Sobel and Raimo, *Bio. Dir. of Governors*, vol. 3; Weathers, *Cleveland Co. History*. PRIMARY SOURCES: Hoey Papers, Duke.

## WILLIAM WOODS HOLDEN
### 1865; 1868-1871

*W*illiam Woods Holden (1818-1892), the illegitimate son of Thomas Holden and Priscilla Woods, was born on November 24, 1818, near Hillsborough. From age six, he lived with his father and stepmother, Sally Nichols Holden. With only a year or two of formal education, he learned to read and write. The remainder of his schooling came through his apprenticeship with Dennis Heartt, editor of the *Hillsborough Recorder*, to whom he was assigned at age ten. Following brief stints with newspapers in Milton, North Carolina, and Danville, Virginia, he moved to Raleigh to work for the *Star* in 1836. Holden married twice. His first wife was Ann Augusta Young whom he wed in 1841. After her death, he married Louisa Virginia Harrison. He fathered a total of eight children.

Holden studied law at night and received his license in 1841, but he preferred the newspaper business to legal practice. He arranged to purchase the *North Carolina Standard*, the Raleigh-based organ for the Democratic Party, and in 1843, became sole owner and editor. Borrowing from his earlier Whig leanings, he promoted reform, equal suffrage in voting for state senators, internal improvements for all sections of the state, continued development in education, and better working conditions in the factories and mills. Holden, more than any other individual, revived the Democratic Party and led it to dominance during the decade of the 1850s.

In the sectional crisis, William W. Holden termed himself a "national" man, one who advocated the Union over secession while agreeing with southern interests in most other cases. As resistance reached futility in the Convention of 1861, he accepted and voted for secession. Having broken with the Democratic Party leadership, Holden used the *Standard* to promote a new Conservative Party, which in 1862 nominated Zebulon B. Vance for governor. With his influential newspaper spearheading the campaign, Holden led Vance to victory. The editor and the governor disagreed on how to conduct the war, however, and faced off as opponents in the 1864 election. Holden's campaign rested on his belief that the Confederacy was doomed, and that North Carolina should seek a separate peace on the best terms possible. He had a sizable following, but most citizens agreed with Vance that continuing the war was preferable to the dishonor of deserting sister states. Holden suffered a humiliating defeat.

On May 20, 1865, President Andrew Johnson called Holden to Washington and appointed him provisional governor of North Carolina effective May 29. Challenged with a state in economic and social chaos, he made more than three thousand appointments in an effort to reorganize state, county, and local governments. He set the schedule for amnesty oaths and supervised their administration, took some steps towards economic recovery, and was a principal figure in the revision of the state constitution to meet federal requirements. Holden urged the newly freed slaves to exercise their rights and make the most of their opportunites "aided as you will [be] by the superior intelligence of the white race."

The 1865 convention called for a gubernatorial election on November 9. The Conservatives selected Jonathan Worth, whom Holden had appointed state treasurer, to oppose the provisional governor. Attacking Holden's Civil War role and federal government relationship, Worth won the contest by almost six thousand votes, but he could not assume duties until December 2, after North Carolina ratified the Thirteenth Amendment. Holden resumed editorship of the *Standard* and set

about establishing the Republican Party in North Carolina. Meanwhile, Radical Republicans had seized control of Congress and put into effect their own plan of Reconstruction.

Radical Reconstruction of the South provided the perfect venue for William W. Holden to make another bid for governor. With freedmen now possessing the vote, he successfully attained his goal in 1868. In his inaugural address on July 4, Holden called for unity to rebuild the state and for the people to accept northern immigration and capital as parts of that effort. He spoke of challenges facing the state: reorganization of government at all levels, re-establishment of the schools, the need for a state penitentiary, development of the devastated economy, expansion of internal improvements, and equal justice for all persons. The last was emphasized by his warning that armed resistance to national authority would be treason, and that an organized and armed militia would be necessary to "execute the laws and suppress riots or insurrections."

Social problems and political discontent brought into existence the Ku Klux Klan (KKK), a secret organization dedicated to the control and intimidation of blacks and Republicans. Holden vowed to destroy the Klan and made some ill-advised decisions capped by the "Kirk-Holden War" that ended his political career. The Conservatives recaptured the General Assembly in 1870 and brought charges of "high crimes and misdemeanors" against the governor for actions involved in his battle with the KKK. Notified that he had been impeached by the House of Representatives, Holden turned over duties of his office to Lt. Gov. Tod R. Caldwell on December 20. The trial began on January 30, 1871, and lasted nearly three months. On March 22, the North Carolina Senate found Holden guilty on the most serious charges and ordered him removed from office, adding that he never again would be allowed to hold a state position. He was the first governor in the nation's history to be impeached and removed from office, and the only one to bear that burden in North Carolina.

For a while Holden edited the *Daily Chronicle* in Washington, D.C., then accepted the job of postmaster in Raleigh. A paralytic stroke on April 2, 1882, forced his retirement from public service. No longer able to write, he dictated his memoirs; the day after completion in February 1889, a second stroke shattered his faculties. He died on March 1, 1892, and was buried in Oakwood Cemetery in Raleigh.

REFERENCES: *ANB,* vol. 11; Boyd, *Holden Memoirs*; *DNCB*, vol. 3; Harris, *William Woods Holden*; Raper, *Holden Papers*, vol. 1; Raper, *William W. Holden.* PRIMARY SOURCES: Holden Papers, Duke; Holden Papers, NCSA.

# GABRIEL HOLMES
## 1821-1824

*G*abriel Holmes (1769-1829) adopted a Jeffersonian view of the importance of agrarian life. He was the father of Theophilus H. Holmes, a Confederate general. Born in present-day Sampson (then Duplin) County, Gabriel Holmes was one of the seven children of Gabriel and Mary Caison Holmes. He received his preparatory education at Zion Parnassus Academy and later attended Harvard College. Returning to North Carolina, he studied law under future chief justice John Louis Taylor, was admitted to the bar, and began the practice of law in Sampson County. Holmes married Mary Hunter of Wake County, daughter of Revolutionary leader Theophilus Hunter. Their marriage produced six children.

Holmes represented Sampson County in the lower house of the General Assembly from 1793 to 1795 and subsequently in the upper house in 1797, 1801, 1812, and 1813. On eight occasions he was appointed to the Council of State. From 1801 to 1804, and from 1817 until his death, he also served as a trustee of UNC.

Holmes was defeated for the governorship by Jesse Franklin in 1820, but emerged victorious the following year in a sharply contested election requiring numerous ballots. Inaugurated on December 7, 1821, he began the first of the maximum three terms allowed under the existing constitution.

In his initial address to the General Assembly as governor, Holmes emphasized themes that would come to characterize his years in office. Chief among these were the allocation of limited public monies for education, improved transportation by land and water, and the encouragement of agriculture. Much like President Thomas Jefferson, he vigorously promoted the interests of the common man and the agrarian way of life. While governor, he also served as president of the board of trustees at UNC. In that role, he pressed for the introduction of agricultural courses and the establishment of a model farm to demonstrate more progressive farming methods. In full accord with the Jeffersonian view, he stressed the productive and practical uses to which higher education could be put. In 1822, at his urging, the General Assembly provided for the distribution of funds to counties throughout the state to promote the work of local agricultural societies.

In 1825, following the expiration of his third term, Holmes was elected to the U.S. House of Representatives, where he served until his death. His committee work involved, among other things, militia affairs and the postal system. Like former governor John Branch, who served concurrently in the Senate, he was closely associated in Washington with the interests and policies of Vice-President John C. Calhoun of South Carolina. Holmes died at his home near Clinton on September 26, 1829, and was interred on the grounds.

REFERENCES: Coon, *Beginnings of Public Education*; *DNCB*, vol. 3; Sobel and Raimo, *Bio. Dir. of Governors*, vol. 3.

## JAMES EUBERT HOLSHOUSER JR.
### 1973-1977

*T*he first Republican elected governor of North Carolina in the twentieth century, James E. Holshouser Jr. (1934- ) extended rural health care, expanded kindergarten and community college programs, acquired park lands, reformed highway fund allocation, and instituted an efficiency study of state government. A native of Boone, Holshouser was born on October 8, 1934, to James E. Holshouser, an attorney and district court judge, and the former Virginia Dayvault. Up to the seventh grade Holshouser suffered from severe asthma; in high school a

Gov. James E. Holshouser (*right*), the first Republican elected governor in the twentieth century, accepts soil samples from James Graham, the commissioner of agriculture.

chronic kidney infection kept him from taking part in athletic activities. He served as sports editor for the student newspaper at Davidson College where he graduated in 1956. While in law school at UNC at Chapel Hill, he developed his first serious interest in politics. In 1961 Holshouser, a Presbyterian, married Patricia Hollingsworth; they would have one daughter.

On completion of his studies at Chapel Hill in 1960, Holshouser returned to Watauga County to practice law. In 1962 he was elected to the first of four terms in the state House. He served as that body's minority leader in the 1965 session and chaired the state Republican Party from 1966 to 1972. In 1968 he directed Richard M. Nixon's presidential campaign in the Tar Heel State.

In the fiercely waged 1972 Republican race for governor, the moderate and shy Holshouser met conservative and flamboyant James C. Gardner, who had been the nominee four years earlier. In the first primary Gardner led by a slim margin over Holshouser and two minor candidates; Holshouser defeated Gardner in the second primary by 1,800 votes. In the fall Holshouser defeated Democratic nominee Hargrove ("Skipper") Bowles. His victory was aided considerably by Richard M. Nixon's 600,000-vote margin over Democrat George McGovern in North Carolina.

Holshouser, at thirty-eight the youngest chief executive in the twentieth century, faced Democratic majorities in both houses of the legislature and state employees still adjusting to reorganization. As his first executive order, Holshouser established the Governor's Efficiency Study Commission chaired by Archie K. Davis. After months of study that board recommended seven hundred cost-saving changes. These included measures such as five-year license plates, use of compact cars by state agencies, and centralized printing services. At the close of his term Holshouser estimated that the changes saved $80 million annually. New initiatives included an ombudsman and "People's Days" to permit direct contact with the governor.

The kindergarten program that extended to 3,427 students in 1973 had expanded to cover the entire state by 1977. Area Health Education Centers and Rural Health Centers received the governor's backing. Holshouser took measures to deal with the energy crisis by lowering speed limits and the heat in state buildings. The board of transportation instituted a seven-year program for highway expansion and a more equitable formula system for allocation of secondary road funds. Ten new state parks were established, more than doubling the acreage of state park land. Moves were taken to protect the New River, Jockeys Ridge, and the Cape Lookout National Seashore. The Coastal Area Management Act was enacted in 1974.

Holshouser presided over events related to the nation's bicentennial in 1976. In that year he served as southern chairman of President Gerald Ford's campaign. After Ford's defeat in the North Carolina primary by Ronald Reagan, Holshouser was denied a seat in the state delegation to the Republican convention by party conservatives.

At the end of his term as governor, Holshouser split his time between law practices in Boone and Southern Pines. In 1978 he moved to the Moore County town, and since 1979 he has served on the UNC Board of Governors.

REFERENCES: *Charlotte Observer*, October 29, 1972; Mitchell, *Holshouser Papers*; National Governors Association, *Education of a New Governor*; Sobel and Raimo, *Bio. Dir. of Governors*, vol. 3.

# THOMAS MICHAEL HOLT
## 1891-1893

*T*aking office upon the unexpected death of Gov. Daniel G. Fowle, Thomas Michael Holt (1831-1896) employed skills developed as a textile leader to captain the ship of state. The second of Edwin Michael and Emily Farish Holt's ten children, the future governor was born on July 15, 1831, at Locust Grove, the family home in

Orange (now Alamance) County. The Holt family helped to pioneer the textile industry in North Carolina. Young Holt studied at the Caldwell Institute in Hillsborough and entered UNC in 1849 but left the next year. With the approval of his father, he sought more practical business experience as a salesman and book-keeper in a large dry goods store in Philadelphia.

Changes in the structure of his textile business prompted E. M. Holt to call his son home in 1851 to run the mill on Alamance Creek. According to the elder Holt's diary, it was his son who, employing the techniques of a French designer, discovered the dyeing process leading to the famous "Alamance Plaid." Thomas Holt married Louise Moore in 1855; they had six children. Throughout the Civil War, Holt supplied clothing and textiles to the Confederacy. After the war he and his partner, Adolphus Moore, built a larger factory on the Haw River that eventually employed 175 people and supported a village of forty homes, a school, and a church.

Holt had been affiliated with the Whig Party in the antebellum years but listed himself as a Democrat while serving as Alamance County commissioner, 1872-1875. He won election to the 1876-1877 session of the state senate and served three terms in the North Carolina House of Representatives beginning in 1883. He was Speaker of the House during the 1885 session. Running on the ticket with Daniel G. Fowle in 1888, he was elected lieutenant governor.

Long interested in education, Holt, prior to serving as governor, promoted the establishment of present-day North Carolina State University and served on the boards of trustees at UNC and Davidson College. He supported establish-ment of a normal school for white women (now UNC at Greensboro), college-level facilities for blacks (present-day North Carolina A&T State University and Elizabeth City State University were chartered by the 1891 legislature), and a new state institution for the deaf at Morganton. He advocated additional funding for Oxford Orphanage, the state mental institutions, and an expansion of the common schools. Holt also supported the growing movement to return elective control of local governments to the residents by repealing the law that gave the legislature the power to select justices of the peace.

Given a strong start by a revolutionary "farmers" legislature that concluded work just before he assumed office in 1891, the governor achieved virtually all of his goals. The people regained control of local governments; an increased tax rate assisted the public schools; and the appropriations for the state hospitals and the university system were increased. As a former president of the North Carolina Railroad, however, Holt did not favor the creation of an unrestrained railroad commission. His thirteen years as president of the Grange and a longtime association with the State Fair afforded him an understanding of the farmers' viewpoint.

Holt's health weakened during his administration, and he chose not to run for reelection in 1892. He retired to private life but could manage his interests only on a part-time basis. A Presbyterian, he died on April 11,

1896, at his home on Haw River and was buried in Linwood Cemetery in Graham.

REFERENCES: *Cyclopedia of Eminent and Representative Men*, vol. 2; *DNCB*, vol. 3; Henderson and others, *North Carolina*, vol. 4; Holt, *Edwin Michael Holt*. PRIMARY SOURCES: Holt Papers, SHC.

# JAMES BAXTER HUNT JR.
## 1977-1985; 1993-2001

The first North Carolina governor elected to consecutive four-year terms and the state's longest serving chief executive with sixteen years in office, James B. Hunt Jr. (1937- ) assumed the moderately progressive mantle of his Democratic predecessors by placing emphasis on education, economic development, and highways. In his third and fourth terms, Hunt, by then jokingly called by some "governor for life," championed child care and, acceding to perceived wishes of the voters, recast himself as a conservative with an increased emphasis on cutting taxes and reducing crime.

Jim Hunt was born on May 16, 1937, in Greensboro to soil conservationist James Baxter Hunt and the former Elsie Brame, a schoolteacher. When he was still of preschool age, the family moved to a farm at Rock Ridge outside Wilson. Raised in the Free Will Baptist Church, Hunt joined the Presbyterian Church as an adult. In 1959 and 1962 he earned degrees from North Carolina State College, completing a master's thesis that dealt with the economics of tobacco production. In 1964 Hunt earned a law degree at UNC at Chapel Hill. He and his wife, the former Carolyn Leonard whom he married in 1958, then moved to Nepal where for two years he worked as an economic adviser to the government under a Ford Foundation grant. Jim and Carolyn Hunt are the parents of four children.

Observers of politics routinely comment on Hunt's ambition and desire to win, reflected in his early political drive. Eleven-year-old Hunt helped his family campaign for Kerr Scott. At N.C. State he took part in the Terry Sanford campaign, and while in law school he worked for Richardson Preyer. On passing the bar Hunt joined a law firm in Wilson. In 1968 he served as president of the state's Young Democrats. In 1970 Gov. Robert W. Scott appointed him to chair a commission to revise the state party's rules. In 1972, a year when Republicans took the presidency, the governorship, and a U.S. Senate seat, Hunt was elected lieutenant governor. In that office he helped guide expansion of the kindergarten program through the legislature. In 1976 Hunt defeated businessmen Edward O'Herron and Thomas Strickland and legislator George Wood in the Democratic gubernatorial primary without a runoff. He gained 65 percent of the vote against Republican David Flaherty in the general election.

In a brief, 450-word inaugural address in 1977, Hunt called for a "new beginning" and citizen involvement in government. The governor established a Primary Reading Program as part of his education reforms that included teacher pay raises and competency testing for teachers and students. The N.C. School of Science and Mathematics, a residential high school for gifted students and a Hunt innovation, opened in 1980. The governor launched efforts to recruit high technology businesses and established the Microelectronics Center in 1980. Hunt declined to stay executions in capital punishment cases and in 1978 reduced the prison sentences of the "Wilmington Ten," convicted of a firebombing related to racial unrest in the port city.

In 1977 voters approved an amendment to the state constitution permitting the governor to serve two consecutive four-year terms. In 1980 Hunt ran for reelection and withstood a primary challenge from former governor Robert W. Scott. In the fall he defeated Republican nominee I. Beverly Lake Jr., son of 1960 and 1964 contender I. Beverly Lake Sr. In 1981 Hunt created North Carolina 2000, a commission chaired by former UNC president William C. Friday, to study future needs of the state. With Hunt's backing the legislature, after a divisive debate, in 1983 approved a

Gov. James B. Hunt, a tireless promoter of education reform, highlights his reading program by reading to young children in 1982. In his sixteen years as governor, Hunt stressed childhood development and promoted his signature program, "Smart Start."

three-cent gasoline tax increase with the funds earmarked for highway improvements. Economic development remained central to Hunt's agenda in his second term. In 1984 Hunt oversaw the 400th anniversary commemoration of the Roanoke voyages. The state zoo expanded, and the film office oversaw increased production.

In 1984 Governor Hunt challenged Senator Jesse Helms for the U.S. Senate seat held by Helms since 1972. The contenders spent over $26 million on the race, mostly on television advertising, making it the costliest Senate campaign in the nation to that date. The two met in a notable series of televised debates. In the end Helms triumphed by a 52 percent to 48 percent margin. Editors of the *Almanac of American Politics* reasoned that the state's voters "preferred Helms's principled advocacy over Hunt's pragmatic problem-solving." Out of office for the first time in twelve years, Hunt returned to the practice of law and spent more time on his Wilson County farm. As governor Hunt had established a national reputation as an education reformer, and as a private citizen he remained active in that movement.

In 1992 Hunt defeated Attorney General Lacy Thornburg in the Democratic primary and Republican lieutenant governor James C. Gardner in the general election to regain the governor's office. In his third inaugural address Hunt stressed childhood development and touted a program tagged "Smart Start," whereby counties create and implement plans to improve child care. Early in his term he called a special session of the legislature devoted to crime. The Republican gains in the 1994 legislative elections, giving the GOP a majority in the state House, led Hunt to seek common ground with the new lawmakers.

In 1996 Hunt defeated Congressman Robin Hayes in his bid to retain his seat. A constitutional amendment approved that same year made him the first North Carolina governor with veto power, an authority he did not exercise in his final four years. In his fourth term Hunt pushed to raise teacher pay to the national average and to increase student test scores. Unprecedented damage caused by Hurricane Fran in 1996 and Hurricane Floyd in 1999 tested Hunt's leadership skills. After a generation in the public eye, he left office in 2001 as one of the most familiar and durable actors ever on the stage of North Carolina politics.

REFERENCES: Barone and Ujifusa, *Almanac of American Politics; Greensboro News and Record*, December 31, 2000-January 2, 2001; Grimsley, *James B. Hunt Jr.*; Mitchell, *Hunt Papers; N.C. Manual*, 1993; Poff, *Hunt Papers*; Poff and Crow, *Hunt Papers*; Raimo, *Bio. Dir. of Governors of U.S.*; Snider, *Helms and Hunt; Who's Who in American Politics; Winston-Salem Journal*, December 31, 2000.

## EDWARD HYDE
## 1711-1712

Edward Hyde (1667-1712) was the first governor of the colony of North Carolina separate and distinct from South Carolina. His brief tenure was dominated by turmoil and violence owing to a revolt led by former governor Thomas Cary and a war with the Tuscarora Indians. The Hyde family was part of the landed gentry and related to two English monarchs, Queen Mary II and Queen Anne. Hyde was born to Robert Hyde and Phillis Snyed Hyde of Cheshire County, England; however, Hyde was an orphan by the age of three. His grandmother raised him along with his two sisters. Hyde entered Oxford University in 1683 at sixteen, but did not complete his degree. He married Catherine Rigby in 1692. One of Hyde's contemporaries, William Byrd, referred to Hyde's wife as an "abundance of life."

Hyde began his public life when, in 1702, Queen Anne appointed him Jamaica's provost marshal. Hyde worked at the post from England and found that it gave him no financial security. Hyde and his family left England and arrived in Virginia in August 1710. At first Gov. Thomas Cary, who had seized the governorship from William Glover, refused to yield the government to Hyde, who held a commission from the Lords Proprietors. By early 1711, Hyde was in the chief executive office but did not possess the skill necessary to restrain the Anglicans or dissenter factions. In the events growing out of his attempt to overthrow the government, Thomas Cary was arrested and sent to England for trial, but he was eventually freed without receiving any punishment. As a result, Hyde no longer had to contend with Cary, but he faced a greater challenge when Indians rose up against the colonists.

In late September 1711, the Tuscarora and smaller tribes attacked colonists in Bath County in retribution for the recent taking of land along the Neuse, Trent, and Pamlico Rivers and apparently for many years of frustration of being poorly treated by whites. The brutal and destructive attack caught the colonists by surprise, and Hyde faced a serious problem. He was unable to raise a large army because of resentment caused by Cary's Rebellion and the refusal of Quakers to bear arms or even lend them to others. In this desperate situation, Hyde appealed for help from Virginia and South Carolina. Virginia did not send any troops, but South

Carolinians, their Indian allies, and some North Carolinians defeated the Tuscarora and negotiated a peace treaty by early 1712. The treaty was not recognized by the assembly, and the peace proved to be short-lived. By the summer, the Tuscarora had resumed the war. The Tuscarora were effectively defeated by a combined force in 1713, but raids continued for several years.

While the conflict with the Indians was raging, the proprietors commissioned Hyde in January 1712 as governor of North Carolina, a chief executive no longer subordinate to a governor in Charles Town, South Carolina. Hyde received the commission in May but did not remain governor long enough to enjoy the commission or to lead troops against the Tuscarora. On September 8, 1712, Hyde, after suffering for a week, died of yellow fever, a victim of an epidemic that had swept through North Carolina.

REFERENCES: *ANB*, vol. 11; Booth, *Seeds of Anger*; *DNCB* vol. 3; Parker et al., *Colonial Records*, vols. 5 and 10; Parramore, "The Tuscarora Ascendancy"; Paschal dissertation, "Proprietary N.C."; Saunders, *Colonial Records of N.C.*, vols. 1 and 2; Skaggs, "First Boundary Survey between the Carolinas"; Swindell and Turner, *Edward Hyde*; Todd, *Graffenried's Account of the Founding of New Bern*; Wright and Tinling, *Secret Diary of William Byrd*.

# JAMES IREDELL JR.
## 1827-1828

*J*ames Iredell Jr. (1788-1853) was born in Edenton on November 2, 1788, to parents of the highest social and political standing. His father, James Iredell Sr., was a prominent Federalist leader and associate justice of the U.S. Supreme Court. His mother, the former Hannah Johnston, was the sister of Gov. Samuel Johnston of Edenton and niece of royal governor Gabriel Johnston. Because young Iredell was only ten years of age when his father died, it is probable that his uncle Samuel, the former governor, exercised a powerful and lasting influence over the boy's development. Iredell's wife was the former Frances Johnston Tredwell of Edenton. Their marriage produced seven children.

Iredell received his early education locally at the Edenton Academy. Later he attended the College of New

Jersey (now Princeton University), from which he graduated in 1806. Returning to North Carolina, he pursued the study of law and was admitted to the bar in 1809. During the War of 1812 he commanded a company of volunteers in the defense of Norfolk; and in 1815 he was commissioned a brigadier general in the North Carolina militia. In 1813 he was elected from Edenton to the lower house of the General Assembly, where he again represented the town from 1816 to 1820 and from 1823 to 1828. During five of these legislative sessions, he served as either Speaker or Speaker pro tempore. On December 5, 1827, he was elected governor by his fellow assemblymen, but less than a year later resigned to fill the U.S. Senate seat vacated by Nathaniel Macon, patriarch of North Carolina's congressional delegation.

Because of its brief duration, Iredell's governorship left only a shallow imprint on the state's history. Significantly, it came during a period when the progressive Whig Party was emergent, and when there were growing demands for constitutional reform, internal improvements, and public education. Like his predecessors, Iredell stressed the need for improved roads and waterways and for the encouragement of industry and agriculture. He expressed frustration, however, that so little had been accomplished in comparison with other states. By way of contrast, his address to the General Assembly contained only one passing reference to public education. Quite probably, this relative lack of emphasis stemmed from the state's poor financial condition and especially that of the

Literary Fund. Indeed, investigations following the death of treasurer John Haywood during the previous year had revealed an unexpected shortage of more than $28,000 in the fund, so that the state was hardly in a position to launch new or comprehensive educational initiatives.

Following his single term in the U.S. Senate, Iredell returned to North Carolina and established a law practice in Raleigh. During the next quarter century he served as a commissioner to revise the state's laws, reported cases for the North Carolina Supreme Court, conducted a law school, and published an authoritative three-volume digest of court cases in the state from 1778 to 1845. Iredell died in Edenton on April 13, 1853, and was buried in the Johnston family cemetery at Hayes Plantation.

REFERENCES: Coon, *Beginnings of Public Education*; *DNCB*, vol. 3; Sobel and Raimo, *Bio. Dir. of Governors*, vol. 3. PRIMARY SOURCES: Iredell Books, SHC; Iredell Family Papers, NCSA; Iredell Papers, Duke; Johnson Collection, NCSA.

◈ ◈ ◈

# THOMAS JARVIS
## 1691-1694

Thomas Jarvis (d. 1694), deputy governor of North Carolina following the Lords Proprietors' appointment of Philip Ludwell as the governor of the Carolina province, was among the earliest settlers in North Carolina. For two decades, he played an active role in colonial politics. Nothing survives to tell about Jarvis's birth or parentage. Jarvis was married to a woman named Dorcas and had a son named Foster and a daughter named Dorcas. He was living in the Albemarle region by 1663. A land grant in that year issued by Virginia governor William Berkeley to John Jenkins mentioned Jarvis's land, near the Perquimans River and Albemarle Sound in an area that became known as Harveys Neck (present-day Perquimans County). He also owned a plantation on Whites Island (present-day Currituck County).

Jarvis began his political career in 1672 as a member of Gov. Peter Carteret's council. In 1677 he served in the rebel assembly that met following Culpeper's Rebellion. From 1683 through 1689 Jarvis was on the council during tenures of governors Seth Sothel and John Gibbs. Jarvis was acting chief executive when former governor John Gibbs decided to rebel against Ludwell's authority by disrupting a court and taking two magistrates as prisoners. In response to Gibbs's actions, Jarvis and the council called out the militia to end the mutiny. They sent a letter to Virginia authorities seeking permission to send the militia into that colony to apprehend Gibbs. Furthermore, Jarvis and the council wrote to Ludwell, who was probably in Virginia, requesting him to come to Albemarle and asking him to seek help from Virginia in capturing Gibbs.

When the proprietors commissioned Ludwell as governor of the Carolina province in 1691, Ludwell appointed Jarvis as deputy governor of North Carolina. In that capacity, Jarvis served as acting governor when Ludwell, who maintained permanent residence in Virginia, was out of the colony. Jarvis officially held the governorship until his death in 1694. In a report provided to royal officials, Edward Randolph provided a biased observation of North Carolina under Jarvis's leadership. He described North Carolina as having "sixty or seventy scattered families, but under no regular government."

Very little is known about Jarvis's private life. Jarvis's 1694 estate inventory provided a glimpse at his life away from politics. He apparently made his primary residence on Whites Island and raised an abundance of livestock, especially cattle. Jarvis possessed whale tools, meaning he was possibly involved in the hunting of whales along the coast. He owned at least seven slaves: two Indians, three blacks, and two of mixed race. His inventory showed a large amount of personal items including silverware, a looking glass, and numerous furnishings. In 1694 Jarvis's son Foster and son-in-law Charles Neal appeared before the General Court seeking a division of Jarvis's estate. Neal was representing his wife Dorcas and daughter Dorcas. The court ordered the division of Jarvis's estate between Foster Jarvis and the widow.

REFERENCES: *DNCB*, vols. 3 and 4; Parker et al., *Colonial Records*, vols. 1 and 7; Raimo, *Bio. Dir. of Col. and Rev. Governors*; Rankin, *Upheaval in Albemarle*; Saunders, *Colonial Records of N.C.*, vol. 1. PRIMARY SOURCES: SS Council Minutes.

## THOMAS JORDAN JARVIS
## 1879-1885

*T*homas Jordan Jarvis (1836-1915) has the distinction of sharing his name with an ancestor, proprietary governor Thomas Jarvis, whose tenure extended from 1691 to 1694. While serving as lieutenant governor in 1879, Jarvis became governor when Zebulon B. Vance resigned to serve in the U.S. Senate; the following year he was elected to his own full term. The son of Bannister Hardy and Elizabeth Daley Jarvis, he was born on January 18, 1836, at Jarvisburg in Currituck County. The "Plough Boy of Currituck" graduated with honors from Randolph Macon College in 1860. A captain in the Eighth Regiment, Jarvis received a crippling arm wound at Drewry's Bluff. After the war, he moved to Columbia where he set up law practice. Jarvis flirted with politics as a delegate to the 1865 convention and in 1868 won a seat in the legislature from

Tyrrell County. Reelected in 1870, he was the party's choice for Speaker of the House and used his power to reduce government costs, investigate railroad frauds, and oversee the impeachment trial of William Woods Holden.

In 1872 Jarvis moved to Greenville and two years later married Martha Woodson; the couple had no children. Having worked his way into the hierarchy of the Democratic Party, Jarvis received the nomination for lieutenant governor on the successful ticket with Zebulon B. Vance in 1876. Two years into the term, Vance resigned to serve in the Senate, thrusting Jarvis into the governorship on February 5, 1879. Jarvis's agricultural background instilled sympathy to the plight of farmers; the Industrial Revolution brought pressures for government intervention. Against both groups Jarvis pitted his commitment to reduce the costs of government, eliminate corruption, and lower taxes. His personal view was that state government's only responsibility in economic development should be provision of an honest and efficient environment for all interests. Consequently, as governor, he sold the state's interest in several railroads to private enterprise, urged state agencies to make use of convict labor, and initiated scrutiny of the expend- itures for county administration.

Jarvis persuaded the legislature to establish five normal schools for teachers; played a major role in the creation of the State Board of Health; pushed for funding for the Deaf and Dumb Asylum and for Oxford Orphanage; and proposed new mental health facilities in Goldsboro and Morganton. Some projects incurred delays as the legislature responded to Jarvis's inaugural appeal and reduced tax rates. In his full term he pushed for increased aid to education and professional standards for teachers. He secured permission from the assembly to build a new governor's mansion.

President Grover Cleveland in 1885 appointed Jarvis U.S. minister to Brazil, an office from which he resigned in 1888 to return to law practice in Greenville. The next year he turned down an offer to be the first president of the North Carolina College of Agriculture and Mechanical Arts (present-day North Carolina State University). Gov. Elias Carr appointed him to fill the Senate seat vacated by the death of Zebulon Vance in 1894. There he promoted a graduated income tax, tariff reduction, and involved himself with other monetary problems. Jarvis hoped to gain a full term in the Senate by challenging incumbent Matt Ransom rather than try for the two years remaining in Vance's term. He failed, but out of his effort came his interest in free coinage of silver.

By the early 1900s elder statesman Jarvis quietly withdrew from public life and concentrated on his legal practice. In 1904 he declined the deanship of the newly created law school at Trinity College (present-day Duke University). In 1907 he and William Ragsdale helped push through the legislature a law establishing a teachers' training school in Greenville (present-day East Carolina University). Thomas Jarvis, a Methodist, died on June 17, 1915,

and was buried in Cherry Hill Cemetery in Greenville.

REFERENCES: *BDC*; Crittenden et al., *100 Years, 100 Men*; *Cyclopedia of Eminent and Representative Men*, vol. 2; *DNCB*, vol. 3; Yearns, *Jarvis Papers*. PRIMARY SOURCES: Jarvis Papers, Duke; Jarvis Papers, NCSA.

◈ ◈ ◈

# JOHN JENKINS
## 1672-1675; 1676-1677; 1678-1679; 1680-1681

John Jenkins (d. 1681) served more times as proprietary governor than any other person, taking the seat no fewer than four times. He achieved power with the backing of the anti-proprietary faction (pre-1663 settlers) of which he was a leader. Jenkins, a native of England, married a woman named Johanna. By the 1650s he evidently lived on four hundred acres in Northampton County, Virginia, known as Egge Neck, receiving the land in return for bringing eight settlers to Virginia. By 1662 he had moved to the Albemarle region. In September 1663 Virginia governor William Berkeley issued a seven hundred-acre grant to Jenkins on Harveys Neck for bringing fourteen people to Virginia. Jenkins had been involved in maritime activities since 1653 when the English Council of

State licensed him to command the ship *King of Poland* to take twenty-three men and one hundred pairs of shoes to Bermuda.

Jenkins began his governmental career as a member of Gov. Samuel Stephens's council. Gov. Peter Carteret appointed Jenkins acting governor in April 1672. Carteret then sailed to London to meet with the Lords Proprietors to seek redress for Albemarle's problems. Carteret never returned, so Jenkins remained in charge.

By the fall of 1674 Jenkins and other officials were governing with expired commissions since the Lords Proprietors never renewed the four-year commissions issued in 1670. Jenkins remained as de facto governor for about a year. In September 1675, as stipulated by the Fundamental Constitutions, the colonists elected a new assembly. The proprietary faction (post-1663 settlers) gained control of the assembly and elected Thomas Eastchurch as Speaker. Eastchurch, who wished to be governor, had Jenkins arrested and imprisoned for "several misdemeanours." Eastchurch assumed the role of governor, but not the official title.

In the spring of 1676 the anti-proprietary faction forcibly released Jenkins and restored him as governor. Both Jenkins and Eastchurch tried to lead Albemarle for a time. Eastchurch departed for London to appeal to the Lords Proprietors.

By the fall of 1676, Jenkins was in control after he and his followers forcibly dissolved the assembly and overturned the leadership. Jenkins's second tenure lasted until July 1677 when he relinquished power to Thomas Miller. The colonists disliked Miller because of his abuse of power. The anti-proprietary faction overthrew the government and imprisoned Miller and his followers in the series of events known as Culpeper's Rebellion. The rebel government with Jenkins as its leader presided over Albemarle through 1678.

Following his appointment by the proprietors, John Harvey assumed the position of chief executive in July 1679. Harvey was highly respected and backed by the anti-proprietary faction. With his untimely death, Harvey's tenure lasted only six months. The council chose Jenkins to become acting governor. During Jenkins's fourth time as governor, Albemarle was fairly quiet, and the government was relatively stable. He remained in the post until his death on December 17, 1681.

REFERENCES: Butler, "The Governors of Albemarle County"; *DNCB*, vol. 3; Nugent, *Cavaliers and Pioneers*, vol. 1; Parker, "Legal Aspects of Culpeper's Rebellion"; Parker et al., *Colonial Records*, vol. 1; Powell, *Ye Countie of Albemarle*; Raimo, *Bio. Dir. of Col. and Rev. Governors*; Rankin, *Upheaval in Albemarle*; Sainsbury, Fortescue, and Headlam, *Calendar of State Papers, Colonial Series*; Saunders, *Colonial Records of N.C.*, vol. 1; Smith thesis, "Culpeper's Rebellion."

## GABRIEL JOHNSTON
### 1734-1752

$G$abriel Johnston (ca. 1698-1752) served longer than any governor in North Carolina's history, eighteen years. Even more remarkable is that, because of problems collecting the quitrents that paid his salary, he was uncompensated for thirteen of those years. Gabriel Johnston was born in Southdean, in the Scottish lowlands, to the Reverend Samuel Johnston and the former Isobel Hall. Records indicate that he was baptized on February 28, 1698. He was educated at the University of Edinburgh and the University of St. Andrews, receiving a master's degree from the latter. He studied medicine briefly at the University of Leiden, in Holland, leaving there in 1722 to accept an appointment to teach Hebrew and Oriental languages at St. Andrews. In 1740 Johnston made an advantageous match with his first wife, Penelope Golland, the thrice-widowed step-daughter of former governor Charles Eden. Before her death in 1741 they had one child, Penelope. Shortly thereafter he married Frances Button. His will mentions two other children, Henry and Carolina, believed to have been born out of wedlock. A fourth child, Polly, predeceased her father.

Around 1728 Johnston moved to London, where he lived in the home of Lord Wilmington, president of the Privy Council. During the time he wrote political articles and met many influential men. It is likely the London connections that helped Johnston to secure the governorship of North Carolina in 1733. He arrived at his post in October 1734 in a colony that welcomed new leadership. After three turbulent years under George Burrington, colonists still condemned many of the realities of being a royal colony, such as heavy, inflexible quitrents and a less powerful lower house. After years of a relatively lenient proprietary government, North Carolinians were resistant to strict royal authority.

Blank land patents were another vestige of the proprietary period to which the colonists clung. Proprietary land agents had sold blank patents, allowing the purchaser to fill in locations and amounts of land. Many such patents were never properly registered or taxed. Johnston's plan to end this practice was not popular with the wealthy men from the southern counties who owned thousands of acres from blank patents. The governor ultimately compromised and recognized many of these patents, provided the owners could provide some measure of documentation. He angered many of the same men when he advocated the establishment of Newton in 1735, later named Wilmington. Johnston facilitated the opening of a port and ordered several government offices and courts to move there, taking commerce away from Brunswick, which would never recover its status in North Carolina.

Johnston's term saw many changes in North Carolina, including the first printer and the first newspaper and printed laws, new agricultural techniques, and the building of several forts. Most notably, North Carolina's population tripled, thanks in part to Johnston's efforts to encourage immigration, especially from his native Scotland. As a result North Carolina's settlements expanded westward, and Johnston saw several new counties formed. Johnston died on July 17, 1752, and was buried at the plantation he inherited from Penelope, Eden House, near Edenton.

REFERENCES: *ANB*, vol. 12; *DNCB*, vol. 3; Ekirch, *"Poor Carolina"*; Saunders, *Colonial Records of N.C.*, vol. 4.

❖ ❖ ❖

## SAMUEL JOHNSTON
## 1787-1789

*S*amuel Johnston (1733-1816), prominent voice for the Patriot cause,

lived at Hayes, the family estate at Edenton. He was born on December 15, 1733, in Dundee, Scotland, the son of Samuel Johnston and the former Helen Scrymsoure. While still an infant, Johnston emigrated with his family to North Carolina and Onslow County, probably at the invitation of their kinsman, Gabriel Johnston, royal governor of the colony from 1734 to 1752. Johnston married Frances Cathcart in 1770; their union produced nine children, four of whom lived to maturity.

Young Johnston attended Yale College (now University), but left prior to graduation. Returning to North Carolina, he established his residence in Edenton in 1753 and pursued the study of law under prominent attorney and merchant, Thomas Barker. Admitted to the bar in 1756, Johnston began his steady rise to prominence in both North Carolina and the nation. In 1759 he was elected to the colonial assembly, where he would serve continuously as a representative from either Edenton or Chowan County until 1775 and the eve of the American Revolution.

As a leader of the Patriot cause, Johnston served from 1774 to 1776 as a member of North Carolina's provincial council. During the same period he was a delegate to the first four provincial congresses, serving as president of both the third and fourth. In addition, he was treasurer of North Carolina's Northern District from 1775 to 1777, with major responsibilities for funding and supplying the Revolutionary War effort. In 1779 Johnston was reelected to the state legislature as a senator from Chowan County. During the following year he entered national politics as a delegate to the Continental Congress. Indeed, in July 1781 he was nominated for the presidency of that body, but declined in order to return to North Carolina for family and business reasons.

Through his years in public service, Johnston already won wide respect for his character, wisdom, and dedication to principle, even from his political opponents. When North Carolina's first constitutional convention met in Hillsborough in 1788, Johnston, a leading Federalist, was elected president, even though the majority of delegates were opposed to ratification. Again he served as president during the following year at Fayetteville, when the assembled delegates voted in favor of ratification.

On December 12, 1787, Johnston was elected to his first term as governor, even though he was not a member of the legislature. Although twice reelected on subsequent occasions, he served just over two full terms. His third term ended after less than two weeks, when he resigned to accept election to the U.S. Senate. As governor, Johnston campaigned successfully with other prominent Federalists for ultimate ratification of the Federal Constitution, promoted national as well as state interests, and exercised a cautious restraint with regard to fiscal and monetary affairs.

Returning to North Carolina following his single term in the U.S. Senate, Johnston retired for a while from public life, resuming the practice of law and overseeing his several plantations. He returned to the state legislature, however, as a senator from Martin County in 1798-1799; and in 1800-1803, he sat on the bench as a superior court judge. Finally, at the age of seventy, he retired permanently from public life. He died thirteen years later, on August 17, 1816, and was buried in the cemetery of his Edenton plantation, Hayes.

REFERENCES: *DAB*, vol. 10; *DNCB*, vol. 3; Gilpatrick, *Jeffersonian Democracy in N.C.* PRIMARY SOURCES: Hayes Collection, NCSA; Hayes Collection, SHC; Johnson Collection, NCSA.

# WILLIAM WALTON KITCHIN
## *1909-1913*

*M*ember of a Halifax County family prominent in North Carolina politics for three generations, William Walton Kitchin (1866-1924) focused the state's attention on economic reform just as his predecessor Charles B. Aycock had concentrated on educational improvements. Born on

October 9, 1866, near Scotland Neck to William Hodge ("Buck") Kitchin and his wife, the former Maria Arrington, "Little Buck" was educated in local schools, among them Vine Hill Academy. His father, an officer of the Twelfth North Carolina Regiment taken prisoner at Spotsylvania Courthouse in 1864, served a single term in the U.S. House in 1879-1881. His brother Claude served in the U.S. House from 1901 to 1923, and rose to majority leader. Young W. W. Kitchin, upon graduation from Wake Forest College in 1884, for one year edited the *Democrat* in Scotland Neck. He then studied law with his father and at UNC. In 1888 he entered practice in Roxboro. In 1892 he married Musette Satterfield of Person County; they had five children.

W. W. Kitchin, a Democrat, entered politics at a point when his party's fortunes were at a low ebb. He began his career in 1890 as party chairman in Person County. In 1892 he unsuccessfully ran for the state senate. In 1896 he competed for the U.S. House seat in the Fifth District against incumbent Republican Thomas Settle, and the two engaged in a notable series of debates. Kitchin was the sole Democrat elected to either house of Congress from North Carolina in the fall 1896 election. As a congressman Kitchin served on the Committee on Naval Affairs and the Democratic Party's Congressional Campaign Committee. He defended the white supremacy and suffrage amendments and took a progressive stance toward other issues, advocating direct election of senators, regulation of business, and an income tax.

In the 1908 race for governor, U.S. senator Furnifold Simmons and ex-governor Aycock backed Locke Craig.

Gov. William W. Kitchin (*in dark suit under sign*), a lawyer by trade, called for economic reform to strengthen antitrust laws, set a ten-hour workday in factories, and prohibit work by children under the age of thirteen. A parade in Person County welcomes Kitchin home.

In the party convention Kitchin, then in his twelfth year in Congress, was the candidate of those opposed to the "Simmons machine." He triumphed on the sixty-first ballot over Craig and Ashley Horne, but only after an informal agreement was reached that Craig would be the nominee four years later. Campaigning largely on an antitrust platform and as the "people's choice," the liberal Kitchin soundly defeated Republican J. Elwood Cox. Voices were raised warning of the radical nature of Kitchin's positions, some even indicating that his plans were socialist.

As governor Kitchin increased expenditures for education, public health, care for the mentally handicapped, and drainage of swamp lands. In line with the national efforts to break up trusts and regulate business, Kitchin backed legislation to strengthen antitrust laws, require better sanitation and set a ten-hour workday in factories, prohibit work by children under the age of thirteen, and license foreign corporations that did business in the state. During his term 1,300 miles of roads were constructed; his administration favored study of road needs before setting a comprehensive construction policy.

In 1912 four influential Democrats competed for the nomination for the U.S. Senate. Incumbent Simmons, who controlled the conservative wing of the party, withstood challenges from Governor Kitchin, state supreme court chief justice Walter Clark, and ex-governor Aycock, who split the liberal vote (Aycock died during the campaign). Kitchin returned to the practice of law, setting up a partnership in Raleigh with James S.

Manning. In 1919 a stroke forced him into retirement, and he returned to Scotland Neck. A stroke also felled his brother Claude, and the two spent much time together in their final years. William W. Kitchin died on November 9, 1924, and was buried in the Baptist Cemetery in Scotland Neck.

REFERENCES: *BDC*; *DAB*, vol. 10; *DNCB*, vol. 3; Hunter, *Governor Kitchin*; *News and Observer*, November 10, 1924; *Proceedings of the Bar Association* (1925); Sobel and Raimo, *Bio. Dir. of Governors*, vol. 3; Wright, *Person Co. History*. PRIMARY SOURCES: Kitchin Papers, SHC.

◈ ◈ ◈

# RALPH LANE
## 1585-1586

Ralph Lane (ca. 1528-1603), a professional soldier, served as governor of the first colony attempted by the English in America. At that time, the region that encompassed Sir Walter Raleigh's land patent was called Virginia in honor of Queen Elizabeth I, the Virgin Queen. The first colony was organized as a military venture from which the Spanish, colonial rival of the English, could be harassed and to serve as a base for the exploration of the new land. In the end, the first colony was abandoned, and the survivors returned to England. It failed because of the settlement's poor location and the colonists' undue suffering; nevertheless, Lane's colony provided the English with valuable knowledge and experience for future endeavors.

Lane, born to Sir Ralph Lane and Maud Parr Lane of Northhampton, attended Oxford University in 1554 and served in the English Parliament in the late 1550s and early 1560s. He evidently never married. By 1563 Lane was serving in Queen Elizabeth's court, marking the beginning of a career of service to queen and country. Lane participated in a force that suppressed a rebellion in Scotland in 1569 where he gained accolades for his military skill. By the early 1570s, Lane had involved himself in maritime affairs that included a queen's commission to seize ships in 1571. By the late 1570s and early 1580s, he was developing plans and offering his services in helping England struggle with Spain. In 1583, Lane received a commission to go to Ireland and direct the construction of forts.

In 1585 the queen recalled Lane from Ireland, and he was given command of the colony that Sir Walter Raleigh was organizing to sail to Virginia (Roanoke Island). Raleigh evidently personally invited Lane to command the land expedition. The company was organized as a military expedition with soldiers and support personnel but also included artist John White and scientist Thomas Harriot. In April 1585, seven ships with about six hundred men under the overall command of Sir Richard Grenville left England. After a storm scattered the fleet and reduced it to five ships, the company regrouped. They arrived at the Outer Banks by June. By August, the colony had come ashore and built a fort following an invitation from the Indians. Grenville's fleet left at the end of August after being unable to secure a good harbor.

Lane's colony of 107 men lasted for only eight months. Lane's men explored the countryside with the intent of finding a better site for settlement. The colony suffered because of a lack of supplies and Lane's lack of skill in dealing with the Indians. Eventually, Lane decided to abandon the colony. The conditions for success were not favorable because of the colony's small size and the ravages of storms. On June 18 or 19, 1586, a fleet led by Sir Francis Drake left Roanoke carrying the first English colonists back home.

Lane was never involved in another colonization expedition but remained active in service to his country. He provided the foreword to Thomas Harriot's *A Briefe and True Report of the New Found Land of Virginia* (1588), and his account of the colony appeared in Richard Hakluyt's *Principal Navigations* (1589). Lane was back in Ireland in 1592 serving as "muster master general" and "clerk of the check of the garrison" and remained in that country for the rest of his life. By 1601 Lane's physical weakness had made him unfit as muster master. Lane died in Dublin, Ireland, and was buried October 28, 1603 at St. Patrick's Church.

REFERENCES: *ANB*, vol. 13; *DAB*, vol. 9; *DNB*, vol. 32; *DNCB*, vol. 4; Durant, *Ralegh's Lost Colony*; Hale, "Life of Sir Ralph Lane"; Kupperman, *Roanoke*; Quinn, *Set Fair for Roanoke*; Quinn and Quinn, *First Colonists*.

## PHILIP LUDWELL
## 1689-1691

*P*hilip Ludwell (ca. 1638-1723) was a career public servant who served both Virginia and Carolina. In Virginia Ludwell was a secretary of state, commander of the militia, and a member of the House of Burgesses. In 1689 the Lords Proprietors commissioned Ludwell as chief executive "of that part of our Province of Carolina that lyes north and east of Cape feare." Ludwell's appointment marked the foundation of North Carolina as a colony with Albemarle being a part of the expanded colony. In time the proprietors chose Ludwell as the first governor of the Carolina province. Born in Bruton Parish, Somersetshire, England, Ludwell was the son of Thomas and Jane Cottington Ludwell. The young man immigrated to Virginia around 1660. He was married to the twice-widowed Lucy Higginson Burwell Bernard around 1667; they had two children, a daughter Jane and a son Philip. His first wife died in 1675. In October 1680 he married Lady Frances Culpeper Stephens Berkeley, the widow of Albemarle governor Samuel Stephens and Virginia governor William Berkeley.

In Virginia Ludwell acquired several plantations and became active in politics. In 1675 he was a member of Governor Berkeley's council, and he served briefly as secretary of state. During Bacon's Rebellion of 1676, Ludwell supported Berkeley's harsh response to Nathaniel Bacon and his followers. As a colonel, he led the militia in capturing several of the rebellion's leaders. Even after Berkeley's recall to England and his subsequent death, Ludwell continued to support the measures that Berkeley took against Bacon and his followers. In 1689 Ludwell traveled to London as an agent for the House of Burgesses to present grievances to the royal government.

While he was in London, Ludwell met with the Lords Proprietors. On December 5, 1689, the proprietors commissioned Ludwell as governor of an expanded northern colony in the Carolina province. As governor, Ludwell was given the responsibility of bringing order to a region that had been inadequately led by Seth Sothel. He established his new government in North Carolina by May 1690. As chief executive, Ludwell maintained his residence in Virginia but traveled often to the colony. John Gibbs, who was serving as governor following Sothel's departure, objected to Ludwell's commission. Gibbs refused to concede power to Ludwell and challenged Ludwell's authority. To settle the problem, Ludwell and Gibbs went to London to present their cases to the Lords Proprietors. The proprietors ruled in Ludwell's favor, upholding his appointment as governor.

In November 1691 the Lords Proprietors appointed Ludwell "Governor and Comander in Cheif [*sic*] of Carolina" with the authority "to apoint [*sic*] a Deputy Governor of North Carolina." Thomas Jarvis was chosen as the deputy governor. With Jarvis in North Carolina, Ludwell concentrated on affairs in South Carolina. Yet, Ludwell acted in some capacity as chief executive of North Carolina beyond 1691. He most likely assumed North Carolina's leadership while Thomas Jarvis was in poor health. During this second unofficial tenure, Ludwell helped to improve the problematic land policies. He sought to honor the validity of the Great Deed of Grant of 1668 that provided land on favorable terms as was given in Virginia. In time Ludwell returned to Virginia politics. Around 1700 he permanently retired to England and apparently died around 1723. Ludwell was buried in a family vault at Stratford-le-Bow Church in Middlesex, England.

REFERENCES: *ANB*, vol. 14; *DAB*, vol. 11; *DNCB*, vol. 4; Parker et al., *Colonial Records*, vol. 2; Raimo, *Bio. Dir. of Col. and Rev. Governors*; Saunders, *Colonial Records of N.C.*, vol. 1; Sirmans, *Colonial N.C.*

## ANGUS WILTON McLEAN
## 1925-1929

*W*ith a background in finance and business, Angus Wilton McLean (1870-1935) introduced into state government sound fiscal management, substantially revising the budget process and reorganizing state agencies. The "Businessman's Governor" was of Scotch ancestry and developed an interest in genealogy; his research was published posthumously by terms of a bequest in his will. He was born on April 20, 1870, in Robeson County to Confederate veteran and farmer Archibald McLean and the former Caroline Purcell. After graduation from local public schools and McMillan Military Academy, young McLean studied law beginning in 1890 at UNC. In 1892 he was admitted to the bar and joined a practice in Lumberton. McLean married Margaret French in 1904; they had three children.

In addition to his legal pursuits, McLean was among Lumberton's leading businessmen, involved with the founding of the town's first bank, three textile mills, and the Virginia and Carolina Railroad, for which he served as president. Long active in the Democratic Party, McLean served on the state executive committee and as a delegate to national conventions. In 1919 President Woodrow Wilson appointed him one of four directors of the War Finance Corporation; in 1920 the president named him assistant secretary of the treasury.

McLean, with the support of the political machine of Sen. Furnifold Simmons, defeated Josiah Bailey for the Democratic gubernatorial nomination in 1924 and in the fall easily defeated Republican Isaac M. Meekins.

In his inaugural address, McLean recommended thorough revision of the budget system for state government. A month later the legislature adopted his plan, making the governor the head of the Advisory Budget Bureau in charge of preparing a biennial budget. The Department of Revenue was created during McLean's term. A daily deposit system enacted by the legislature required the direct

Gov. Angus W. McLean was known as the "Businessman's Governor." He poses with his wife Margaret, in front of the Executive Mansion during his term in office.

deposit of all state funds in order to reap the maximum interest. In the campaigns with Bailey and Meekins, attention had been drawn to the bonded debt accumulated under Governor Morrison. With conservative management of the revenue McLean concluded his term with a $2½ million surplus, a cushion that would aid his successor during the Depression.

McLean continued the highway improvements initiated by his predecessor, with new bond issues of $20 million issued in 1925 and $30 million in 1927. During his term of office, the Department of Conservation and Development replaced the old Geological and Economic Survey. That agency, the duties of which have since been assumed by successor departments, promoted economic development and the protection of natural resources. The Corporation Commission was established to supervise the regulation of business. A classification system and uniform wage and salary schedule were put in place for state employees. At the recommendation of the governor, the General Assembly enacted laws to change the structure of county government, with budgetary procedures and roles for commissioners defined by law.

McLean withheld his support from progressive labor measures, among them bills to secure workmen's compensation and extended child labor legislation. An avid outdoorsman, McLean was the first modern chief executive to leave the state for extended stays. The first statewide game law was passed during his administration. McLean in 1927 endorsed the legislation necessary to establish the Great Smoky Mountains National Park.

Upon the conclusion of his term as governor, McLean returned to his law practice in Lumberton and soon opened a second office in Washington, D.C. In deference to his friend Furnifold Simmons he declined to run for the U.S. Senate in 1930. In April 1935 he suffered a stroke in Raleigh and died two months later on June 21, 1935. His body was returned to Lumberton for burial.

REFERENCES: Connor et al., *History of N.C.*, vol. 5; Corbitt, *McLean Papers*; Curry, *Highland Scots*; *DNCB*, vol. 4; Lawrence, *The State of Robeson*; McLean et al., *Lumber River Scot*; *News and Observer*, June 22, 1935; *Proceedings of the Bar Association* (1935); Sobel and Raimo, *Bio. Dir. of Governors*, vol. 3; Underwood dissertation, "Angus Wilton McLean." PRIMARY SOURCES: McLean Papers, SHC.

## CHARLES MANLY
### 1849-1851

Charles Manly (1795-1871) presided over the decline and fall of the Whig Party in North Carolina. The son of Basil and Elizabeth Maultsby Manly, he was born on May 13, 1795, at Oak Mont, the family home near Pittsboro. His early education came from black educator John Chavis, who was hired by Basil Manly to teach his sons, and at Pittsboro Academy run by William Bingham. He enrolled at UNC in 1811 and graduated with honors in 1814. While studying law in Raleigh, Manly earned a living tutoring the children of state treasurer John Haywood. He was admitted to the bar in 1816. In 1817 Manly married Charity Hare Haywood of Raleigh. They would be the parents of eleven children.

In 1823 Manly served as clerk to the commission to settle claims against Great Britain under the Treaty of Ghent. The following year he was appointed assistant clerk to the House of Commons, an office he held until 1830 when he was made the principal clerk. He tended to that duty for the next seventeen years except for the 1842-1843 session. Meanwhile, he was serving as treasurer of the board of trustees for UNC (1821-1849) and was invited to deliver the first annual address to the Alumni Association in 1838.

Manly joined the Whig Party at its formation and was the choice to succeed Gov. William A. Graham in 1848. He narrowly defeated David S. Reid in the general election and took the oath of office on January 1, 1849. His administration was not particularly notable since most of the Whig initiatives had been started under the three previous administrations. Manly maintained support for internal improvements and public education while also calling for a statewide geological survey. He assisted efforts to preserve the state's colonial history by collecting documents housed in London. He also proclaimed the first Thanksgiving Day in North Carolina: Thursday, November 15, 1849. His message to the General Assembly in 1850 foreshadowed the dilemma facing many Whigs in North Carolina. He warned of dangers in the separation of the South from the Union and urged state leaders to avoid secession. Yet, at the same time, he vowed that the South should never surrender its constitutional and moral rights in an effort to change southern destiny.

Charles Manly's election in 1848 was the last victory for the Whig

Party. His bid for re-election in 1850 failed as Democrat David S. Reid won by almost 3,000 votes. With his political career over, Manly returned to a successful law practice in Raleigh. He was again selected as secretary–treasurer of the board of trustees for UNC in 1851 and served until the Reconstruction government took control of the university in 1868. He held that post for a total of forty-five years.

In retirement Manly lived on his Ingleside Plantation, comprising 1,060 acres, east of Raleigh. In April 1865 troops under command of Gen. William T. Sherman pillaged his home and storehouses. After a long illness, one that left him blind, Manly died at his mansion on May 1, 1871. He was buried in the City Cemetery with only his name and life dates inscribed on a simple tombstone.

REFERENCES: Angley, Cross, and Hill, *Sherman's March*; Ashe et al., *Biographical History*, vol. 6; *Cyclopedia of Eminent and Representative Men*, vol. 2; *DNCB*, vol. 4; Murray, *Wake: Capital County*, vol. 1; Osborn and Sturgill, *Chatham County Architectural Heritage*.

# ALEXANDER MARTIN
## 1782-1784; 1789-1792

*A*lexander Martin (ca. 1739-1807) served nonconsecutive terms as governor in the late eighteenth century. He was born in Hunterdon County, New Jersey, the eldest son of Hugh Martin and the former Jane Hunter. Following a preparatory education in Connecticut, he attended the College of New Jersey (now Princeton University), where he received A.B. and A.M. degrees in 1756 and 1759 respectively. Although he never married, he left a son, Alexander Strong Martin, whom he had publicly acknowledged.

About 1760 Martin moved to North Carolina and established himself as a merchant and lawyer in Salisbury. By 1766 he had become a justice of the peace and county attorney. In 1770 he was one of several county officials attacked by Regulators at Hillsborough, and during the next year he was reproved by Gov. Josiah Martin for unauthorized negotiations with Regulators near Salisbury. In 1773 Martin relocated to a tract of land along the Dan River in present-day Rockingham (then Guilford) County. Rising quickly to local prominence, he represented Guilford County in the colonial assembly in 1773-1774 and in the second and third provincial congresses in 1775. He later served in the state senate from 1778 to 1782. He was chairman of the Board of War in 1780, and Speaker of the senate from 1780 to 1782. Following the Revolution, Martin returned to the state senate in 1785, 1787, and 1788, again serving as Speaker.

Martin's brief military career during the Revolution was marred by controversy. Named to succeed Robert Howe as commander of the Second Regiment of the North Carolina Continental Line, he was later court-martialed for cowardice following the Battle of Germantown. Though acquitted, he resigned his commission and returned to North Carolina. In 1787 Martin was one of five delegates from North Carolina to the Constitutional Convention in Philadelphia. He took little part in the deliberations and returned home well before the Constitution was adopted. Moreover, he was the only member of the North Carolina delegation not strongly committed to the Federalist position. Martin, as Speaker of the senate, in 1781 assumed the office of governor during Thomas Burke's period of captivity, and on April 22,

1782, he was elected over Samuel Johnston to the first of three consecutive terms in his own right. Seven years later, on December 5, 1789, he was again elected to the first of three consecutive terms. As chief executive, Martin steered a moderate course between Federalist and Anti-Federalist extremes, seeking consensus on major issues while defending the interests of western residents. His repeated election to the governorship bears ample testimony to his practicality, political skills, and personal popularity. Major accomplishments during his two administrations included the close of the Revolution, collapse of the breakaway "State of Franklin," chartering of UNC, and the establishment of Raleigh as the permanent state capital.

At the end of his last term, Martin was elected to the U.S. Senate where he served for the next six years. While there he advocated open sessions, limited government, and economic restraint. Defeated for reelection in 1798, he returned to North Carolina and to his Rockingham County home, "Danbury." In 1804 and 1805 he again returned to the state senate, serving during the latter year as Speaker. Martin died at his home on November 2, 1807, and was interred on the grounds.

REFERENCES: *DAB*, vol. 12; *DNCB*, vol. 4; Gilpatrick, *Jeffersonian Democracy in N.C.*; Sobel and Raimo, *Bio. Dir. of Governors*, vol. 3.

## JAMES GRUBBS MARTIN
## 1985-1993

The election of Republican James G. Martin (1935- ) to two consecutive four-year terms as governor reflected the fact that North Carolina was no longer a one-party state. A political moderate and the first Ph.D. to hold the office, Martin pursued initiatives with respect to economic development, education, transportation, and the environment but met blunt resistance to his programs in the General Assembly, dominated by Democrats. Born in Savannah, Georgia, on December 11, 1935, James Grubbs Martin was the son of Arthur Morrison Martin, a Presbyterian minister, and the former Mary Julia Grubbs. Raised in Winnsboro, South Carolina, young Martin attended public schools, where he took part in sports and played the tuba (as an adult Martin composed music). He attended Davidson College, graduating in 1957, and earned a doctorate in chemistry from Princeton University in 1960. In 1957 he married Dorothy Ann McAulay; they would have three children.

In 1960 Martin joined the faculty of his alma mater and taught chemistry at Davidson until 1972. From 1966 to 1972 he served on the Mecklenburg County Board of Commissioners, for three years as chair. In 1972 voters of the Ninth District elected Martin, who lived at Lake Norman, to the U.S. House. In six terms in Congress Martin chaired the House Republican Research Committee and the Republican Task Force on Health and Environment. Also a member of the Ways and Means Committee, Martin was recognized for his expertise on food additives and toxic waste. In the Republican primary for governor in 1984, Martin easily defeated Ruby Hooper and in the fall defeated the Democratic nominee, Attorney General Rufus L. Edmisten. In 1988 Martin defeated his Democratic opponent, Lt. Gov. Robert B. Jordan III. James C. Gardner became the first Republican elected lieutenant governor in the twentieth century in the same election.

As a candidate Martin, an advocate of supply-side economics, campaigned on a pro-business platform, and as governor, benefiting from the prosperity of the mid-1980s, Martin boosted industrial development by reducing business taxes and recruiting out-of-state companies. In proposing his Strategic Highway Corridor plan in 1987, whereby a four-lane highway would pass within 96 percent of the state's residents, Martin stressed economic benefits. He forwarded the concept of a global air cargo industrial complex and held to his promise to see I-40 completed. In the Coastal Initiative and Mountain Area Planning System, the administration sought to strike a balance between development and environmental protection. Martin led an unsuccessful bid to land the Superconducting Super Collider.

Martin contended that education was his first priority and, toward that end, increased spending on public schools and teacher salaries. An advocate of a career ladder for teachers, Martin clashed with the legislature over provisions of the Basic Education Program, adopted in 1985. The governor instituted special training in foreign languages, a day care initiative, and a campaign against illiteracy. Martin launched campaigns against infant mortality and substance abuse and advocated an accelerated prison construction program.

In his first inaugural address Martin spoke of "One United State" and improvements to the quality of life. A proponent of open government, he reduced the number of state employees subject to political firing. Other initiatives pursued by the

Gov. James Martin, the first Republican elected to two consecutive terms, boosted industrial development by reducing business taxes and recruiting out-of-state companies. Governor Martin threshes hay at the Old Threshers' Reunion held in Denton, North Carolina. The annual event celebrates historical farming techniques through demonstrations of farm machinery, craft exhibits, and musical festivals.

administration included the Adopt-a-Highway program, the planting of wildflowers along the highways, aquaculture research, improved beach access, estuarine study projects, reinstituted passenger rail service, and an expanded film industry.

By 1993 the Republican Party had established broad appeal to middle-class voters in North Carolina. Martin, advocate of the gubernatorial veto and appointment of judges, laid the groundwork for subsequent political changes. After his self-pronounced retirement from officeholding, Martin became chairman of the Research Develop- ment Board at the Carolinas Medical Center in Charlotte.

REFERENCES: Mullaney, *Bio. Dir. of Governors*; Poff, *Martin Papers*, vols. 1 and 2; *Who's Who in American Politics, 1979-1980*. PRIMARY SOURCES: Martin Papers, SHC.

◈ ◈ ◈

## JOSIAH MARTIN
## 1771-1775

*J*osiah Martin (1737-1786), the last royal governor of North Carolina, aroused sentiment for independence in North Carolina through his inflexible loyalty to the Crown. He was born in April 1737 in Dublin, Ireland, to Col. Samuel and Sarah Wyke Irish Martin of Greencastle,

Antigua. He spent most of his first fifteen years in Ireland and England, traveling with his tutor to the West Indies in 1752. He did not care for the tropical climate in Antigua, however, claiming that it affected his health. In 1756 Martin reported to London to study law. There his older half brother Samuel, a member of Parliament, used his influence to help Josiah gain favorable positions. Forsaking the study of law, young Martin for a time pursued a military career. Josiah Martin married his first cousin Elizabeth Martin in New York in January 1761. They had eight children, four of whom survived to maturity, but none of whom married.

His brother Samuel's efforts on his behalf finally paid off when Lord Hillsborough, the secretary of the colonies, was shuffling leadership posts. North Carolina's governor, William Tryon, transferred to New York to assume its governorship. Josiah Martin, at age thirty-four, was named to succeed Tryon in December 1770. He did not receive the notification, however, until March 1771. By that time he was undergoing medical treatment in New York. It would be several months before he could move south.

Martin inherited numerous problems from Tryon, among them the fallout from the War of the Regulation, an ongoing boundary dispute with South Carolina, and a controversy over the colonists' rights over non-resident debtors. His term initially showed promise, as he was able to calm discordant feelings resulting from the War of the Regulation. The governor and the assembly worked together to produce legislation in 1771 to resolve the war debt. Yet, Martin's loyalty to the Crown was without question. The assembly in 1773 tacked a foreign attachment clause onto the court law bill permitting colonists to recover debts owed by non-residents who owned property in North Carolina. Martin vetoed the bill because the attachment clause was unfavorable to the Crown. The veto left the colony without a court system. For this the colonists blamed royal authority.

North Carolinians, holding Martin in contempt, convened the First Provincial Congress in New Bern in 1774. This convention recommended that counties form committees of safety, a move to supplant royal authority. Within the year, Martin sent his family to New York, fearing for their safety. He fled from New Bern to Fort Johnston, in present-day Southport. There he stayed until, hearing of a plot to take the fort, he moved headquarters offshore to the war sloop *Cruizer*.

Martin stayed with his family in New York from 1776 to 1779, during which time his wife died, and all of his property in North Carolina was sold by order of the assembly. Late in the war, still hopeful that he could regain his post, he joined Lord Charles Cornwallis to try to rally Loyalist troops in North Carolina. Citing health reasons, Martin left for England in 1781 with all but one of his children. Martin died on April 13, 1786, and was buried at St. George's Parish Church in London.

REFERENCES: *DNCB*, vol. 4; Stumpf, *Josiah Martin*; Taylor, "The Foreign Attachment Law."

# THOMAS MILLER
## 1677

*T*homas Miller (d. ca. 1685) served as Albemarle's governor for about six months in 1677, during which time his government was overthrown in an uprising known as Culpeper's Rebellion. Miller originally resided in Ireland working as a merchant and apothecary. By 1673 he had settled in Albemarle and become a leader in the proprietary faction. In 1676 the anti-proprietary faction, led by John Jenkins, regained partial control of Albemarle from proprietary leader Thomas Eastchurch. They indicted Miller for treason and blasphemy and for speaking disparagingly of the Lords Proprietors. Miller was imprisoned and later sent to Virginia in May 1676 for trial. The Virginia Council acquitted Miller; he left for London where he joined Eastchurch.

Miller and Eastchurch met with the proprietors in the fall of 1676. They presented their version of the events in Albemarle to the proprietors who accepted their story. The Lords Proprietors issued commissions appointing Eastchurch as governor of Albemarle and Miller as council member and secretary. Miller also received an appointment as customs collector. The two men left for Albemarle in the summer of 1677.

The ship carrying Miller and Eastchurch stopped in the West Indies. During this stopover Eastchurch met a wealthy woman and married her. Wishing to stay longer, Eastchurch commissioned Miller as acting governor. He arrived in Albemarle in July 1677 and claimed the governor's office. He authorized the collection of fees and tried anti-proprietary faction members for various offenses. Miller called for the election of a new assembly but disfranchised the anti-proprietary faction. Miller's assembly imposed fines on the anti-proprietary faction to punish them. Miller caused more antagonism by having the assembly levy high taxes and by using public money to pay his armed guards.

In December 1677 Miller's arrest of Zachariah Gillam for customs violations and his attempted arrest of anti-proprietary leader George Durant sent Albemarle into rebellion. Led by John Culpeper and Valentine Bird, an armed group imprisoned Miller and his followers. Gaining control of the government, the anti-proprietary faction brought Miller to trial. The trial was discontinued when Eastchurch, who was in Virginia, issued a proclamation calling on the colonists to disarm, to free Miller and others, and to restore the rightful government. The proclamation stopped the trial proceedings and saved Miller from the prospect of execution for treason. However, he remained imprisoned for two years before being freed by friends.

Miller went to London and complained to the Lords Proprietors, the Commissioners of Customs, and the Privy Council about what had happened. He obtained the arrest of Zachariah Gillam and John Culpeper when they were in London. But Gillam was released for a lack of evidence, and Culpeper was acquitted of treason. Miller obtained some justice receiving monetary compensation from the royal treasury. He received an appointment as customs collector in Poole, England,

in March 1681. In July 1682 he transferred to a better customs post in Weymouth. In short order he was removed from the position and imprisoned for embezzling. Miller died in prison prior to October 1685.

REFERENCES: Butler, "The Governors of Albemarle County"; *DNCB*, vol. 4; Parker et al., *Colonial Records*, vol. 2; Parker, "Legal Aspects of Culpeper's Rebellion"; Rankin, *Upheaval in Albemarle*; Saunders, *Colonial Records of N.C.*, vol. 1; Smith thesis, "Culpeper's Rebellion."

# WILLIAM MILLER
## 1814-1817

*A*fter his term as governor, William Miller (ca. 1783-1825) was appointed to a diplomatic position in Central America but died en route to the post.

Born in Warren County, he was the second son of Thomas Miller Jr. His mother is thought to have been a daughter of Allen Love of Brunswick County, Virginia. Upon the death of his father in the early 1790s, young Miller inherited a plantation of 930 acres. His early education was apparently at Warrenton Male Academy, under the Reverend Marcus George. He enrolled at UNC in 1802, but left school prior to graduation. By 1809 he was a resident of Warrenton and was engaged in the practice of law. Miller married Lydia Anna Evans in 1816, but their union was to prove only of brief duration. She died in 1818 at her father's home near Petersburg, Virginia. Their only child, William Jr., followed her in death while still a small boy.

In 1810 Governor David Stone named Miller to succeed Oliver Fitts as state attorney general. That same year Miller began the first of four terms in the General Assembly, twice serving as Speaker of the House of Commons. Although returned for a fifth term, he resigned to become governor upon his election to that office.

Miller served three terms as governor (1814-1817), and was the first to occupy the newly completed Executive Mansion at the south end of Raleigh's Fayetteville Street. Within the context of national politics, he supported the military policies of President James Madison during the concluding weeks of the War of 1812 by ordering out additional militia forces for potential service on the southern frontier. With regard to internal affairs in the state, he lent his support to the early efforts to establish a system of public education, improve trade and transportation, and reform the penal code and judicial system. In 1817 he and Archibald D. Murphey joined forces in an unsuccessful effort to establish an independent supreme court. That effort would come to fruition during the following year under Miller's successor. It is of interest to note, as well, that it was during Miller's tenure as governor that the Canova statue of George Washington was commissioned.

Following several years in Warrenton as a private citizen, Miller returned to Raleigh in 1821 as a member of the state senate for Warren County. In 1825 President John Quincy Adams appointed him a diplomatic agent to Guatemala. However, he died of yellow fever on December 10, 1825, at Key West, en route to assume his new post, and was probably buried at sea.

REFERENCES: *DNCB*, vol. 4; Gilpatrick, *Jeffersonian Democracy in N.C.*; Johnson, *Ante-Bellum N.C.*; Sobel and Raimo, *Bio. Dir. of Governors*, vol. 3.

## DANIEL KILLIAN MOORE
### 1965-1969

*W*ith years of experience on the bench, Dan K. Moore (1906-1986) brought to the governor's office during the turbulent 1960s a calm, judicial temperament and a moderately conservative approach to balanced state government, a philosophy he termed "total development." Tagged "Mountain Man" during the 1964 campaign, Moore was born on April 2, 1906, in Asheville. His father Fred Moore, a superior court judge, died when young Moore was two years old, and his mother, the former Lela Enloe, moved the family to Jackson County. In 1927 he graduated from UNC with a business degree and then for a year studied law in Chapel Hill. In 1933 he married Jeanelle Coulter of Pikeville, Tennessee; they would have two children.

From 1931 to 1933 Dan K. Moore was attorney for Jackson County, and for twelve years he was the attorney for the local school board. Moore served a single term in the state House in 1941. In 1943 he entered the U.S. Army as a volunteer and served in Europe. On his return in 1945 he was elected solicitor, and in 1948 Gov. R. Gregg Cherry appointed Moore to the North Carolina Superior Court. Two years later Judge Moore was elected to a full term and served until his resignation in 1958, when he moved to Canton and became counsel and assistant secretary of Champion Paper.

Moore retained his strong interest in politics and in 1964 entered the contest for the Democratic nomination for governor. After the first primary the leader was L. Richardson Preyer, who had the support of Gov. Terry Sanford and was the most liberal of the three major candidates. Third-place finisher I. Beverly Lake, the most conservative, threw his support to the moderate Moore in the runoff where Moore bested Preyer. In the fall Moore defeated Republican Robert L. Gavin, who had also lost to Sanford in 1960.

As governor Moore employed a reasoned, deliberate approach to issues and, a number of times, appointed study commissions to assist in decision-making. In the closing days of the 1963 session, the General Assembly enacted a law barring Communists from speaking on state campuses. Moore's nine-member commission, headed by David Britt, recommended that trustees at each institution set policy with respect to speakers. A special session of the legislature in 1965, called by Moore, endorsed the idea. In 1968 a federal court declared the original law unconstitutional.

In his inaugural address Governor Moore introduced his concept of "total development," that is, his aim to develop all of the state's resources without emphasis or detriment to one. His agenda included a $300 million road bonds package approved by voters in 1965, increased teacher and state employee salaries, court-ordered reapportionment of legislative and congressional districts, institution in 1967 of "brown-bagging" as opposed to liquor by the drink, an

emphasis on highway safety, and creation of a Law and Order Committee to deal with racial unrest. Following the assassination of Martin Luther King Jr. in 1968, Moore deployed the National Guard and Highway Patrol to curb violence. During his administration Charlotte College became UNC at Charlotte, the School of the Arts opened, a zoo study commission was created, the State Court of Appeals was established, and the first state welcome centers were built.

After his term as governor, Moore joined a Raleigh law firm and in 1969 was named by Gov. Robert W. Scott as an associate justice on the North Carolina Supreme Court. He was elected to a full term in 1970 and served until 1978. The following year Gov. James B. Hunt Jr. named Moore to chair a commission on transportation needs and financing, a board that recommended a motor fuels tax increase later approved by the legislature. Moore, a Methodist, died on September 7, 1986, and is buried in Oakwood Cemetery in Raleigh.

Gov. Daniel K. Moore exhibits some of the postcards he received from all over the world (ca. 1970). The cards were sent by members of the North Carolina Air National Guard as they performed flight missions in support of the Vietnam War.

REFERENCES: *Asheville Citizen*, September 8-9, 1986; Henderson and others, *North Carolina*, vol. 4; Mitchell, *Moore Papers*; *News and Observer*, September 8-9, 1986; Powell, *North Carolina Lives*; Sobel and Raimo, *Bio. Dir. of Governors*, vol. 3; Spence, *The Making of a Governor*. PRIMARY SOURCES: Moore Collection, NCSA.

## JOHN MOTLEY MOREHEAD 1841-1845

John Motley Morehead (1796-1866), builder of the magnificent Blandwood estate in Greensboro and the first governor inaugurated in the present Capitol, presided over an era of industrial development and, after his term, promoted construction of the North Carolina Railroad. The son of John and Obedience Motley Morehead, he was born in Virginia on July 4, 1796, but his parents moved to Rockingham County when he was two. Young John studied at David Caldwell's school near Greensboro and then entered UNC with the class of 1817. He completed his education by studying law with Archibald D. Murphey and set up an office in Wentworth in 1819. In 1821 Morehead had married Ann Eliza

Lindsay of Greensboro; they would have eight children.

Morehead represented Rockingham County in the 1821 session of the House of Commons and Guilford County for two successive sessions beginning in 1826. His political views were honed by residency in a then western county and his early association with the visionary Archibald D. Murphey. Owing to the former he witnessed the domination of a majority by a minority with special interests and the need for constitutional reform, and from the latter he had learned of the potential benefits of internal improvements, a stronger banking system, expanded education, and a government active in the public sector. As a delegate to the 1835 Constitutional Convention, he sided with his fellow westerners and fought for legislative representation based on population. As a proponent of education and the father of five daughters, he took upon himself the establishment in 1840 of Edgeworth Female Seminary.

Morehead's activity and high visibility made him a logical choice of the Whig Party, which sought to continue the progressive program begun during the previous administration. Though popular enough to be elected governor in 1840 and again in 1842, Morehead found himself facing a legislature controlled by conservative Democrats. He pushed for a broad program of internal improvements but made little headway. His one achievement was a law establishing a school for the deaf. The blind, whose education he also advocated, were not admitted until years later; nevertheless, the long operating school for the sight-impaired still bears his name.

After his terms as governor, Morehead became the state's foremost promoter of railroads, particularly the North Carolina Railroad, which he served as president from 1850 to 1855. To him must go much of the credit for its construction. He also invested in a cotton mill at Leaksville and other manufacturing enterprises, and he was on the board of trustees of UNC. Morehead again represented Guilford County in the House in 1858-1859. He returned for the next session as a member of the state senate. As the secession crisis mounted, Morehead favored maintaining union and attended the Washington "Peace Conference," hoping to avert the impending conflict. With its failure, he viewed secession as an unavoidable necessity and threw his allegiance to the South. He was elected as a delegate to the Confederate Provincial Congress in 1861 and served until it completed its work in 1862. His public service to his state was over, and he returned to Greensboro. He died in Alum Springs, Virginia, four years later on August 27, 1866. His grave remains in the yard of the First Presbyterian Church in Greensboro.

REFERENCES: *ANB*, vol. 15; Arnett, *Greensboro*; Caldwell, *Founders and Builders of Greensboro*; Connor, "John Motley Morehead"; *DAB*, vol. 13; *DNCB*, vol. 4; Konkle, *John Motley Morehead*.

# CAMERON MORRISON
## 1921-1925

*I*n a public career spanning fifty years, Cameron Morrison (1869-1953) served as U.S. senator and representative as well as governor, but is best remembered for highway and school improvements financed by bond issues, initiatives that earned North Carolina a reputation as the most progressive southern state in the 1920s. The "Good Roads Governor" was born on October 5, 1869, in Richmond County to Confederate veteran and local officeholder Daniel Morrison and the former Martha Cameron. Educated in schools in Ellerbe Springs and Rockingham, young Morrison did not attend college but in 1892 studied law with Judge Robert P. Dick of Greensboro. The same year he passed the bar and returned to Rockingham to practice. In 1905, the year he moved his practice to Charlotte, Morrison married Lottie May Tomlinson of Durham; of their four children, only their daughter Angelia survived infancy. Lottie Morrison died in 1919, on the eve of his gubernatorial bid. While governor, on April 2, 1924, Morrison married Sarah Ecker Watts, widow of Durham financier George Washington Watts.

Morrison switched from the Republican to Democratic Party in 1891 and expended much effort opposing what he viewed as abuses of the political system by Republicans

Under the tutelage of Gov. Cameron Morrison, North Carolina earned a reputation as the most progressive southern state in the 1920s. He was called the "Good Roads Governor" for the improvements made on the state highways. Governor Morrison takes a walk on a mountain trip in July 1920.

and their allies in the 1890s. As a leader of the "Red Shirts" in his home county, he promoted white supremacy with tactics that included harassment of and threats of violence against blacks. Morrison, who served as mayor of Rockingham, was defeated in a bid for the state senate in 1896 but was elected to a single term in 1900. With the support of the political machine of U.S. senator Furnifold Simmons, Morrison won the Democratic nomination for governor in 1920, besting Lt. Gov. O. Max Gardner and former congressman Robert N. Page in a close and hard-fought contest. In the fall he defeated Republican John J. Parker by a wide margin.

Morrison devoted almost half of his inaugural address to highways, endorsing practically all of the goals of the Good Roads movement. With his backing and grass-roots organization, the 1921 legislature enacted an act providing for a $50 million bond issue (followed in 1923 by an additional $15 million). To be financed by receipts from automobile and gasoline taxes, the bonds funded construction of 5,500 miles of hard-surface roads. The swift action and fiscal daring shocked Morrison's conservative backers, who warned that the plan would bankrupt the state. His administration ended with a deficit of $9 million that was repaid during his successor's term.

The legislature, on the governor's recommendation, funded $20 million in bonds for improvements for higher education and the state's charitable institutions. During Morrison's administration the state assumed operation of the orthopedic hospital at

Gastonia and elevated the North Carolina College for Negroes in Durham (now N.C. Central University) to four-year status. Despite his earlier history, Morrison sought to improve race relations and all but ended lynching in the state. A Presbyterian, Morrison was a traditionalist on social issues, endorsing Prohibition and opposing the teaching of evolution in the public schools. His principal defeat during his term came at the hands of voters in 1924, when they rejected his proposal for an $8 million bond issue to finance state port terminal facilities.

In 1925 Morrison returned to Charlotte and his Morrocroft estate, then under construction. In 1930 Gov. O. Max Gardner appointed him to fill an unexpired U.S. Senate term on the death of Lee S. Overman. Two years later, Robert R. Reynolds defeated Morrison in his bid for a full term in a campaign where the political novice ridiculed the veteran for his wealth acquired through marriage. In 1942 Morrison was elected to the U.S. House but two years later was defeated by Clyde R. Hoey in another bid for the Senate. Morrison died in Quebec on August 20, 1953, and is buried in Elmwood Cemetery in Charlotte.

REFERENCES: Brown, *State Highway System of N.C.*; *DNCB*, vol. 4; Graham, "Cameron Morrison"; Magruder dissertation, "Cameron Morrison"; Puryear, *Democratic Party Dissension*; Richardson and Corbitt, *Morrison Papers*; Sobel and Raimo, *Bio. Dir. of Governors*, vol. 3.

## ABNER NASH
### 1780-1781

*A*bner Nash (ca. 1740-1786) succeeded Richard Caswell to become the second governor of the young state. He was born in present-day Prince Edward (then Amelia) County, Virginia. Of Welsh extraction, he was the son of John Nash and the former Ann Owen. Though little is known of his educational background, he began the practice of law in 1757 and in 1761-1762 represented Prince Edward County in the House of Burgesses. Nash was first married to Justina Davis Dobbs, the widow of Gov. Arthur Dobbs. His second marriage was to Mary Whiting Jones of Chowan County.

Soon after leaving the Virginia legislature, Nash moved to North Carolina, residing briefly in Hillsborough and Halifax. Experiencing success in both law and politics, he represented the town of Halifax and

Halifax County in the North Carolina Assembly in 1764-1765 and 1771, respectively. In the early 1770s, Nash relocated to New Bern, the seat of royal government, where his professional and public careers prospered. Moreover, as tensions with Great Britain mounted, Nash distinguished himself as a leading and zealous advocate for the Patriot cause. Indeed, when Gov. Josiah Martin fled from New Bern for his own safety, he singled out defiant Nash for special censure.

From 1774 to 1776 Nash was a delegate to each of North Carolina's five provincial congresses, while also serving as a member of the provincial council. In 1777 he represented New Bern in North Carolina's first General Assembly as an independent state, serving as Speaker of the House of Commons. During the two following years, he remained in the lower house of the legislature as a representative of Craven County. In 1779 and 1780 Nash sat for neighboring Jones County in the state senate, serving briefly as Speaker. On April 20, 1780, he resigned his seat upon his election as governor.

As chief executive Nash drew upon every resource to support the national war effort, while protecting North Carolina against British attack from the south. Like Caswell before him, he found his constitutional powers woefully inadequate to the task that lay before him. Responding to his pleas, the legislature created an emergency Board of War to assist him; but Nash soon found that the board's creation had weakened his powers even further. Bitterly, he complained that "men, not knowing whom to obey, obeyed nobody."

In August 1780 the disastrous defeat of Patriot forces at Camden rendered circumstances still more desperate, for North Carolina now lay open to invasion by Cornwallis's army. Eventually, the tide of war began to turn following the battles of King's Mountain and Guilford Courthouse, but the exhausted and frustrated Nash had no desire to serve longer in a position he considered untenable. When nominated for reelection in June of 1781, he cited "excessive Fatigues" and "want of health" in asking that his name be withdrawn from consideration.

Despite his departure from the governorship, Nash remained active in public life on both the state and national levels. He returned to the House of Commons in 1782 and 1784-1785; and three times accepted election to the Continental Congress (1782, 1783, and 1785), where he came to recognize the pressing need for a stronger central government. It was while attending Congress that Nash died in New York City, on December 2, 1786. Initially buried there in St. Paul's churchyard, he was later moved to the cemetery of his Craven County plantation, Pembroke.

REFERENCES: *DAB*, vol. 13; *DNCB*, vol. 4.

## JOHN OWEN
### 1828-1830

John Owen (1787-1841) presided over advances in internal improvements and education while governor and, post-term, turned down an offer to be the Whig vice-presidential candidate. Born in Bladen County in August 1787, he was the son of Eleanor Porterfield and Col. Thomas Owen, Revolutionary Patriot, legislator, and prosperous landowner. Little is known of Owen's youth or early education, but in 1804 he was a student at UNC. Though he did not graduate from UNC, he would serve for more than twenty years as a trustee. Owen married Lucy Brown of Bladen County, daughter of Gen. Thomas Brown. Their marriage produced a daughter, Lucy.

Owen represented Bladen County in the House of Commons from 1812 to 1814 and in the senate in 1819, 1820, and 1827-1828. From 1824 to 1827 he also served on the Council of State under governors Hutchins G. Burton and James Iredell Jr. On December 8, 1828, Owen was elected governor after several ballots, narrowly defeating Richard Dobbs Spaight Jr. He was elected again in 1829, but declined to seek a third term during the following year for personal reasons.

Owen's two terms as governor brought significant initiatives in county government, internal improvements, and education. Sheriffs and clerks of court in the various counties were made subject to election by all qualified voters rather than by justices of the peace alone. In the area of internal improvements, Owen's progressive leadership led to sizable appropriations for improvements on the Roanoke River at Weldon, and for the recurring scheme to create a navigable inlet through the Outer Banks near Roanoke Island.

Owen's positions on education were especially progressive, particularly with regard to primary schools. In addressing the General Assembly, he stressed the constitutional obligations of government and the moral utility of public education in reducing not only ignorance, but poverty and crime as well. While other states had forged ahead, North Carolina, in his view, had been guilty of "a manifest dereliction of duty" in failing to instruct its young people. Moreover, Owen believed that sufficient funds for educating the poor should be obtained through taxing the rich.

It was during Owen's governorship that related regional and racial tensions reached crisis proportions. In 1830, only one year prior to the Nat Turner rebellion, Owen warned the General Assembly and the public at large of abolitionist attempts to "sow sedition" among the state's slave population. In light of the growing public concern, the General Assembly that same year strengthened the existing patrol system to further restrict the movement and free association of bondsmen.

Owen returned to Bladen County following his second term as governor, but did not retire from public life. He was a leading member of the Constitutional Convention of 1835, where he opposed the disfranchisement of free blacks and a continuance of the religious test for officeholders. In the fall of 1839, he presided over the first Whig Party convention in the state and also over the Whigs' national convention in Harrisburg, Pennsylvania. Indeed, during the national convention, he declined to run as vice-president on the ticket headed by William Henry Harrison. Had he accepted the nomination, and the election results remained the same, he would have become president following Harrison's early death in April 1841. Owen died while in Pittsboro on October 9, 1841, and was buried there at St. Bartholomew's Episcopal Church.

REFERENCES: Coon, *Beginnings of Public Education*; *DNCB*, vol. 4; Johnson, *Ante-Bellum N.C.*; Sobel and Raimo, *Bio. Dir. of Governors*, vol. 3. PRIMARY SOURCES: Owen Papers, NCSA.

◈ ◈ ◈

# THOMAS POLLOCK
## 1712-1714; 1722

Thomas Pollock (1654-1722), one of North Carolina's wealthiest and largest landowners during the proprietary period, served as chief executive following the deaths of governors Edward Hyde and Charles Eden. His initial tenure was marked by the conflict with the Tuscarora Indians, while his second term was foreshortened because he died after five months in office. Over his lifetime Pollock was a merchant, lawyer, planter, soldier, church leader, and politician. His influence in North Carolina extended beyond the office of governor. Pollock was born on March 5, 1654, in Glasgow, Scotland, to Thomas Pollock. He first came to Maryland and eventually settled in North Carolina in June 1683 to serve as a proprietary deputy. In June 1690, he married the widowed Martha Cullen West; they had eight children. Later, Pollock married the widow Esther Wilkinson (d. prior to July 1716); his second marriage produced no children.

In North Carolina, Pollock established himself as an attorney and large planter, owning land along the Chowan, Roanoke, Neuse, and Trent Rivers. Pollock named a plantation located along Salmon Creek (in present-day Bertie County) Balgra after his Scottish ancestral home. At the time of his death, Pollock bequeathed over 50,000 acres to his sons.

He owned black as well as Indian slaves (his will listed around seventy slaves), and evidently hired indentured servants to work his lands. On his lands, Pollock had horses, hogs, and cattle and exported them in exchange for tar and pitch.

Pollock was an astute merchant who involved himself in business ventures that included shipping and moneylending. Christoph von Graffenried, the founder of New Bern, referred to Pollock as "one of the wealthiest men in North Carolina" and as the "strictest creditor." Pollock co-owned sailing vessels that brought molasses, sugar, and rum from Barbados into North Carolina.

Pollock held a variety of public offices in his long career in government. In 1689 he was a member of the assembly, and, in 1694, the Executive Council made Pollock the coroner and customs collector. Pollock served on the Executive Council almost continuously from 1693 until his death in 1722 and worked as a justice on several courts. A devout Anglican, Pollock disliked Quakers and supported both governors William Glover and Edward Hyde in their disputes against dissenters (non-Anglican Christians) for control of North Carolina's government. Pollock's home along the Chowan River was the site of the attempted coup by forces led by Thomas Cary, but it was repulsed by Hyde's forces.

On the heels of Cary's Rebellion, North Carolina in September 1710 was plunged into war against the Tuscarora Indians and their Indian allies. Initially, the Tuscarora attack overwhelmed the white colonists. As major general of the militia, Pollock organized a force of 150 men. A year into the Tuscarora War, Governor Hyde died on September 8, 1711, from yellow fever. Four days later, the Executive Council chose Pollock to serve as governor. In May 1714, Charles Eden presented his commission as governor, and Pollock returned to the Executive Council. Eden remained as governor until his death on March 26, 1722. Again, the Executive Council turned to Pollock to serve as governor, unanimously electing him on March 30, 1722. Pollock's second tenure was peaceful compared to his first. Pollock died on August 30, 1722, and was buried next to his first wife at his plantation; their remains were later moved to St. Paul's Episcopal Church in Edenton.

REFERENCES: *DNCB*, vol. 5; Hindale, "Governor Thomas Pollock"; Lawson, *New Voyage*; Parker et al., *Colonial Records*, vols. 2, 3, 5, 7, and 10; Paschal dissertation, "Proprietary N.C."; Saunders, *Colonial Records of N.C.*, vols. 1 and 2; Todd, *Graffenried's Account of the Founding of New Bern*. PRIMARY SOURCES: Pollock Papers, NCSA.

# WILLIAM REED
## 1722-1724

William Reed (ca. 1670-1728) began serving as a proprietor's deputy and member of the council in 1712, and from October 7, 1722, until his death was president of the council. As president, he served in the capacity of acting governor from the time of his selection until the arrival of George Burrington in January 1724. Little is known about Reed's early life or, in fact, his personal life in general, since there were several William Reeds in the colony at the time, and it is difficult to distinguish them in extant records. Reed was married twice; the first wife was named Christian and the second, Jane. With his wife Christian, he had two sons, Christian and Joseph, and with Jane he had William.

It has been presumed that the William Reed who appears as a witness in Currituck Precinct court in 1692 and as a juror in 1697 was the future acting governor. It is likely the same William Reed who was chosen as a vestryman for the Church of England in the Currituck Precinct in 1715. Gov. Charles Eden appointed Reed and two other men to the Virginia-North Carolina Boundary Line Commission on October 30, 1718. While this group began its survey the following year, the dispute over the line was not settled until 1729, after Reed's death.

William Reed's tenure as acting governor was relatively uneventful. He seems to have fulfilled the duties of his office, as well as participated in some land speculation. There was a complaint in a 1726 report of the Committee of Grievances, Pasquotank Precinct, claiming that in 1724 Reed levied and collected an unfair tax and assumed the power to appoint commissioners and assessors. When Burrington took the oath of office in 1724, Reed continued as president of the council.

As president, Reed did not get along with either of the proprietary governors with whom he served. He also had grievances with several of the councillors. While not, to judge from surviving records, overly combative, Reed did not tolerate disrespect from the council, demanding on one occasion to be referred to as President Reed instead of Mr. Reed. Despite quarrels, William Reed served as president of the council until his death in 1728. There is even a letter to the king in which he and the council complain about the state of North Carolina's government at the hands of Sir Richard Everard, which was dated and sent the day after his death. He was contentious until the end. Reed died at his home in Pasquotank County on December 11, 1728.

REFERENCES: *DNCB*, vol. 5; Parker et al., *Colonial Records*, vol. 7.

## DAVID SETTLE REID
### 1851-1854

*D*avid Settle Reid (1813-1891), in addition to being governor, served in both houses of Congress; his long political career extended beyond the era of Reconstruction. The oldest son of Reuben and Elizabeth Settle Reid, David Reid was born on April 19, 1813, in Rockingham County and was raised in a community that in time became the city of Reidsville. Forced to earn his keep at a young age, in 1829 he was appointed postmaster at the age of sixteen. On December 19, 1850, Reid married Henrietta Settle, daughter of Thomas Settle Sr., and they were parents of four children.

Through hard work, Reid rose quickly in wealth and popularity. In 1835 he achieved two goals, being elected colonel of the county militia and a state senator at the age of twenty-two, where he was a leader of the Democratic Party. Reid played an influential role in passage of the 1839 public school law. The state's first public school opened in Rockingham County in 1840. Aided by realignment, he won his second bid for election to the U.S. House in 1843. There he supported the expansionist policies of President James K. Polk, including statehood for Texas, resolution of the Oregon dispute, war with Mexico, and subsequent Mexican territorial cession.

As the Democratic choice for governor in 1848, Reid agreed to run only if permitted to introduce the issue of elimination of the property requirement to vote for state senators. Narrowly defeated by Charles Manly, Reid ran again in 1850 on the same issue, defeating Manly and sending the Whig Party into eclipse. Other planks in Reid's campaign called for "judicious" internal improvements, more support for public schools, and defense of southern rights. The last was paramount in his inaugural address on January 1, 1851. While professing loyalty to the Union, Reid declared that the suppression of states' rights would violate the Constitution and negate such allegiance.

Reid's two terms as governor were marked by expanded internal improvements; appointment of Calvin H. Wiley as the first superintendent of the Common Schools; initiation of the geological survey; and confirmation of land titles held by Cherokee Indians who had remained in North Carolina. Reid also proposed replacing the land and poll tax with one based on the value of one's estate, but it was not seriously considered by the legislature.

On November 24, 1854, the General Assembly elected David S. Reid to fill a vacancy in the U.S.

Senate, and he turned over gubernatorial duties to Warren Winslow. During his term in the Senate, he spoke in defense of states' rights, reflected in support for the Kansas-Nebraska Act. Defeated for re-election in 1858, Reid retired to private life, stepping back into the public arena occasionally to defend southern rights. His last political venture came in the Convention of 1875 where, from behind center stage, he directed Democratic Party activity and influenced constitutional reform. Reid suffered a severe stroke in May of 1881 that left him paralyzed. He fought failing health for a decade before succumbing on June 18, 1891. He was buried in Reidsville.

REFERENCES: *BDC*; Butler, *Reid Papers*, vols. 1 and 2; *Cyclopedia of Eminent and Representative Men*, vol. 2; *DAB*, vol. 15; *DNCB*, vol. 5. PRIMARY SOURCES: Reid Family Papers, Eden; Reid Papers, Duke; Reid Papers, NCSA.

◈ ◈ ◈

## NATHANIEL RICE
### 1734; 1752-1753

*N*athaniel Rice (d. 1753) came to North Carolina from England in 1731 with commissions as royal councillor and provincial secretary. He had procured these through the influence of his brother-in-law Martin Bladen for the purpose of infiltrating the government of the first royal governor, George Burrington. In 1730 Burrington turned in his list of appointments to the royal council to the Board of Trade, having left the two most senior slots for the board to fill. Bladen, a longtime adversary of Burrington's who served on the board, took the list and wrote in his own selections for those positions, including Nathaniel Rice as secretary. The board accepted this list despite Burrington's appeal. The circumstances of his appointment, and the resulting autonomy, caused tremendous conflicts between Rice and Burrington.

There is no evidence to indicate that Nathaniel Rice lived in North Carolina prior to his appointment to the royal council. Once in the colony, however, he accumulated a large estate, including at least seventeen slaves and 6,340 acres of land, primarily in Bladen, Onslow, and New Hanover Counties. His residence was in New Hanover County. Rice likely visited South Carolina prior to his appointment to North Carolina's council, perhaps as early as 1725, and purchased lands there, as well. He is reported to have gone to South Carolina in September of 1731 to collect his family and bring them back to North Carolina.

Nathaniel Rice seized control of the colony as acting governor in 1734. The situation is unclear, for while the group claimed that Burrington had "departed" North Carolina, there are no documents to substantiate the claim. It is possible that he was simply in poor health or even on one of his many explorations within the colony. Depending on the circumstances, this was a questionable, if not illegal, move since Rice did not follow the procedures for such an assumption of power, appointing himself the acting governor in the presence only of his associates.

Following his return, Burrington dismissed Rice from the council alleging an attempt by Rice and others to murder him. Rice was restored to the council and the office of secretary upon Gabriel Johnston's assumption of the governorship in November of 1734. Under Johnston, Rice continued to support causes in which he believed, even if they were in opposition to the governor. When Johnston died in July of 1753, Rice, still president of the council, again became acting governor. This tenure was unremarkable except that it was the period in which Bishop August Gottlieb Spangenburg visited North Carolina and chose lands for the Moravian settlement.

On January 29, 1753, feeble and long suffering from the gout, Nathaniel Rice died. He left a wife, Mary, and a son, John. He is presumed to have been buried on his property near Rice's Creek in New Hanover County.

REFERENCES: *DNCB*, vol. 5; Ekirch, *"Poor Carolina"*; Price, "Men of Good Estates"; Price, "A Strange Incident"; Saunders, *Colonial Records of N.C.*, vols. 3 and 4. PRIMARY SOURCES: Moore Papers, NCSA; New Hanover Co. Deeds; SS Land Grants; SS Wills.

◇ ◇ ◇

# MATTHEW ROWAN
## 1753-1754

$M$atthew Rowan (d. 1760), long-time member of the Executive Council, became president of the council and acting governor upon the death of Nathaniel Rice and served in that capacity for nearly two years. He was born to the Reverend John Rowan and the former Margaret Stewart in County Antrim, Ireland. It is unclear exactly when Matthew Rowan immigrated to the colonies. His first appearance in extant records is as a church warden in Bath in 1726, where he was a merchant and was involved in shipbuilding. He became a member of the assembly in 1727 and was named to the Executive Council in 1731, actively serving from 1734 until his death in 1760. In 1735 Rowan was part of the team that surveyed the boundary line between North and South Carolina, and two years later was appointed surveyor-general of the colony.

Matthew Rowan married Elizabeth, the widow of his brother Jerome, in 1742. Together they had no children, although she brought with her four daughters, Elizabeth, Anna, Esther, and Mildred. Rowan did father one child, a son called John Rowan, with Jane Stubbs of Bath. He always acknowledged the child and, indeed, left John significant real and personal property in his will.

The majority of his time in North Carolina was spent in the Lower Cape Fear region near the Brunswick

120

County community now known as Northwest. By the time of his death in 1760, he owned at least twenty-six slaves and 9,401 acres of land in that area. Rowan is often associated with the western Piedmont because during his service as acting governor, a large county was established in that region, what was then the frontier. It was named Rowan County in his honor.

Matthew Rowan recognized that the militia of North Carolina was in need of reorganization, since it had virtually dissolved under former governor Gabriel Johnston, but was not able to boost its strength during his tenure. His attempt to create a company of cavalry in each county failed. The musters lagged behind in numbers because many eligible men were exempted owing to their occupations and lacked potential because many men who joined did not have the arms and supplies to contribute. Despite tensions with the Indians and the threat of war with the French, the militia would not be augmented until Arthur Dobbs arrived in 1754 with supplies and money.

Matthew Rowan died at some point between the signing of his will, on April 18, 1760, and an Executive Council meeting held on the twenty-second of that month, which he missed. He was likely buried on his Brunswick County plantation known as Rowan, now Roan.

REFERENCES: *DNCB*, vol. 5; Lee, *Lower Cape Fear*; Price, "Men of Good Estates"; Saunders, *Colonial Records of N.C.*, vol. 5.

# DANIEL LINDSAY RUSSELL JR.
## 1897-1901

*D*aniel Lindsay Russell Jr. (1845-1908) was elected to office by the uneasy "Fusion" alliance of Republicans and Populists in the bitter and racially charged election of 1896. The "Maverick Republican" was the son of Daniel Lindsay and Caroline Sanders Russell, born on August 7, 1845, at Winnabow Plantation in Brunswick County. At age six, he went to live at Palo Alto, the Onslow County home of his grandfather. Educated first by private tutors, Russell at age twelve left to study at the Bingham School in Orange County. Three years later he entered UNC; the war cut short his education. In 1862 he returned to

Brunswick County to form an artillery unit. His military career ended when he barely escaped a court-martial for beating a fellow officer. Daniel L. Russell married a cousin, Sarah Amanda Sanders, in 1869; they had no children.

Russell was nineteen when he was elected in 1864 to the first of two terms in the state House. With the advent of Radical Reconstruction, Russell sided with the new Republican regime and won election as a superior court judge, remaining in that position for six years. While Russell maintained a law office in Wilmington, his residence was in Brunswick County from which he was returned to the legislature in 1876. Two years later he entered the Third District congressional race and served a single term. He did not seek re-election in 1880 and returned to his law practice. Out of political office and doubtful of returning, Daniel Russell often spoke candidly. He castigated the Democrats for their unabated use of the racial issue, charging that blacks had been innocent victims of white barbarity.

By the early 1890s agrarian unrest and economic depression split the state's Democratic Party. The schism widened, giving the Republicans a long awaited opportunity. An alliance with Populists resulted in victories in 1896 that removed control of the legislature from the Democrats and placed Republican Russell in the governor's office. A number of advances were made during Russell's administration: the Railroad Commission gave way to a Corporation Commission; a new law provided for popular election of the commissioner of agriculture; and a Department of Insurance was established. Some of the greatest gains came in education: an 1897 law restored the office of county superintendent; school districts were required to vote on local school taxes until approved; and a legislative appropriation of $50,000 aided school districts in complying with the tax law.

One of Russell's greatest disappointments concerned his inability to recover the North Carolina Railroad from its lease to the Southern Railway. Bipartisan support for the lease and the influence of railroad tycoon J. P. Morgan forced Russell to abandon his efforts. Frustration followed disappointment in the last two years of his term as a reorganized Democratic Party resurrected the racial issue in 1898 and staged the "Red Shirt" campaign, capturing the legislature and many state offices. The Democrats virtually negated any gubernatorial powers, witness Russell's ineffectiveness in using state troops to quell the "race riot" in Wilmington. Further insult followed when Russell was forced to accept the "Grandfather Clause" effectively prohibiting blacks from voting.

Not only was Russell's political career over in 1901, but the failure of his farms had also drained his financial resources. He returned to Belville in Brunswick County to try to recoup his losses, resting his hopes on speculation in repudiated state bonds. The scheme was a failure, and at his death on May 14, 1908, his estate cleared only $1,000. Russell is buried in a family plot at Belgrade in Onslow County.

REFERENCES: Brown, *Onslow Co. History*; Crow and Durden, *Maverick Republican*; *DNCB*, vol. 5. PRIMARY SOURCES: Russell Papers, NCSA; Russell Papers, SHC.

# JAMES TERRY SANFORD
## 1961-1965

*J*ames Terry Sanford (1917-1998), the youngest governor since Charles B. Aycock and the first born in the twentieth century, heralded a "New Day" for the state in his inaugural address. He was elected the same day that John F. Kennedy was elected president and, like his fellow Democrat, launched a host of progressive programs, notably a series of education initiatives. Born in Laurinburg on August 20, 1917,

Terry Sanford was the son of Cecil Sanford, a merchant and realtor, and the former Elizabeth Martin, a teacher. A 1941 graduate of UNC, Sanford served briefly as a special agent for the Federal Bureau of Investigation before joining the U.S. Army. Trained as a paratrooper, Lieutenant Sanford saw action in Italy, France, Belgium, and Germany during World War II. After the war he returned to Chapel Hill where he completed a law degree in 1946 and served as assistant director of the Institute of Government for two years. In 1942 he married a college classmate, Margaret Rose Knight of Hopkinsville, Kentucky; they would have two children.

With the establishment of a law practice in Fayetteville, Sanford remained active in the National Guard through 1960. A Methodist, he was the first trustee chairman of Methodist College. Gov. Kerr Scott appointed him to the State Ports Authority in 1950. In 1952 he was elected to a single term in the state senate. In 1954 Sanford managed Kerr Scott's successful campaign for the U.S. Senate. Scott died in 1958.

Sanford had the support of Scott's organization in the bid for governor in 1960. The field of four candidates for the Democratic nomination was reduced to two after the first primary. I. Beverly Lake, the remaining contender and a former assistant attorney general, campaigned largely on a segregationist platform. Sanford defeated Lake in the runoff and Republican Robert L. Gavin in the fall.

In the campaign Sanford advocated increased spending on education and, days after his inauguration, outlined what he termed his "Quality Education Program." He urged the legislature to support $100 million in improvements for public schools and, in his most controversial action, proposed financing by removing sales tax exemptions, including that on food. Sanford stumped the state on behalf of the proposals, and the 1961 General Assembly approved the measures. Two years later the legislature endorsed Sanford's proposals for education beyond high school, including the creation of senior public colleges in Wilmington, Charlotte, and Asheville, and a community college system. Specialized education initiatives included the Governor's School, for gifted and talented high school students; the School of the Arts, a high school for study of the performing arts; Operation Second Chance, for retraining of dropouts; the Advancement School, for underachieving students; and the Learning Institute, for research on education.

Sanford in 1963 created the North Carolina Fund, with Ford Foundation and other private money, to combat poverty. He established the Center for the Study of Mental Retardation and the State Board of Science and Technology. During his term the legislature underwent reapportionment, and the court system was reformed. Sanford advocated "first-class citizenship" for all races and established the biracial Good Neighbor Council to deal with race relation issues. He promoted food processing industries as a way to boost agriculture.

After his term as governor Sanford led a two-year study, based at Duke University, into the role of state governments. From 1969 to 1985 he served as president of Duke University, there gaining among the students the nickname, "Uncle Terry." In 1972 and 1976 he was a candidate for the presidential nomination of the Democratic Party. In 1986 Sanford defeated James T. Broyhill in a race for the U.S. Senate; six years later Lauch Faircloth defeated Sanford in his bid to retain the seat. Sanford returned to the practice of law. In his last years he spearheaded an effort to construct a performing arts center in the Triangle. Sanford died on April 18, 1998, and was buried in Duke Chapel on the university campus.

Gov. Terry Sanford, the first governor born in the twentieth century and veteran of World War II, launched a host of progressive programs upon his election. Sanford (*left*) receives a shooting lesson from "Carbine" Williams, famed gunmaker.

REFERENCES: Covington and Ellis, *Terry Sanford*; Drescher, *Triumph of Good Will*; Mitchell, *Sanford Papers*; *News and Observer*, January 6, 1961, and April 18, 1998; Powell, *North Carolina Lives*; Ragan, *The New Day*; Sobel and Raimo, *Bio. Dir. of Governors*, vol. 3. PRIMARY SOURCES: Sanford Papers, Duke; Sanford Papers, SHC.

# ALFRED MOORE SCALES
## 1885-1889

Alfred Moore Scales (1827-1892) served with distinction in the Confederate army, in the legislature, and in Congress before his election as governor in 1884. The son of Robert and Jane Bethel Scales, he was born on November 26, 1827, at Ingleside, the family plantation east of Reidsville in Rockingham County. He attended Caldwell Institute in Greensboro before entering UNC in 1845. Scales studied law at the university but never earned enough credits for graduation.

He left school, continued private study under Judge William H. Battle, and passed the bar exam in 1852. He established his practice in Madison in western Rockingham County. Scales married twice, but little is known about his first wife, Margaret Smith of Louisiana, because she refused to move to North Carolina. The legislature finalized Scales's request for a divorce in 1858. In 1862 he married Katherine Henderson, daughter of former state supreme court chief justice Leonard Henderson, who survived him. They had no children but raised a niece, Kate Lewis Scales, as if she were their daughter.

The year 1852 proved to be memorable for Scales. He also served as solicitor for the county and, with the Democratic Party's resurgence, won election to the state House. Rockingham County sent him back to the House for the 1856-1857 session, and at the end of the term, he left for Washington as the Sixth District representative in Congress. With the end of that session in 1859, Scales returned to his law practice in Madison but shortly thereafter became involved in the highly partisan presidential election of 1860. As a southern Democrat he supported John C. Breckinridge and served as a presidential elector on his behalf.

Alfred M. Scales volunteered for Confederate service a month before North Carolina seceded from the Union. He joined the "Rockingham Guards," and, when that unit became Company H of the Thirteenth Regiment, Scales was elected captain. Through promotion and appointment he rose to the rank of brigadier general, seeing action in some of the war's principal encounters. He received serious wounds at Chancellorsville and Gettysburg (there seeing action in all three days of the battle) but completed his service with high honors. After the war Scales moved to Greensboro to continue his law practice. Politics called again in 1875 when he was elected to the Forty-fourth Congress. Re-elected four times, he served through December 1884. One of his particular concerns was the negative treatment afforded the Indian nations, which offended his personal motto of "duty and honor go hand in hand."

Democrats nominated Scales for governor in 1884. His Republican opponent, Tyre York of Wilkes County, hoped to use the still heated prohibition issue against his opponent, but Scales steered clear of the controversy and appealed to the need for party unity. Scales defeated York by 20,000 votes, indicating that the people wanted to bury bitterness and enter a period of peace and quiet. Scales's administration followed that pattern. No major legislation came forth, but neither did major confrontation. For the most part, the governor recommended improvements to already functioning facilities, such as repairs to railroads and highways, a greater quantity and quality of schools with a longer school year, and new directions for the Department of Agriculture to assist farmers. Scales persuaded the United States Coast and Geodetic Survey to study the North Carolina oyster beds with a view to improving that industry in the state. Scales returned to Greensboro in 1889 to serve as president of the Piedmont Bank. He

died on February 9, 1892, and was buried in Green Hill Cemetery in Greensboro.

REFERENCES: *BDC*; Caldwell, *Founders and Builders of Greensboro*; *DNCB*, vol. 5; *Prominent People of N.C.* PRIMARY SOURCES: Scales Papers, ECU; Scales Papers, NCSA.

# ROBERT WALTER SCOTT
## 1969-1973

*T*he second governor (after Richard Dobbs Spaight Jr.) to follow his father into office, Robert W. ("Bob") Scott (1929- ) reorganized state government and restructured the state's system of higher education. The heir to the Scott mantle was born on January 13, 1929, in the Haw River community of Alamance County, where his forebears had farmed and worshipped at Hawfields Presbyterian Church for generations.

His grandfather, Robert W. ("Farmer Bob") Scott, for whom he was named, served in the legislature. His father, Kerr Scott, served as state agriculture commissioner, U.S. senator, and governor from 1949 to 1953. Young Robert W. Scott attended Duke University and graduated from North Carolina State College in 1952. In 1951 he married Jessie Rae Osborne; they would have five children, one of whom, daughter Meg Scott Phipps, was elected commissioner of agriculture in 2000 (she resigned in 2003 and subsequently pleaded guilty to charges of extortion and conspiracy).

Robert W. Scott, upon graduation, returned home to manage his father's dairy farm at Haw River. From 1953 to 1955 he was a special agent for the Counter Intelligence Corps of the U.S. Army and served in the Far East. At the end of his tour he returned to the farm just as he would throughout his political career. In 1961 Scott served as master of the State Grange. Gov. Terry Sanford appointed him to serve on the State Board of Conservation and Development. In 1964 Scott was successful in his bid for lieutenant governor, his first elective office, and held that post, presiding over the state senate, during the governorship of Dan K. Moore. In the Democratic gubernatorial primary in 1968, Scott met J. Melville Broughton Jr., son of the former governor, and Dr. Reginald Hawkins, the first African American to seek the

Gov. Robert W. Scott reorganized state government and restructured the state's system of higher education during his tenure in the office. Scott observes a "Demonstration of Moonshine Whiskey" at the National Park Centennial, Doughton Park along the Blue Ridge Parkway on June 30, 1972. Left to right: Lt. Wayne Keeter (the governor's security aide), Gen. Dixon Watson (father of folksinger "Doc" Watson), Gov. Robert W. Scott, Dr. H. G. Jones (head of the Department of Archives and History), and Charles W. Bradshaw Jr.

office. Broughton declined to call for a runoff after Scott led the voting but failed to gain a majority in the primary. In the fall Scott defeated Congressman James C. ("Jim") Gardner, the Republican nominee. In an additional irony of history, Hoyt Pat Taylor Jr. was elected lieutenant governor in 1968. His father had served in that post from 1949 to 1953 while Kerr Scott was governor.

Like O. Max Gardner, governor from 1929 to 1933, Scott left his imprint principally through reorganization and consolidation of governmental functions. From 300-plus state agencies and offices Scott created seventeen cabinet-level departments, effectively changing the basic structure of the executive branch. Over strong opposition Scott championed the concept of a single governing board for the state's institutions of higher education. In 1971 the legislature created the sixteen-campus University of North Carolina system with a single president and thirty-two-member board of governors.

During Scott's term North Carolina instituted a kindergarten program and increased vocational education in the high schools. The legislature increased taxes on gasoline, tobacco, and soft drinks to support highway construction and new programs. The governor placed an emphasis on planning and established the Council on State Goals and Policy and a system of multi-county planning regions toward that end. During his administration the Good Neighbor Council, an innovation of Governor Sanford, became the Human Relations Commission. The Citizens Committee on the Schools dealt with resolution of conflicts arising from court-ordered busing to achieve racial integration. Governor Scott deployed the National Guard and Highway Patrol to control unrest on college campuses. In national forums he supported President Richard M. Nixon's concept of revenue sharing.

At the close of his term as governor, Scott became vice-president of the N.C. Agribusiness Council. He co-chaired the Appalachian Regional Commission from 1977 to 1979. In 1980 he unsuccessfully challenged Gov. James B. Hunt Jr. in the Democratic primary for governor. From 1983 to 1994 he served as president of the state's community college system. Scott's governorship marked the end of the seventy-two-year Democratic monopoly on the office.

REFERENCES: Clay, *The Long View*; Mitchell, *Robert Scott Papers*; Powell, *North Carolina Lives*; Roberts and Roberts, *The Governor*; Sobel and Raimo, *Bio. Dir. of Governors*, vol. 3; Turner, *The Scott Family of Hawfields*. PRIMARY SOURCES: Robert Scott Papers, NCSA.

## WILLIAM KERR SCOTT
### 1949-1953

Agricultural leader and champion of rural North Carolinians or, as his supporters were known, the "Branchhead Boys," W. Kerr Scott (1896-1958) inaugurated a new era of progressive reforms, chief among them the hard-surfacing of farm-to-market roads across the state. "The Squire of Haw River" was born in that Alamance County community on April 17, 1896, to Robert Walter Scott and the former Elizabeth Hughes. His father, known as "Farmer Bob," was a leader of the Farmers' Alliance and served on the State Commission of Agriculture and in both houses of the legislature. Kerr Scott, who completed a degree in agriculture at North Carolina State College in 1917, remained a farmer and dairyman with close ties to his home and church, Hawfields Presbyterian, all of his life. In 1919,

on return from brief service as an artilleryman in World War I, Scott married Mary Elizabeth White. Their three children included Robert Walter Scott, governor of North Carolina from 1969 to 1973.

From 1920 to 1930, Kerr Scott worked as agricultural agent in Alamance County and from 1930 to 1933 served as master of the North Carolina State Grange. He was regional director of the Farm Debt Adjustment Program of the Resettlement Administration, with duties extending to seven southern states, from 1934 to 1936. In 1936 Scott fulfilled a promise made to his father by successfully running for state agriculture commissioner, unseating incumbent William A. Graham. As commissioner Scott was a leading proponent of rural electrification and led the successful fight to rid the state of Bang's disease among cattle. He forced manufacturers of feed and fertilizer to eliminate sawdust and sand from their products.

With a political base among the state's farmers, Scott met State Treasurer Charles Johnson, who had the backing of what remained of O. Max Gardner's political machine, and liberal Raleigh attorney R. Mayne Albright in a field of six in the 1948 Democratic gubernatorial primary. In the runoff Scott defeated Johnson, ending almost fifty years of Democratic politics dominated first by the organization of Sen. Furnifold Simmons and then by that of Gardner. Reformers, frustrated throughout the New Deal by the conservative, cautious approach of North Carolina governors, hailed the victory. In the fall Scott easily defeated Republican George Pritchard, becoming the state's first farmer-governor since Elias Carr was elected in 1892.

In his inaugural address Kerr Scott, who had charged in the campaign that over $100 million in surplus funds was "lying idle" in state banks, proposed investment of those monies and massive spending programs. Those proposals, which he labeled his "Go Forward" program, met resistance in the legislature, but with a series of radio addresses, Scott took his case to the people. In June 1949 voters approved referenda to issue $200 million in road bonds and $50 million in school bonds. Over four years the state paved more roads than had been paved up to 1949. The governor prodded the utilities commission to extend electricity and telephone service to rural areas. The 1949 legislature, on Scott's recommendation, funded construction of deep water ports at Morehead City and Wilmington. Scott's appointments included the first black member of the State Board of Education, Harold Trigg, and the first female superior court judge, Susie Sharp. In 1949 he appointed UNC president Frank Porter Graham to the U.S. Senate.

In 1953 Scott, known for his bushy eyebrows, cigar, and red rose in his lapel, left Raleigh to return to his farm at Haw River. The following year he was elected to the U.S. Senate where he served on the Agriculture Committee and where he helped

Gov. W. Kerr Scott inaugurated a host of new progressive reforms during his term, chief among them the hard-surfacing of farm-to-market roads across the state. Scott, who remained a farmer his entire life, uses a stone-grinding wheel on his farm in Haw River.

frame legislation to finance the interstate highway network. His death on April 16, 1958, left North Carolina, for the first time in history, with no living ex-governors.

REFERENCES: Albright, "O. Max Gardner"; *ANB*, vol. 23; Coon thesis, "Kerr Scott"; Corbitt, *Kerr Scott Papers*, *DNCB*, vol. 5; *News and Observer*, April 17-18, 1958; Scott, "A Report to the People"; Sobel and Raimo, *Bio. Dir. of Governors*, vol. 3; Turner, *The Scott Family of Hawfields*. PRIMARY SOURCES: Kerr Scott Papers, NCSA.

## BENJAMIN SMITH
### 1810-1811

*B*enjamin Smith (1756-1826) owned what is now Bald Head Island and was once known as Smith's Island. Born on January 10, 1756, in present-day Brunswick (then New Hanover) County, he came from a family of considerable wealth and social standing. His father Thomas was a prosperous planter and the grandson of Landgrave Thomas Smith of South Carolina. His mother Sarah was the daughter of "King Roger" Moore, owner of Orton Plantation and longtime member of the colonial Council of State. Little is known of Smith's early youth or education, but in 1774 he was admitted to the Middle Temple of London's Inns of Court. Benjamin Smith's wife was the former Sarah Rhett Dry, daughter of Col. William Dry, collector for the Port of Brunswick. They were the parents of two adopted children.

After returning from London, Smith fought with distinction in the Revolution, serving under George Washington in New York and with William Moultrie in South Carolina. By the war's end, he had risen to the rank of colonel. In 1784 he was elected to the Continental Congress, but there is no evidence of his attendance. During that same year he represented Brunswick County in the upper house of the General Assembly. Later he was elected to the state constitutional conventions of 1788 and 1789. Smith represented Brunswick County in the state House from 1789 to 1792 and in the senate from 1792 to 1800, from 1804 to 1810, and once again in 1816. From 1795 to 1799 he served as Speaker of the senate. Strongly affiliated with the Federalists throughout his early years in the legislature, Smith was later associated with the Republican Party.

When UNC was chartered in 1789, Smith was named to the original board of trustees and donated 20,000 acres of land in present-day Tennessee to the school as an endowment. Thereafter, he remained a trustee until 1824. During much of the period he was under contract with the federal government to rebuild and expand Fort Johnston at Smithville (now Southport), the town established and named in his honor in 1792. In 1789 he purchased the tract at the mouth of the Cape Fear River that came to be known as Smith Island, and in 1794 he sold the federal government land for construction of the first lighthouse on that landmass. In 1797 he was promoted to major general in the state militia; in 1807 he served as the state's adjutant general.

Smith was elected governor on December 1, 1810. He served a single term, declining to stand for reelection. As chief executive, he advocated reforms in the penal system, encouragement of industry, revitalization of the militia, and the establishment of an educational system "within the reach of every child in the state." His complaint that the governor's accommodations in Raleigh were not "fit for the family of a decent tradesman" may well have hastened construction of the first executive mansion, which was completed three years later.

Following his governorship, Smith returned to Brunswick County and to the life of a prosperous planter. His once enormous wealth, however, was increasingly ravaged by financial misfortunes, personal extravagance, and long-term debt obligations. Though once the owner of Orton Plantation, he only retained residences at Smithville and at his Belvedere Plantation near Wilmington. It was at his dilapidated Smithville residence that he died, a virtual pauper, on January 26, 1826. Initially buried at Smithville, he was later reinterred in the churchyard of St. Philips at Brunswick Town.

REFERENCES: *DNCB*, vol. 5; Gilpatrick, *Jeffersonian Democracy in N.C.*; Sobel and Raimo, *Bio. Dir. of Governors*, vol. 3. PRIMARY SOURCES: Smith Papers, NCSA; Smith Papers, SHC.

# SETH SOTHEL
## 1678; 1682-1683; 1686-1689

*S*eth Sothel (d. ca. 1694), known to history as among the most corrupt of chief executives, was commissioned by the Lords Proprietors in 1678 but did not serve. His tenure in office came four years later when those same men persuaded him to lead Albemarle in the aftermath of Culpeper's Rebellion. They believed that Sothel had the ability to remedy the disorder, but he turned out to be a dreadful governor. In 1675 Sothel, "a person of considerable estate" in England, planned to acquire land in Carolina and establish a town, yet those plans never came to realization. Two years later Sothel purchased the Earl of Clarendon's proprietorship.

While Sothel was sailing for Albemarle in 1678, Algerian pirates captured his ship and took him to Algiers where they enslaved him. The English government offered two pirates in exchange for Sothel. However, the Algerians also demanded 6,000 pieces of eight. Two Englishmen living in Algiers provided the bond for the ransom, and Sothel was released returning to England in 1681. Sothel refused to pay the ransom and ended up in debtor's prison. Upon release Sothel left for Albemarle.

By 1682 Sothel was in Albemarle. In his private life, he was a large landowner married to the twice-widowed Anna Willix. They had no children and resided in a two-room dwelling at a plantation at Salmon Creek (present-day Bertie County). On his plantation, Sothel established a trading post for conducting business with Indians. Sothel, an owner of Indian and black slaves, cultivated tobacco and raised cattle, sheep, and hogs.

As governor, he was accused of placing rebels on the council. The governor ignored the proprietors' instructions to establish a court to try people involved in the "late disturbances." Sothel also inappropriately used public money and protected pirates. The governor imprisoned George Durant, a prominent leader, for libeling his character and confiscated land belonging to Durant. Sothel illegally imprisoned two traders by claiming they were pirates. When one of the men died, Sothel refused to recognize the dead man's will and seized his property. When Thomas Pollock, the executor of the estate, threatened to contact the proprietors about Sothel's actions, the governor placed him in jail. Furthermore, Sothel accepted bribes, seized estates and slaves, and stole items.

Finally, the colonists had enough of Sothel's escapades. In 1689 the colonists imprisoned the governor. The assembly tried Sothel and found him guilty of numerous charges.

The assembly banished Sothel from Albemarle for one year and forbade him from holding public office. In December 1689, the proprietors, upon hearing of the charges, suspended Sothel's governorship and commissioned Phillip Ludwell as governor.

In 1690 Sothel exercised his right as a proprietor to claim the southern colony's governorship and once again commenced his dishonest ways. In 1691 the Lords Proprietors decided to rid themselves of Sothel by suspending the Fundamental Constitutions and Sothel's governorship and commissioning Ludwell governor of the Carolina province. Ludwell arrived in Charles Town in 1692. At first, Sothel opposed the new governor, but he relinquished his power from a lack of supporters. Sothel left the southern colony and died around 1694. He was possibly buried at his Salmon Creek plantation.

REFERENCES: *ANB*, vol. 20; *Bertie Ledger-Advance*, July 10, 1997; Booth, *Seeds of Anger*; Butler, "The Governors of Albemarle County"; *DNCB*, vol. 5; Grant et al., *Acts of the Privy Council*, vols. 1 and 2; Hill and Wilde-Ramsing, "Historical Research Report"; Lounsbury, "Domestic Architecture in Albemarle Region"; Parker et al., *Colonial Records*, vols. 2 and 3; Powell, *Proprietors of Carolina*; Riddell, "Half Told Story"; Sainsbury, Fortescue, and Headlam, *Calendar of State Papers, Colonial Series, 1675-1676, Also Addenda, 1574-1674*; Saunders, *Colonial Records of N.C.*, vol. 1.

# RICHARD DOBBS SPAIGHT
## 1792-1795

$\mathcal{R}$ichard Dobbs Spaight (1758-1802), a signer of the U.S. Constitution and the first native-born governor, was the father of Richard Dobbs Spaight Jr., who served as governor, 1835-1836. Of Irish extraction, the elder Spaight was born in New Bern on March 25, 1758, to Richard and Elizabeth Wilson Spaight, and was distantly related to Gov. Arthur Dobbs. Orphaned as a boy of nine, Spaight received his preparatory education in Ireland and is thought to have graduated from the University of Glasgow. His wife was the former Mary Jones Leech of New Bern, whom he married in 1788.

Returning to North Carolina during the early stages of the Revolution, Spaight served as a military aide to Gov. Richard Caswell. Early on, however, his energies and ambitions were directed primarily toward politics rather than warfare. From 1779 through 1783 and the winning of independence, Spaight represented New Bern in the state House of Commons. Following two years as a delegate to the Continental Congress (1783 to 1785), he returned to the House of Commons from 1785 to 1787 and in 1792. In 1785 he served as Speaker of the House. Following his governorship, he served in the state senate in 1801 and 1802.

As a prominent Federalist leader, Spaight was one of five delegates from North Carolina to the Constitutional Convention in Philadelphia in 1787. Following an active role in the Convention, he signed the Constitution; and in 1788 he argued forcefully but unsuccessfully for its ratification at the state Constitutional Convention in Hillsborough. Spaight was never a robust man, and his poor health forced him from public life from 1788 to 1792, when he was returned to the state House for a final term. On December 11 of that year, he was elected governor by his fellow assemblymen after four days of balloting. Twice reelected, he served the maximum three consecutive terms.

Spaight was the first governor to convene the General Assembly in Raleigh. Much of his role as chief executive was played against the backdrop of war between England and France. Although he supported President George Washington's proclamation of neutrality, strong Republican support for France existed in the state's seaports, especially in Wilmington. In 1794 Spaight's appeal to the General Assembly resulted in the mobilization of the state's militia forces and the strengthening of coastal fortifications. Other issues during Spaight's administration included the ongoing settlement of financial accounts with the federal government, the negotiation of lingering border disputes with South Carolina, and the threat of Cherokee uprisings in the mountain region. In 1795 he presided over the official opening of UNC.

Post-term, Spaight returned to New Bern and the life of a wealthy planter, but in 1798 he was elected to the U.S. House of Representatives. There he remained until 1801 and his election to the state senate. For several years following ratification of the federal Constitution, Spaight had found himself increasingly inclined toward Jeffersonian Republicanism. His final conversion to that political philosophy stemmed largely from his opposition to the Alien and Sedition Acts. In 1802 he became embroiled in a bitter personal rivalry with the ardent Federalist and fellow New Bernian, John Stanly. On September 5th of that year the two men fought a duel in which Spaight was seriously wounded. He died on the following day, in the forty-fifth year of his life, and was buried in the family cemetery at Clermont Plantation.

REFERENCES: Andrews, "Richard Dobbs Spaight"; *DAB*, vol. 17; *DNCB*, vol. 5; Gilpatrick, *Jeffersonian Democracy in N.C.*; Sobel and Raimo, *Bio. Dir. of Governors*, vol. 3; Watson, *Richard Dobbs Spaight*.

# RICHARD DOBBS SPAIGHT JR. 1835-1836

Richard Dobbs Spaight Jr. (1796-1850) was the son of Richard Dobbs Spaight, governor from 1792 to 1795, and was the last governor to be elected by the General Assembly. His mother was the former Mary Jones Leech of New Bern. The younger Spaight was educated at New Bern Academy and UNC, graduating with high honors from the latter institution. In 1818 he was admitted to the bar and the following year represented Craven County in the House of Commons. Spaight then served in the state senate from 1820 to 1822, U.S. Congress from 1823 to 1825, and again in the state senate from the time he returned from Washington until he became governor in 1835. He never married.

At the state constitutional convention of 1835, while still a state senator from Craven County, Spaight served as chairman of the Rules Committee. Although the convention altered the way in which the governor would be elected in the future, the General Assembly was to elect the chief executive one last time. They elected Spaight. The following year, in 1836, as the Democratic gubernatorial nominee in the first popular election under the new constitution, Spaight was defeated by Edward Dudley. Typical of many candidates of that era who attempted to portray their interest in public office as a reluctant willingness to serve, Spaight declined invitations to banquets and rallies. The result was an unenthusiastic campaign that was not well received by the voting public.

After his gubernatorial loss, Spaight retired from politics and returned to his law practice in New Bern. He never held another public office. Income from his farms and other real estate holdings furnished him with the means necessary to practice law, primarily for charitable purposes. It was said that he continued his law practice not for professional success but because he enjoyed intellectual discussions of legal matters with colleagues. Spaight was an active Mason from 1822 through his governorship and beyond. He remained devoutly active in the state's Grand Lodge when his local St. John's Lodge fell into periods of inactivity. Spaight served the Freemasons as Grand Lecturer from 1833 through 1838 and as Grand Master in 1830 and 1831. He held various other offices and served on committees in St. John's and the Grand Lodge, being as well versed in

Masonic law as with the laws of the state. Spaight was also a member and vestryman of Christ Episcopal Church in New Bern.

Richard Dobbs Spaight Jr. died on November 17, 1850, and was buried in the family plot at Clermont Plantation, across the Trent River from New Bern. When the General Assembly members meeting in Raleigh learned of Spaight's death, they respectfully adjourned in his memory.

REFERENCES: Ashe et al., *Biographical History*, vol. 4; Carraway, *Years of Light*; *DNCB*, vol. 5; Hoffmann, "Election of 1836 in N.C."; Watson, *Richard Dobbs Spaight*.

◈ ◈ ◈

# SAMUEL STEPHENS
## 1662-1664; 1667-1670

Samuel Stephens (ca. 1629-1670), appointed in 1662 as "commander of the southern plantation" and in 1667 the second governor of Albemarle County, became leader of a colony suffering from disease and natural disasters. The colonists were divided into two camps: the anti-proprietary faction consisting mostly of pre-1663 charter settlers and the proprietary faction containing post-1663 charter settlers. To compound the situation, the Lords Proprietors provided Stephens with confusing directives that increased tensions.

Stephens, the son of Richard and Elizabeth Piersey Stephens, was born in Virginia. The elder Stephens was a member of the Virginia House of

Burgesses and Council. Stephens married Frances Culpeper in 1652; they had no children. He owned vast acreage in Albemarle, including Roanoke Island, as well as a sizable estate in Virginia. One year prior to the implementation of the Carolina Charter of 1663, Stephens was appointed the "commander of the southern plantation." His commission, issued by the Virginia Council and dated October 9, 1662, placed him in charge of the Albemarle region that became part of the Carolina grant to the Lords Proprietors. He remained as commander until the appointment of William Drummond of Virginia as the first proprietary governor of Albemarle County in 1664. Stephens became the second governor by virtue of his October 8, 1667, commission from the proprietors.

Natural disasters and diseases created difficulties for the colonists during Stephens's tenure. A hurricane devastated the Albemarle region in August 1667, destroying crops and buildings. The following year, a three-month drought followed by a month of excessive rain ruined crops. Another hurricane hit the region in 1669. To further aggravate misfortunes, diseases devastated the population and wiped out large numbers of livestock.

During Stephens's administration, the Lords Proprietors made their restrictive land policies more liberal in response to a petition from the settlers requesting that land be granted in Albemarle on the same basis as in Virginia. The proprietors responded with the Great Deed of Grant giving the Albemarle settlers similar rights but soon thereafter rescinded many of those same rights. Legislation enacted by the assembly preventing colonists from collecting on debts or enforcing contracts and restricting the sale of imported goods caused problems for the governor.

Stephens apparently witnessed little dissension early in his tenure. In October 1668 it was reported that the colonists were "well-satisfied with Mr. Stephens for their governor." Unfortunately, this situation did not last. The conditions became so vicious that some people drew their swords against the governor. However, according to Virginia's governor William Berkeley, Stephens withstood the challenges owing to his mild demeanor and did not punish his adversaries.

Stephens died in office around February or March 1670. In a March 1670 letter from Governor Berkeley to the Albemarle Council, Berkeley acknowledged Stephens's death and referred to him as "a man of approved courage, great integrity, and a lover of the colony and had many other personal virtues which usually make men loved and desired by those that know them." Stephens's widow, Frances, married Berkeley in June of that year.

REFERENCES: Butler, "The Early Settlement of Carolina"; Butler, "The Governors of Albemarle County"; *DNCB*, vol. 5; Parker, et al., *Colonial Records*, vols. 2 and 7; Powell, *Ye Countie of Albemarle*; Raimo, *Bio. Dir. of Col. and Rev. Governors*.

## MONTFORT STOKES
### 1830-1832

Montfort Stokes (1762-1842) served in the U.S. Senate prior to his term as governor, a post from which he resigned in 1832 to accept President Andrew Jackson's appointment as chairman of a federal Indian commission. Stokes was born in Lunenburg County, Virginia, on March 12, 1762, the eleventh child of planter David Stokes and the former Sarah Montfort. He went to sea as a youth of thirteen, and during the Revolution enlisted in the Continental navy. Following the Revolution, he settled briefly in Halifax and then in Salisbury, where he read law under his brother John and began a lifelong and politically important friendship with Andrew Jackson. His first wife was Mary Irwin of Tarboro, whom he married in 1790. His second wife, whom he married in 1796, was Rachel Montgomery of Salisbury. Together, the two marriages produced eleven children.

From 1786 to 1790 and from 1799 to 1816, he served, respectively, as assistant clerk, and clerk of the state senate. In 1804 he declined an opportunity to complete an unexpired term in the U.S. Senate, and on numerous occasions was chosen a presidential elector on the Republican ticket. Stokes moved to Wilkes County about 1810, and during the War of 1812 held the rank of major general in the state militia. In 1816 he was selected by the General Assembly to fill the Senate seat vacated by James Turner's resignation, after which he served in his own right until 1823. As a senator, his committee work focused on the District of Columbia and on postal and military affairs. Initially identified with the policies of John C. Calhoun, he later embraced Jacksonian democracy. Conspicuously more liberal than his Senate colleague from North Carolina, Nathaniel Macon, he opposed the further extension of slavery in the Missouri Compromise, and expressed his support for a constitutional amendment to abolish slavery. In 1823 he was replaced in the Senate by former governor John Branch.

Returning to North Carolina, Stokes chaired the reform convention of 1823, and in 1824 was defeated for the governorship by Hutchins G. Burton. In 1826-1827 and in 1829-1831, he represented Wilkes County in the upper and lower houses, respectively, of the General Assembly. Stokes was elected to his first term as governor on December 17, 1830, defeating Richard Dobbs Spaight Jr. of New Bern. Despite strong opposition from the eastern part of the state, he won election to a second term the following year.

As governor, Stokes was strongly identified with the interests of western North Carolina, political and constitutional reform, internal improvements, and a sound banking system. Only secondarily did he lend his support to the tentative efforts under way to provide for public education. During the widespread hysteria following the Nat Turner uprising of 1831, he acted with firmness and moderation to minimize violence. Against the backdrop of national politics, Stokes was a strong supporter of Andrew Jackson and a vocal opponent of nullification. Repeatedly he denounced that doctrine as inimical to the Union.

In November 1832 Stokes resigned his governorship to accept President Jackson's appointment as chairman of a federal commission charged with the resettlement of Indians from the southeastern U.S. Relocating to Fort Gibson in present-day Oklahoma, he continued to work with Indian affairs for the remainder of his life. Stokes died at Fort Gibson on November 4, 1842, and was buried near the post.

REFERENCES: *DAB*, vol. 18; *DNCB*, vol. 5; Foster, "Career of Montfort Stokes in N.C."; Sobel and Raimo, *Bio. Dir. of Governors*, vol. 3. PRIMARY SOURCES: Stokes Papers, NCSA.

# DAVID STONE
## *1808-1810*

*D*avid Stone (1770-1818), a follower of Thomas Jefferson politically, was the builder of the now-restored Hope Plantation near Windsor. Born in Bertie County on February 1, 1770, he was the only son of Zedekiah Stone and the former Elizabeth Hobson. Little is known of his early education, but in 1788 he graduated from the College of New Jersey (now Princeton University) with honors. Stone's first wife was Hannah Turner of Bertie County, whom he married in 1793. She died in 1816; six of their eleven children reached adulthood. In 1817 he married Sarah Dashiell of Washington, D.C.

Stone studied law under William R. Davie at Halifax and was

admitted to the bar. He served as a Federalist at the Fayetteville convention of 1789 that ratified the federal Constitution, and was subsequently elected to the state House of Commons, where he represented Bertie County from 1790 to 1795. Following four years as a superior court judge, he was elected to the U.S. House of Representatives, where he served from 1799 to 1801. It was while in Congress that Stone switched his political affiliation from Federalist to Republican, supporting Thomas Jefferson for president in 1800. The following year he resigned from the House to accept a seat in the U.S. Senate. There he remained until 1807. In both chambers of Congress, Stone generally supported Jeffersonian policies while still maintaining a high degree of political independence.

Stone returned to North Carolina and to the state judiciary in 1807, and on November 28th of the following year, was elected to the first of two terms as governor. As chief executive, he struggled to protect property owners from the land claims of Lord Granville's heirs; encouraged broad-based education; and urged improvements in agriculture, transportation, and finance. It was during his second term as governor (1810) that the State Bank was chartered.

Declining to stand for a third term, Stone ended his governorship in December 1810 but returned to the state House of Commons in 1811 and 1812. During the latter year he was again elected to the U.S. Senate, where he served for two additional years. As senator, Stone's persistent opposition to the War of 1812 provoked a resolution of censure from the North Carolina General Assembly, whose members supported the Madison administration and the war by a substantial margin. Stone vigorously defended his actions as based on principle, but in 1814 resigned his Senate seat and returned to North Carolina as a private citizen and gentleman planter. His landholdings were quite extensive, through both inheritance and acquisition, his principal plantation residences being Hope in Bertie County and Restdale near Raleigh. Renewing his earlier interest in internal improvements, he endeavored during his last years to improve navigation along the upper reaches of the Neuse River. Stone died at his Wake County plantation on October 7, 1818, and was buried there on the grounds.

REFERENCES: *ANB*, vol. 20; *DAB*, vol. 18; *DNCB*, vol. 5; Gilpatrick, *Jeffersonian Democracy in N.C.*; Iobst research report, "David Stone"; Lemmon, *Frustrated Patriots*; Sobel and Raimo, *Bio. Dir. of Governors*, vol. 3. PRIMARY SOURCES: Stone Papers, NCSA.

## DAVID LOWRY SWAIN
## 1832-1835

*D*avid Lowry Swain (1801-1868) had a long tenure as president of UNC (1835-1868) after his service as the state's chief executive. He was born in Buncombe County on January 4, 1801, the youngest child of George Swain and Caroline Lane Lowry. After attending Newton Academy, he briefly enrolled at UNC and then began the study of law under Chief Justice John Louis Taylor. He returned to Buncombe County in 1823 to begin his practice. Swain's wife was the former Eleanor White, granddaughter of Revolutionary governor Richard Caswell; they had five children.

Established as an attorney in Asheville, Swain was elected in 1824 to the state House for the first of five terms. In that body he became recognized as an advocate for western interests, internal improvements, and progressive government. Non-committal with respect to party, he was associated with a coalition of National Republicans and others opposed to Andrew Jackson and to the dominance of eastern Democrats. On December 1, 1832, the General Assembly elected Swain to his first term as governor, even though he had not been regarded as a leading contender for the office. His support came from the disparate coalition opposed to Jackson and to the leading Democratic candidate for governor, Richard Dobbs Spaight Jr. The next two years he was reelected governor, openly associating himself with the new Whig Party and with forces of reform.

From the outset Swain played a more active role as governor than his predecessors, even though the constitutional powers of the office remained constrained. Repeatedly and forcefully, he advocated sweeping reforms in the areas of education, banking, taxation, and internal improvements, carrying his message beyond the halls of the legislature. By 1834, he began to focus on constitutional reforms, convinced that progressive measures hinged upon the defeat of the eastern establishment.

Swain ushered through the General Assembly a bill calling for a constitutional convention, which met in Raleigh in July 1835. Swain himself sat as a delegate and served as chairman pro tempore. To him, more than anyone else, belongs the credit for the accomplishments of that meeting, including crucial reforms in the methods of representation and the election of governors by popular vote. With the political impediments to progress finally broken down, railroad construction, public education, and other progressive measures became realities under Whig leadership.

In 1835 Swain was elected president of UNC by its board of trustees. Though lacking in academic credentials, he won the respect of both students and faculty for his administrative ability, personality, and integrity. Moreover, as university president, he redoubled his persistent search for documentary materials relating to the state's history. By 1860, the university had become the largest institution of higher learning in the South, with course offerings, a physical plant, and enrollment all having grown under Swain's leadership.

Though facing severe hardships during the Civil War, Swain managed to keep the university open. As Sherman's army approached Raleigh in the spring of 1865, Swain played a role in surrendering the state capital and in securing assurances that the university would not be harmed. He remained as university president until July of 1868, when he and his entire faculty were removed by the new board of trustees. Swain died on August 29, 1868, as the result of a buggy accident. Initially buried at his Chapel Hill home, he was later reinterred in Raleigh's Oakwood Cemetery.

REFERENCES: *ANB*, vol. 21; *DAB*, vol. 18; *DNCB*, vol. 5; Coon, *Beginnings of Public Education*; Jones, *For History's Sake*; Sobel and Raimo, *Bio. Dir. of Governors*, vol. 3; Wallace, "David Lowry Swain." PRIMARY SOURCES: Swain Papers, NCSA; Swain Papers, SHC.

## WILLIAM TRYON
## 1765-1771

*W*illiam Tryon (1729-1788), royal governor of both North Carolina and New York, served the two colonies during times of controversy and conflict. Tryon was born in Surrey, England, to Charles Tryon and the former Lady Mary Shirley. Though not formally educated, Tryon advanced militarily and politically by virtue of being wellborn and well married. A professional soldier, he was first commissioned as a lieutenant in 1751 and rose erratically through the ranks thereafter. William Tryon married Margaret Wake on December 26, 1757. Together they had two children. Their daughter Margaret died in England, unmarried, at age thirty, and their son died in infancy in North Carolina.

Tryon was related by marriage to Lord Hillsborough, Lord of Trade and Plantations. It is likely that Hillsborough was behind Tryon's appointment as lieutenant governor of North Carolina in 1764 when Arthur Dobbs requested retirement from the governorship. Tryon, his wife, and young daughter arrived in the colony in October 1764. He assumed the duties of governor on March 28, 1765, upon Dobbs's death, and received his commission within a few months.

Tryon's first political challenge was the Stamp Act crisis, which erupted in

October 1765 in North Carolina. Sympathetic with the colonists, Tryon understood that the tax would cause great hardship in the colony's cash-poor economy, but in deference to the Crown required the taxes to be paid. Through organized resistance, North Carolinians avoided paying the tax until the act was repealed effective May 1, 1766.

Tryon erroneously believed that the colonists would not object to a tax levied to erect a capitol and governor's residence. The assembly appropriated funds and authorized Tryon to oversee the project, which quickly exceeded the budget. Some North Carolinians felt that injustices in the colony, including the tax for "Tryon's Palace," corrupt officials, and lack of representation for the backcountry, needed regulation. They therefore formed a resistance group known as the Regulators. After several defiant incidents, a special session of the assembly was called that caused further agitation. Tryon organized and led militia into the backcountry in 1768 and 1771, defeating the Regulators on May 16, 1771, in the Battle of Alamance. Following the battle, the governor offered pardons to all who agreed to take the oath of allegiance, with a few named exceptions. Ultimately, six leaders were hanged, and the rank and file were pardoned.

While on the backcountry expedition in 1771, Tryon was notified of his transfer to the governorship of New York. Subsequently, he lost the majority of his personal effects and papers in a fire at his New York residence. Throughout the Revolution, Tryon maneuvered for military position, attaining major general. Feeling underemployed in America, Tryon asked to be excused from the civil governorship and allowed to return to England, which he did in 1780. He continued to pursue military promotions there, reaching lieutenant general. Tryon died on January 27, 1788, and is buried at St. Mary's Church, Middlesex, England.

REFERENCES: *ANB*, vol. 21; *DNCB*, vol. 6; Nelson, *William Tryon and Course of Empire*; Powell, *Tryon Papers*, vols. 1 and 2; Powell, Huhta, and Farnham, *Regulators in N.C.*

◈ ◈ ◈

# JAMES TURNER
## 1802-1805

*J*ames Turner (1766-1824) was a friend and ally of U.S. senator Nathaniel Macon. Turner was born on December 20, 1766, in present-day Warren (then Bute) County, the son of Thomas and Rebecca Turner. Little is known of his early youth or education, but during the late stages of the Revolution he saw service in North Carolina as a private in the army of Gen. Nathanael Greene. Serving in the same company was an older Warren County resident, Nathaniel Macon, with whom Turner formed a lasting and formative friendship. By 1790 Turner had become a moderately successful planter, having acquired two Warren County plantations and some twenty slaves. Turner was married three times and widowed twice. His first wife was Mary Anderson of Warrenton, who died in 1802. His second wife, Anna Cochran, died in 1806. His third wife was Elizabeth Johnston, who survived him. The three marriages together produced six children, two sons and four daughters.

Entering upon a varied career in politics, Turner represented Warren County in the House of Commons from 1798 to 1800 and in the senate in 1800-1801. As a member of the General Assembly, he was affiliated with the so-called "Warren junto," an influential group of conservative Republicans led by Nathaniel Macon, his former comrade in arms. On November 29, 1802, the Republican dominated legislature elected John Baptista Ashe governor. Ashe, however, died less than a week later prior to taking office. In a second election, held December 4, Turner was selected in his place to his first term as governor. Reelected to office on two subsequent occasions, he served the constitutional maximum of three consecutive years.

Turner's tenure came during a period of clear Republican ascendancy in the political life of the state, its erstwhile Federalist leaders having largely died, recanted, or retired. Moreover, fiscal conservatism and distrust of innovation were such prominent features of the political landscape that few accomplishments could reasonably be expected from his administration. Each of his three principal messages to the General Assembly spoke generally of the need for broad-based public education in the state, but specified no concrete steps through which such a goal could be achieved. Other areas of concern during his administration included the lingering border dispute with Georgia and the need for modest reform of the state's judicial system. With respect to business and finance, it should be noted that it was during his governorship that the state's first banks were chartered in New Bern and Wilmington.

In November 1805 Turner resigned the governorship to accept his recent election to the U.S. Senate. There he remained for the next eleven years, generally associating himself with the conservative Republican politics of his mentor, Nathaniel Macon. Turner, however, achieved no distinction or prominence during his years in the Senate, his energies often depleted by poor health. Prevented by illness from returning to Washington in the fall of 1816, Turner submitted his resignation. Largely withdrawing from public life, Turner passed his remaining years quietly at his principal Warren County plantation, Bloomsbury. There he died on January 15, 1824, and was interred on the grounds.

REFERENCES: Coon, *Beginnings of Public Education*; *DNCB*, vol. 6; Gilpatrick, *Jeffersonian Democracy in N.C.*; Sobel and Raimo, *Bio. Dir. of Governors*, vol. 3.

# WILLIAM BRADLEY UMSTEAD
## 1953-1954

*A* veteran of both houses of the U.S. Congress, William B. Umstead (1895-1954) suffered a heart attack two days after his inauguration as governor and spent much of his twenty-two-month term in office confined to bed leading up to his death on November 7, 1954. The son of legislator and Confederate veteran John W. Umstead and the former Lulie Lunsford, a teacher, William B. Umstead was born on a farm near Bahama (Durham County) on May 13, 1895. A 1916 graduate of UNC, Umstead, who excelled as a debater, taught school in Kinston for a year. In 1917 he joined a machine gun battalion of the 81st ("Wildcat") Division, serving in France and rising to the rank of first lieutenant. On his return to civilian life, Umstead studied law at Trinity College and in 1920 began practice in Durham. In 1922 he was elected prosecutor and in five years became solicitor. In 1929 he married Merle Davis of Rutherford County; they would have one child, a daughter also named Merle.

In 1932 the voters of the Sixth District elected Umstead to the first of three terms in the U.S. House. A political moderate, Umstead supported causes of interest to his constituents, such as tobacco, rural electrification, and soil conservation. In 1938 he declined to seek reelection and returned to his law practice. R. Gregg Cherry in 1944 asked Umstead to manage his campaign for governor; after the election he served as chairman of the state Democratic executive committee. In 1946, on the death of Sen. Josiah Bailey, Governor Cherry appointed Umstead to the Senate. Two years later, in his only political defeat, Umstead lost to former governor J. Melville Broughton in the Democratic primary for the Senate seat. In 1952 he defeated Judge Hubert F. Olive in the Democratic primary for governor and in the fall defeated Republican H. F. ("Chub") Seawell.

Umstead's serious health problems appeared without notice, frustrating what should have been the climax to his political career. On inauguration day, January 8, 1953, he was hoarse and appeared to suffer from a cold. The long day's events were tiring, and two days later the governor was admitted to Watts Hospital in Durham where a heart attack was diagnosed. He remained hospitalized until May 21 and then moved to the second-floor bedroom in the Executive Mansion. As his health would permit, he took on responsibilities and met with his staff and with legislators.

Governor Umstead, who in his inaugural address issued a call for a "better tomorrow," continued programs initiated by his predecessor Kerr Scott by endorsing state bond issues to finance school buildings and improve mental institutions. He reorganized the Board of Paroles and put in place uniform and equitable policies. Umstead urged the state to

Gov. William B. Umstead suffered a heart attack two days after his inauguration, causing him to spend much of his time as governor confined to bed. During his short time in office, he supported rural electrification and soil conservation. Umstead provides his signature for a document in 1952.

seek new and more diversified industries. The U.S. Supreme Court decision mandating school desegregation was handed down on May 17, 1954. Unlike other southern governors, Umstead counseled moderation and appointed a nineteen-member biracial panel to make recommendations. Hurricane Hazel lashed the state on October 15, 1954, leading the governor to ask the federal government for a disaster declaration. For a short term in office, Umstead had the unusual distinction of appointing two members of the U.S. Senate. Following the death of Willis Smith he selected Alton Lennon, and on the passing of Clyde Hoey he appointed Sam J. Ervin.

Described by a Raleigh newspaper as "painfully lacking in personality," Umstead was widely admired for his integrity and his commitment to public service. The governor spent three weeks in October 1954 in the hospital. On November 4, weakened by budget hearings, he was hospitalized again and, three days later, became the first chief executive since Daniel Fowle in 1891 to die in office. He was buried at Mount Tabor Methodist Church at Bahama.

REFERENCES: *BDC*; Corbitt, *Umstead Papers*; *DNCB*, vol. 6; *Durham Morning Herald*, November 8-9, 1954; Gill, "Dedication of Umstead Building"; Henderson and others, *North Carolina*; *News and Observer*, November 8, 1954; Sobel and Raimo, *Bio. Dir. of Governors*, vol. 3.

## ZEBULON BAIRD VANCE
### 1862-1865; 1877-1879

Buncombe County solicitor at twenty-one, state legislator at twenty-four, congressman at twenty-eight, Confederate colonel at thirty-one, governor at thirty-two, three times governor of North Carolina, and U.S. senator for fifteen years, Zebulon Baird Vance (1830-1894) was the most popular political leader that the state has produced. Born on May 13, 1830, at the family homestead along Reems Creek in Buncombe County, he was the son of David Vance II and Mira Margaret Baird Vance. Although he received some formal education in local schools, he acquired most of his basic knowledge from his mother who supplemented his schooling in Asheville following his father's death in 1844. Vance entered UNC early in 1851 and for the rest of the year pursued the study of law under Judge William H. Battle and Samuel F. Phillips. More important than the law license he obtained in December 1851, however, were the contacts and friendships that would be influential later in his career.

A few months after setting up his legal office in Asheville in early 1852, Vance was elected solicitor for Buncombe County. The next year he received his license to practice law in the superior courts of the Seventh Judicial District, which covered thirteen mountain counties. Zeb Vance never saw the practice of law as his mission in life. To him it was an entrance to the political arena, and he used courtrooms as opportunities to build a wide reputation and to meet prominent people. He ventured into state politics in 1854, using his personality, oratorical abilities, and mountain wit to eke out a victory over Daniel Reynolds for a seat in the state senate.

Vance equated the Democratic Party with sectionalism, which he believed was dangerous to the best interests of North Carolina and the South. Determined to oppose it, he cast his allegiance with the declining Whig Party. He continued to call himself such after the party had dissolved and he had entered other campaigns as a member of the American or Know Nothing Party. Vance was elected to the House of Representatives in 1858 to fill a vacant seat. His harsh criticism of Democrats as promoters of sectionalism resulted in a hot re-election campaign against David Coleman that almost ended in a duel. Vance served in Congress from 1858 to 1861, during which time he strongly advocated maintenance of the Union. He spoke against the act of secession because he thought it unwise and dangerous, but he never denied the legal right of a state to secede. The firing on Fort Sumter and Lincoln's call to arms forced a choice of loyalty, and he cast his lot with his state and region.

Zeb Vance refused to be nominated as a candidate for the Confederate Congress; instead he raised his own company, the Rough and Ready Guards, of which he was the captain. He was elected colonel of the Twenty-sixth Regiment on August 27, 1861, and saw considerable action. Still, politics was never far from the mind of Zebulon Vance, and he was criticized frequently for mingling politics with his official duties.

Anti-administration opponents had established a loosely knit organization called the Conservative Party, and they picked the popular colonel to head the 1862 gubernatorial contest against Democrat William Johnston. The campaign was fought in the press, and with the full support and vitriolic pen of William W. Holden, editor of the *North Carolina Standard*, Vance was elected by an overwhelming majority, more than 32,000 votes.

His antebellum stance as a strong Unionist had created some fears that his election would bring an effort at reunion, but Vance gave that no encouragement in his inaugural address. He acceded to the judgment of the people in the vote for secession and pledged to continue the war. He appeased Confederate authorities by promising to enforce the unfavorable Conscription Act, while softening the anger of his fellow citizens by questioning the authority of the central government to pass the law.

Governor Vance diligently supported the Confederacy and made every effort to keep North Carolina loyal, but when the consolidation tendencies of the central government created hardships for North Carolinians and endangered its citizens, he took exception and complained bitterly; consequently, he quarreled frequently with President Jefferson Davis. Having abandoned his old Whig nationalism when the South seceded, Vance became a staunch defender of states' rights, particularly regarding civil laws and judicial procedure. These, he reasoned, could not be sacrificed to any cause no matter how well justified.

On the home front, the governor had to deal with a flood of problems caused by the war: scarcity of goods and clothing, high prices, currency depreciation, and sinking morale. With alternatives having been exhausted, he turned to the practice of blockade-running to provide needed supplies for both troops and civilians; he organized and established supply depots in the counties to distribute goods; and he offered sympathy and assurances to the people to boost spirits. Still, there was a sizable element of the population suffering from discontent, frustration, alarm at the growing presence of Union troops in the state, resentment of the Davis government for failure to protect them, and defeatism as the hope of victory slipped further away.

Gov. Zebulon B. Vance, one of the state's most popular politicians, guided the state through the Civil War. He later served in the U.S. Senate for fifteen years. This photo was made when he was inaugurated in 1862.

Led by William W. Holden, who had broken ties with the man that he practically had made governor, the group initiated a peace movement to take the state out of the Confederacy. Holden took the issue to the voters by challenging Vance in the election of 1864, but the governor's efforts on behalf of the people had increased his immense popularity, and he was re-elected by a four-to-one margin.

With the fall of Fort Fisher and Wilmington in January 1865, not even Zebulon Vance could lift morale or persuade the legislature to pass laws to help the dying Confederacy. As Gen. William T. Sherman moved his Union troops closer to Raleigh, the governor began moving military supplies and official records to the west on April 10. Two days later, he left Raleigh. On May 13, 1865, Vance was arrested at his home in Statesville and transferred to Old Capitol Prison in Washington. Although no charges were ever levied, he was held there until July 6.

After the war, Vance moved his law practice to Charlotte. Laboring under political disabilities imposed by the Fourteenth Amendment, which prevented him from taking the U.S. Senate seat to which he was elected in 1870, Vance worked behind the scenes to develop the Conservative Party until his disabilities were removed in 1872. By 1876 the Conservative Party had become the Democratic Party with Zeb Vance at its head. He ran for governor successfully in 1876 in a notable campaign against Thomas Settle. In the first two years of his administration, railroad construction resumed; progress was made in the education of both races; promotion of agriculture and industry brought North Carolina into the era of the New South; the financial structure of the state was placed on a more solid footing; and the last federal troops left the state.

In 1879, with two years remaining in his term, Vance left the governor's office for a seat in the U.S. Senate where he acted as a mediator attempting to heal the sectional wounds caused by the war. He offered explanations of southern motivations and feelings in the difficult times, but he never apologized for the war. Simultaneously, he urged the South to allow its wounds to heal and look forward, not backward, in its relationship with the North. For fifteen years Zebulon Vance represented North Carolina, speaking for the South, yet seeking the best interests of the nation. He died in office on April 14, 1894. His body was returned to his home state and buried in Riverside Cemetery in Asheville. Vance had married Harriette (Hattie) Espy on August 3, 1853, in her home county of Burke. They had four sons. She died on November 3, 1878, and two years later, Senator Vance married Florence Steele Martin who survived him.

REFERENCES: *ANB*, vol. 23; Connor, *Makers of N.C. History*; Crittenden et al., *100 Years, 100 Men*; *DAB*, vol. 19; Hamlin, *Ninety Bits of N.C. Biography*; Johnston, "Zebulon Baird Vance"; Johnston and Mobley, *Vance Papers*, vols. 1 and 2; McKinney, McMurray, and others, *Guide to Microfilm Edition of Vance Papers*. PRIMARY SOURCES: Vance Letters, NCSA; Vance Papers, Duke; Vance Papers, NCSA; Vance Papers, SHC.

◇ ◇ ◇

## HENDERSON WALKER
## 1699-1703

*H*enderson Walker (ca. 1659-1704), during "whose administration ye province injoyed that tranquility which is to be wished it may never want," worked to establish the Church of England as a government-supported religious denomination in North Carolina. Walker was born around 1659 and trained in law. He arrived in Albemarle around 1682. In April 1686 Walker married Deborah Green; they had only one child, a daughter Elizabeth. In February 1694 Walker married Ann Lillington, daughter of Alexander and Elizabeth Lillington. The second marriage produced no children.

In Albemarle Walker led the life of a colonial gentleman. He acquired land, raised and sold livestock, and co-owned the sloop *Debertus* with a Boston merchant. Throughout his life, Walker worked as an attorney. He started out his public career as a clerk of the county courts. Walker held a variety of public offices, including assembly man and customs collector. He became attorney general in October 1695, a position he held briefly, and sat as a justice on the General Court, Court of Chancery, and Admiralty Court. He first joined the colonial council under Gov. Thomas Harvey in 1694. As a council member, Walker was appointed as boundary commissioner by Governor Harvey in March 1699 to help settle the boundary dispute with Virginia. Following the death of Harvey in July 1699, Walker was chosen by the council to serve as chief executive.

During Walker's tenure, North Carolina enjoyed a period of relative peace and growth as people came from Virginia. However, Walker faced his share of problems. Cases were heard in court involving assaults upon colonists by Indians. In 1703, the Meherrin Indians were charged with "destroying their stock and burning their timber and houses refusing to pay tribute or render obedience to the Government." Walker's greatest challenge came from dealing with the royal and Virginia governments. The Crown wanted to gain control of the proprietary colonies in America. It used navigational acts and admiralty courts to undermine the proprietary colonies. Walker was caught between obeying the Crown or the Lords Proprietors. The Virginia government was worried about the large migration of settlers from Virginia to North Carolina, and the two colonies continued to debate the unsettled boundary.

As a devoted Anglican, Walker worked to make the Church of England stronger in North Carolina. In November 1701, a receptive assembly enacted the first law (known as a vestry act) that established parishes and vestries and provided "for building of Churches and establishing a maintenance for Ministers." A poll tax "on every Tythable in the precinct" was evidently the way the Church of England was to support itself. This act was not popular with non-Anglicans.

Walker continued as governor until the summer of 1703 when he relinquished the governorship to Robert Daniel. Walker remained on the council, serving as its president from 1703 to 1704 and continued to sit as a justice.

Walker died on April 14, 1704, and was buried at his plantation "on a point of land not far from the water [Albemarle Sound], and sufficiently elevated above it to command an extensive prospect in every direction." However, the encroachment of the water in time resulted in the governor's remains being moved to the churchyard of St. Paul's Episcopal Church in Edenton.

REFERENCES: Crayon, "N.C. Illustrated"; *DNCB*, vol. 6; Hathaway, "Births, Deaths and Marriages"; Hathaway, "Henderson Walker to the Court"; Hathaway, "Letter from John Lawson"; Marley, "Minutes of the General Court of Albemarle"; Parker et al., *Colonial Records*, vols. 2, 3, 4, 7, and 10; Raimo, *Bio. Dir. of Col. and Rev. Governors*; Saunders, *Colonial Records of N.C.*, vol. 1.

# JOHN WHITE
## 1587-1590

*J*ohn White (b. ca. 1540), artist, surveyor and cartographer, is best known as the governor of the second English expedition to Roanoke Island that ended in the ill-fated "Lost Colony." He created an accurate map of the "Virginia" coast that was incorporated by other European mapmakers in their maps of North America and sketched the first drawings of America's natural life and natives, ones that outclass any other efforts at artistic portrayal of the New World. At one time, it was debated whether White the governor and White the artist were the same person, but historical evidence indicates that the governor and artist were indeed the same person.

White's personal history prior to the Roanoke voyages is obscure, made more so by the fact that John White was such a common name. He was likely born in England possibly between 1540 and 1550 since he was a grandfather by 1587. White attended church in the parish of St. Martin Ludgate in London; he married Tomasyn Cooper in June 1566. The marriage produced two known children: Tom, who died as a young child, and Eleanor. White probably trained as an illustrator under a London master.

By the 1580s, White had become deeply involved with the English efforts to colonize North America. In 1585 White accompanied Sir Ralph Lane's expedition at establishing the first English colony in America. White served as the official artist and mapmaker for the expedition; he worked with scientist Thomas Harriot in recording flora and fauna and native people. In 1588 Harriot published *A Briefe and True Report of the New Found Land of Virginia*; it was not until Frankfort engraver and printer Theodor de Bry published Harriot's book in 1590 that White's images were reproduced. The book was published in four languages and attained wide attention in Europe.

Following the return of the all-male Lane colony, a new scheme emerged to establish another colony in Virginia. The new colony was to be settled with families and would be self-sustaining. The Chesapeake Bay area was the site selected for the colony. Sir Walter Raleigh, who held the land patent for Virginia, gave White the responsibility of organizing the effort. White spent late 1586 obtaining prospective settlers, in time securing 113 people. These included White's daughter Eleanor and son-in-law Ananias Dare (who was also listed as one of White's assistants). On January 7, 1587, a formal plan was established naming "John White of London Gentleman, to be the chief Governor there."

The new colony left for Virginia in May 1587; they arrived at Roanoke Island in late July. The second colony at Roanoke repaired the building left from Lane's colony and constructed new ones. White attempted to establish friendly relations with the Indians, but failed and tensions resulted. On a personal level, White became a grandfather following the birth of Virginia Dare, the first English child born in North America, on August 18. The colonists' situation soon became precarious. They arrived too late to plant crops, and the colonists could not depend on the Indians for help. With their supplies running low, the colonists asked White to return to England for supplies. White departed for England in late August and arrived in November.

White did not return to Roanoke until August 1590 because of various problems, including hostilities between England and Spain. In time, White arranged a relief expedition. However, when he and his party went ashore, they found no sign of life, but discovered that the colonists had constructed a fort. On an entrance post, the group found the word "CROATOAN" carved in it. The word was a predetermined signal that the colonists had gone to Croatoan, Manteo's friendly Indian tribe. Poor weather conditions and a shortage of food and water forced White to give up the search for the colonists. White returned to England, arriving in November 1590. The fate of the "Lost Colony" was never determined. The incident was a personal tragedy for White because he never again saw his daughter, son-in-law, or grand-daughter.

Details of White's life after Roanoke are virtually unknown. By February 1593 he resided in a house in County Cork, Ireland. Beyond this information nothing else survived. The date of his death has not been determined.

REFERENCES: Adams, "An Effort to Identify John White"; *ANB*, vol. 23; Cumming, "The Identity of John White"; *DNCB*, vol. 6; Durant, *Ralegh's Lost Colony*; Hulton, *America, 1585*; Kupperman, *Roanoke*; National Gallery of Art, *Watercolor Drawings of John White*; Neville, *John White*; Quinn, *The Roanoke Voyages*, 2 vols.; Quinn, *Set Fair for Roanoke*.

# HENRY WILKINSON
## 1680

*T*he Lords Proprietors commissioned Capt. Henry Wilkinson (b. ca. 1620) as governor of Albemarle in November 1680 with the hope that he would restore peace. Wilkinson made all the preparations to come to the colony, but he never left England. Born in York, England, around 1620, Wilkinson was a professional soldier who fought for the royalists during the English Civil War. When his military career ended, he tried to work in other occupations but was a failure. Despite his difficulties, Wilkinson refused to seek a pension or an appointment from the royal government. Around 1679 Wilkinson and his family left York for London.

After making the acquaintance of Wilkinson, the proprietors offered him the governorship of Albemarle. Out of a succession of problems created by Thomas Eastchurch and Thomas Miller, the proprietors placed importance on selecting the right man as governor. To the proprietors, Wilkinson seemed to be that man. He was a stranger with no connection to Albemarle's factions. The Lords Proprietors believed that Wilkinson would manage the colony's affairs with moderation and "doe equall justice to all partyes." They also thought he would make sure the king's customs duties were collected. Furthermore, Wilkinson offered traits of loyalty, experience, steadiness, and dependability to the proprietors.

The Lords Proprietors instructed Wilkinson to create his government with the Fundamental Constitutions as its basis. They authorized him to establish an impartial court to settle disputes related to Culpeper's Rebellion. Wilkinson could appoint an acting governor only with the approval of a majority of the council. They also wanted the boundary between Virginia and Carolina properly adjusted and an inquiry into the damages suffered by the king's officials, so they could receive compensation. The proprietors commissioned one of Wilkinson's sons as surveyor and proprietary deputy, and another son as register. Wilkinson received blank deputations to appoint new councilors in case the ones chosen by the proprietors do not "behave as they should, in healing all breaches that have been in the Colony."

Wilkinson made arrangements for his voyage to Albemarle, planning also to transport his family and servants. In August 1680 he petitioned the king for loan of a ship that was "supplied with Guns and ammunition at his

Majesties charge," but his request brought no reply. He secured the ship, *Abigail*, and a captain and ten crewmen in April 1681. The ship languished in harbor from April to August 1681 with Wilkinson paying to maintain it. His outstanding debt led to his arrest, and he was jailed in London. He remained there for nearly two months before being moved to the King's Bench Prison. While in prison, persons looking to incriminate one of the Lords Proprietors, Anthony Ashley Cooper, in a plot to seize King Charles II came to see Wilkinson. They hoped Wilkinson would provide incriminating evidence against Cooper. Even though he was bribed, Wilkinson stated that Cooper told him nothing about a plot to seize the king. Wilkinson remained in prison until November 1681, possibly longer. He never reached Albemarle, and the rest of his life remains a mystery.

REFERENCES: Andrews, "Captain Henry Wilkinson"; Andrews, *Narratives of the Insurrections*; Grant and Mitchell, *Acts of the Privy Council*, vol. 2; Parker et al., *Colonial Records*, vol. 2; Paschal dissertation, "Proprietary N.C."; Rankin, *Upheaval in Albemarle*; Sainsbury, Fortescue, and Headlam, *Calendar of State Papers, Colonial Series*; Saunders, *Colonial Records of N.C.*, vol. 1.

## BENJAMIN WILLIAMS
### *1799-1802; 1807-1808*

*B*enjamin Williams (1751-1814) served as governor in nonconsecutive terms. Born in Johnston County on January 1, 1751, he was the son of John Williams and the former Ferebee Pugh. Through his many years of politics, agriculture played an important role in his life as a private citizen. Williams's wife was the former Elizabeth Jones, whom he married in 1781. Their union produced only one child, a son named Benjamin.

With the approach of the American Revolution, Williams became active in public affairs and in the Patriot cause, representing Johnston County in the colonial assembly in 1775 and in the provincial congresses of 1774 and 1775. Commissioned a lieutenant soon after hostilities began, he rose to the rank of colonel following the Battle of Guilford Courthouse. Remaining active in state politics during the interim periods of his military service, he served in the House from 1779 to 1780 and in the senate from 1780 to 1782. Following the Revolution, Williams returned to the House in 1785 and to the senate every other year from 1784 to 1789. He served in the state constitutional convention of 1788, and was appointed to the original board of trustees of UNC in 1789. From 1794 to 1795 he was active in national politics as a member of the U.S. House of Representatives.

Returning to North Carolina, Williams resided in the fledgling city of Raleigh. It was there that he was living in November 1799, when elected to the governorship. Reelected in each of the next two years, he served the maximum three consecutive terms. In 1807 he was representing Moore County in the state senate when elected to his fourth and final term as governor. A candidate for governor no fewer than six times between 1800 and 1809, Williams enjoyed a broad base of support.

Although sometimes classified as an Anti-Federalist or Republican, Williams should be viewed instead as a marginal or restrained Federalist. Indeed, his initial election as governor in 1799 occurred during the brief resurgence of Federalism produced by the threat of war with France. Thereafter, his successive reelections resulted from the combined support of his fellow Federalists and that of Republicans. As chief executive, Williams provided encouragement to internal improvements and public education, but lacked the effective means of financing. Against the backdrop of national politics, it was his adherence to Federalist principles that eventually eroded his base of bipartisan support. After Congress imposed its embargo on foreign trade in 1807, Williams refused repeated calls to convene a special session of the legislature for the relief of debtors. When the legislature met in regular session the next year, its resentful members not only provided statutory relief to debtors, but also denied Williams reelection to an anticipated fifth term. Williams departed from the governorship in 1808, but not entirely from public life. During the following year he was again elected from Moore County to the state senate, thus concluding his varied career in politics.

Williams's last years were devoted almost entirely to his Moore County plantation, now open to the public as the House in the Horseshoe State Historic Site. He died there on July 20, 1814, and was buried some distance away in the family cemetery. In 1970 he was reinterred in the side yard of his residence.

REFERENCES: Broussard, "The North Carolina Federalists"; Coon, *Beginnings of Public Education*; *DNCB*, vol. 6; Gilpatrick, *Jeffersonian Democracy in N.C.*; Robinson, *Moore Co. History*; Sobel and Raimo, *Bio. Dir. of Governors*, vol. 3.

## WARREN WINSLOW
## 1854-1855

*W*arren Winslow (1810-1862) served as governor for less than one month, the shortest term of any of the state's chief executives. The son of John and Caroline Martha Winslow, he was born in Fayetteville on January 1, 1810. His ancestors, unlike those of many of his political contemporaries, had supported the Crown during the Revolution. His paternal grandfather, Edward Winslow, had been a chaplain in the British army. Nothing is known of his early life, but he may have attended the Fayetteville Academy where his father was one of the original trustees. He graduated from UNC in 1827 and studied law while in Chapel Hill, returning to Fayetteville to set up practice. In January 1834 he married Mary Ivie Toomer, who preceded him

in death by nineteen years. They had no children.

Winslow declared himself a Democrat and, caught up in that party's resurgence, was elected to the state senate in 1854. Intraparty maneuverings and compromises placed him in the position of Speaker. He had barely assumed that role when Gov. David S. Reid accepted election to a vacant seat in the U.S. Senate. Until 1868, the state constitution did not provide for a lieutenant governor; therefore, the Speaker of the senate was next in line for the office of chief executive. Reid turned over duties to Winslow who qualified as governor on December 6, 1854. Thomas Bragg, however, had been elected to the office in November and was to be inaugurated on January 1, 1855. Warren Winslow was governor of North Carolina for all of twenty-five days. Furthermore, he remains one of only two governors since 1776 who was not elected either by the General Assembly or popular vote.

Winslow was elected to represent District Three, which included Cumberland County, in the U.S. Congress in 1855. Though he took little active role in the proceedings, he quietly defended southern rights on the constitutional issues. He left the House of Representatives with the close of the 1861 session.

Winslow's next service was as an adviser and agent of Gov. John Ellis. On April 22, 1861, after the outbreak of hostilities but before North Carolina seceded from the Union, Winslow negotiated the surrender of the arsenal at Fayetteville to the state. He continued in charge of the facility during the spring of that year. In May the legislature created the Military and Naval Board to advise and aid an ailing Governor Ellis in the conduct of his office. Warren Winslow was named chairman of that board. Unfortunately, he delivered to Ellis the unwise and erroneous advice that the coast of North Carolina was adequately protected by the natural shoals and sand bars, and that the forts (Hatteras and Clark) would not need large garrisons. When the forts fell and the northeastern coast succumbed to Union blockade, many citizens blamed Winslow, damaging his influence and prestige.

He had been a delegate to the Convention of 1861 that voted for secession and that acted as the state's legal body for the first year of the war. A few months after the debacle at Hatteras, he resigned his seat and retired to Fayetteville. Winslow died less than a year later on August 16, 1862, and was buried in Cross Creek Cemetery.

REFERENCES: *BDC*; Crabtree and Patton, *"Journal of a Secesh Lady"*; Johnston and Mobley, *Vance Papers*, vol. 1; Oates, *Story of Fayetteville*; Tolbert, *Ellis Papers*, vols. 1 and 2.

# JONATHAN WORTH
## 1865-1868

*J*onathan Worth (1802-1869) found his Quaker upbringing and temperament tested by the trials of Reconstruction. The first of Dr. David and Eunice Gardner Worth's twelve children, Jonathan Worth was born on November 18, 1802, at Center in Randolph County. He received a basic education in local schools and at the Greensborough Male Academy. Worth learned law as a student of Archibald D. Murphey and received his license in December 1824. He moved to Asheboro to establish his practice. Jonathan Worth married Martitia Daniel, niece of Murphey, in 1824; they had eight children, six of whom survived their father.

Worth possessed an inhibited personality and found public speaking distasteful and laborious; consequently, his early law practice floundered.

He was more successful in business, investing in early textile mills as well as navigation and plank road companies. Believing that politics might help him overcome his professional handicaps, he entered the race for the state House in 1830 and was elected. There he voted against resolutions endorsing the administration of President Andrew Jackson yet spoke out strongly against the concept of nullification. Ostracized for standing on his principles, he returned to his law practice and prospered.

During the 1830s, Worth became a devoted member of the Whig Party, viewing Democratic doctrine as subversive to good government based on the federal Constitution. He spent three terms in the state senate between 1840 and 1861 denouncing the Democratic policies. Twice he ran for Congress but was defeated. Worth bitterly opposed secession and refused to be a delegate to the May 1861 convention that took North Carolina out of the Union. He detested war or any form of violence owing to his Quaker heritage but, faced with the inevitable, chose to support his state.

Jonathan Worth frequently disagreed with the Confederate administration but, despite his hatred of war, never became associated with peace movements. He supported the Conservative Party in 1862 and was elected state treasurer on December 3. At the close of the war he was asked by Gov. William W. Holden to continue in that office as part of the provisional government. He resigned on November 15, 1865, to run against Holden for governor in the general election. A combination of Worth's popularity and Holden's lack of it led to Worth's victory by nearly 6,000 votes.

The new governor faced major obstacles: quarreling factions within the state that needed to be reconciled; a president in Washington whose skepticism of North Carolina's sincerity had to be assuaged; and a hostile Congress demanding satisfaction from increasingly stringent rules and regulations. Worth enjoyed moderate success in the first two, but the last proved intractable. He had barely taken the oath of office for his second term when Congress passed the first of the Reconstruction Acts that imposed military rule upon the South. The governor developed a good relationship with Gen. Daniel E. Sickles, who had charge of the Second Military District. Sickles frequently asked for and followed Worth's advice; he was replaced by Gen. Edwin R. S. Canby in August 1867, and the situation changed. Worth found himself working simultaneously to restore North Carolina to the Union while trying to fend off military encroachments upon civil authority. With new elections ordered for 1868, Worth refused to run against Holden, now a Republican, who was certain to win. A military order directed Worth to turn over the governor's office to Holden on July 2. In failing health, he retired to his home, "Sharon," in Raleigh where he died fourteen months later on September 5, 1869. He was buried in Oakwood Cemetery.

REFERENCES: *ANB*, vol. 23; Boyd, *Holden Memoirs*; *Cyclopedia of Eminent and Representative Men*, vol. 2; Hamilton, *Worth Correspondence*, vols. 1 and 2; Zuber, *Jonathan Worth*. PRIMARY SOURCES: Worth Papers, NCSA; Worth Papers, SHC.

# Bibliography

## Published Works

Abrams, Douglas Carl. *Conservative Constraints: North Carolina and the New Deal.* Jackson: University Press of Mississippi, 1992.

Adams, Randolph G. "An Effort to Identify John White." *American Historical Review* 41 (October 1935): 87-91.

Albright, R. Mayne. "O. Max Gardner and the Shelby Dynasty." *The State* (April, July, August 1983).

Alderman, Edwin Anderson. "Charles Brantley Aycock—An Appreciation." *North Carolina Historical Review* (July 1924): 243-250.

Alexander, C. B. "The Training of Richard Caswell." *North Carolina Historical Review* 23 (January 1946): 13-31.

Andrews, Alexander B. "Richard Dobbs Spaight." *North Carolina Historical Review* 1 (April 1924): 95-120.

Andrews, Charles M. "Captain Henry Wilkinson." *Southern Atlantic Quarterly* 15 (July 1916): 216-222.

\_\_\_\_\_., ed. *Narratives of the Insurrections, 1675-1690.* New York: Charles Scribner's Sons, 1915.

Angley, Wilson, Jerry L. Cross, and Michael Hill. *Sherman's March through North Carolina: A Chronology.* Raleigh: North Carolina Division of Archives and History, 1995.

Arnett, Ethel Stephens. *Greensboro, North Carolina: The County Seat of Guilford.* Chapel Hill: University of North Carolina Press, 1955.

Ashe, Samuel A., et al., eds. *Biographical History of North Carolina from Colonial Times to the Present.* 8 vols. Greensboro, N.C.: Charles L. Van Noppen, 1905-1917.

Badger, Anthony J. *Prosperity Road: The New Deal, Tobacco, and North Carolina.* Chapel Hill: University of North Carolina Press, 1980.

Barone, Michael, and Grant Ujifusa, eds. *The Almanac of American Politics, 1994.* Washington, D.C.: National Journal, 1972-1993.

Barrett, John G. *The Civil War in North Carolina.* Chapel Hill: University of North Carolina Press, 1963.

Bell, John L., Jr. *Hard Times: Beginnings of the Great Depression in North Carolina, 1929-1933.* Raleigh: North Carolina Division of Archives and History, 1982.

*Biographical Directory of the United States Congress, 1774-1989.* Bicentennial Edition. Washington, D.C.: United States Government Printing Office, 1988.

Booth, Sally S. *Seeds of Anger: Revolts in America, 1607-1771*. New York: Random House, 1977.

Boyd, William K., ed. *Memoirs of W. W. Holden, 1818-1892*. Durham: The Seeman Printery, 1911.

Brawley, James S. *The Rowan Story, A Narrative History of Rowan County, N.C., 1753-1953*. Salisbury: Rowan Print Co., 1953.

Brown, Cecil K. *The State Highway System of North Carolina: Its Evolution and Present Status*. Chapel Hill: University of North Carolina Press, 1931.

Brown, Joseph Parsons. *The Commonwealth of Onslow, A History*. New Bern, N.C.: O. G. Dunn, 1960.

Broussard, James H. "The North Carolina Federalists, 1800-1816." *North Carolina Historical Review* 55 (winter 1978): 18-41.

[Burke County Historical Society]. *The Heritage of Burke County*. Morganton, N.C.: Burke County Historical Society, 1981.

Bushong, William. *North Carolina's Executive Mansion: The First Hundred Years*. Raleigh: Executive Mansion Fine Arts Committee and Executive Mansion Fund, 1991.

Butler, Lindley S. "The Early Settlement of Carolina: Virginia's Southern Frontier." *Virginia Magazine of History and Biography* 79 (January 1971): 20-28.

_____. "The Governors of Albemarle County, 1663-1689." *North Carolina Historical Review* 46 (summer 1969): 281-299.

_____., ed. *The Papers of David Settle Reid*, 2 vols. Raleigh: North Carolina Division of Archives and History, Department of Cultural Resources, 1993-1997.

Caldwell, Bettie D. *Founders and Builders of Greensboro, 1808-1908*. Greensboro: Stone and Co., 1925.

Carraway, Gertrude S. *Years of Light: History of St. John's Lodge, No. 3 A. F. & A. M. New Bern, North Carolina 1772-1944*. New Bern: Owen G. Dunn Co., 1944.

Cheney, John L., Jr., ed. *North Carolina Government, 1585-1979: A Narrative and Statistical History*. Raleigh: North Carolina Department of State, 1981.

Clark, Walter. "William Alexander Graham." *North Carolina Booklet*, XVI (July 1916): 3-16.

Clarke, Desmond. *Arthur Dobbs Esquire 1689-1765: Surveyor General of Ireland, Prospector and Governor of North Carolina*. Chapel Hill: University of North Carolina Press, 1957.

Clay, Russell. *The Long View: The Administration of Governor Robert W. Scott, 1969-1973. A Summary of Accomplishments during the Four Years.* N.p.: n.p., 1973.

Connor, R. D. W. "John Motley Morehead: Architect and Builder of Public Works." *North Carolina Booklet*, XII, No. 3 (January 1913): 173-193.

_____. *Makers of North Carolina History.* Raleigh: Thompson, 1911.

Connor, R. D. W., and Clarence Poe. *The Life and Speeches of Charles Brantley Aycock.* Garden City, N.Y.: Doubleday, Page & Co., 1912.

Connor, R. D. W., et al. *History of North Carolina.* 6 vols. Chicago: Lewis Publishing Co., 1919.

Coon, Charles L. *The Beginnings of Public Education in North Carolina: A Documentary History, 1790-1840.* Raleigh [N.C.]: Edwards & Broughton Printing Co., 1908.

Corbitt, David Leroy, ed. *Addresses, Letters and Papers of Clyde Roark Hoey: Governor of North Carolina, 1937-1941.* Raleigh: Council of State, 1944.

_____. *Addresses, Letters and Papers of John Christoph Blucher Ehringhaus: Governor of North Carolina, 1933-1937.* Raleigh: Council of State, 1950.

_____. *Public Addresses, Letters and Papers of Joseph Melville Broughton: Governor of North Carolina, 1941-1945.* Raleigh: Council of State, 1950.

_____. *Public Addresses, Letters and Papers of William Bradley Umstead: Governor of North Carolina, 1953-1954.* Raleigh: Council of State, 1957.

_____. *Public Addresses, Letters, and Papers of William Kerr Scott: Governor of North Carolina, 1949-1953.* Raleigh: Council of State, 1957.

_____. *Public Addresses and Papers of Robert Gregg Cherry: Governor of North Carolina, 1945-1949.* Winston-Salem: Winston Printing Company, 1951.

_____. *Public Papers and Letters of Angus Wilton McLean: Governor of North Carolina, 1925-1929.* Raleigh: Edwards & Broughton Printing Co., 1931.

Covington, Howard E., and Marion A. Ellis. *Terry Sanford: Politics, Progress, and Outrageous Ambitions.* Durham: Duke University Press, 1999.

Crabtree, Beth Gilbert, and James W. Patton, eds. *"Journal of a Secesh Lady": The Diary of Catherine Ann Devereux Edmonston, 1860-1866.* Raleigh: North Carolina Division of Archives and History, Department of Cultural Resources, 1979.

Crayon, Porte. "North Carolina Illustrated." *Harper's New Monthly Magazine*. 14 (March 1857): 449.

Crittenden, Christopher, et al., eds. *100 Years, 100 Men, 1871-1971*. Raleigh: Edwards & Broughton Printing Co., 1971.

Crow, Jeffrey J., and Robert F. Durden. *Maverick Republican in the Old North State: A Political Biography of Daniel L. Russell*. Baton Rouge: Louisiana State University Press, 1977.

Cumming, William P. "The Identity of John White Governor and John White the Artist." *North Carolina Historical Review*. 15 (July 1938): 197-203.

Curry, Louise Davis, ed. *Highland Scots in North Carolina: An Unpublished Manuscript by Angus Wilton McLean*. Dallas, Tex.: N.C. Scottish Heritage Society, 1993.

*Cyclopedia of Eminent and Representative Men of the Carolinas of the Nineteenth Century*. 2 vols. Madison, Wis.: Brant & Fuller, 1892.

Daniels, Josephus. "Charles Brantley Aycock–Historical Address." *North Carolina Historical Review* 1 (July 1924): 251-276.

Douglass, Elisha. "Thomas Burke: Disillusioned Democrat." *North Carolina Historical Review* 26 (April 1949): 150-186.

Dowd, Jerome. *Sketches of Prominent Living North Carolinians*. Raleigh, N.C.: Edwards & Broughton, printers, 1888.

Drescher, John. *Triumph of Good Will: How Terry Sanford Beat a Champion of Segregation and Reshaped the South*. Jackson: University Press of Mississippi, 2000.

Durant, David N. *Ralegh's Lost Colony*. New York: Atheneum, 1981.

Edgar, Walter B. and N. Louise Bailey, eds. *Biographical Directory of the South Carolina House of Representatives*. 3 vols. Columbia: University of South Carolina Press, 1974-1981.

Ekirch, A. Roger. *"Poor Carolina": Politics and Society in Colonial North Carolina 1729-1776*. Chapel Hill: University of North Carolina Press, 1981.

Fink, Arthur E. "Changing Philosophies and Practices in North Carolina Orphanages." *North Carolina Historical Review* 48 (October 1971): 333-358.

Foster, W. O. "The Career of Montfort Stokes in North Carolina." *North Carolina Historical Review* 16 (July 1939): 237-272.

Garraty, John A., and Mark C. Carnes, eds. *American National Biography*. 24 vols. New York: Oxford University Press, 1999.

Gill, Edwin. "The Dedication of the William B. Umstead Building." *We the People* (May 1962).

Gill, Edwin, comp., and David Leroy Corbitt, ed. *Public Papers and Letters of Oliver Max Gardner: Governor of North Carolina, 1929-1933.* Raleigh: Council of State, State of North Carolina, 1937.

Gilpatrick, Delbert H. *Jeffersonian Democracy in North Carolina, 1789-1816.* New York: Columbia University Press; London: P. S. King & Son, Ltd., 1931.

Graham, Frank Porter. "Cameron Morrison: An Address, by the Honorable Frank P. Graham." Raleigh, N.C.: n.p., 1955.

Grant, William L., James Munro, and Almeric Fitzroy, eds. *Acts of the Privy Council of England: Colonial Series,* 1613-1783. 6 vols. Hereford, England: Printed for H. M. Stationery Office by Anthony Brothers, 1908-1912.

Grimsley, Wayne. *James B. Hunt Jr.: A North Carolina Progressive.* Jefferson, N.C.: McFarland & Company, 2003.

Hale, Edward E. "Life of Sir Ralph Lane." *Archaelogia Americana: Transactions and Collections of the American Antiquarian Society.* Vol. 4. Boston: John Wilson and Son, 1860.

Hamilton, J. G. de Roulhac, ed. *The Correspondence of Jonathan Worth.* 2 vols. Raleigh: North Carolina Historical Commission, 1909.

Hamilton, J. G. de Roulhac, et al., eds. *The Papers of William Alexander Graham.* 8 vols. Raleigh: North Carolina Division of Archives and History, Department of Cultural Resources, 1957-1992.

Hamlin, C. H. *Ninety Bits of North Carolina Biography.* New Bern, N.C.: Owen G. Dunn Co., 1946.

Harris, William C. *William Woods Holden: Firebrand of North Carolina Politics.* Baton Rouge: Louisiana State University Press, 1987.

Hathaway, J. R. B., ed. "Births, Deaths and Marriages in Berkely, Later Perquimans Precinct, N.C." *North Carolina Historical and Genealogical Register* 3 (April 1903): 199-220.

_____. "The Harvey Family." *North Carolina Historical and Genealogical Register* 3 (July 1903): 478-480.

_____. "Henderson Walker to the Court." *North Carolina Historical and Genealogical Register* 3 (January 1903): 137-138.

_____. "Letter from John Lawson to Gov. Walker, relating to the Bay River Indians." *North Carolina Historical and Genealogical Register* 1 (October 1900): 598.

Haywood, Marshall DeLancey. *Builders of the Old North State, Selected Sketches.* Raleigh, N.C.: n.p., 1968.

Henderson, Archibald, and others. *North Carolina: The Old North State and the New.* 5 vols. Chicago: The Lewis Publishing Company, 1941.

Hindale, Mrs. John W. "Governor Thomas Pollock." *North Carolina Booklet* 5 (April 1906): 219-231.

Hodges, Luther H. *Businessman in the Statehouse: Six Years as Governor of North Carolina*. Chapel Hill: University of North Carolina Press, 1962.

Hoffmann, William S. "The Election of 1836 in North Carolina." *The North Carolina Historical Review* 32 (January 1955): 31-51.

_____. "John Branch and the Origins of the Whig Party in North Carolina." *North Carolina Historical Review* 35 (July 1958): 299-315.

Holt, Eugene. *Edwin Michael Holt and His Descendants, 1807-1948*. Richmond, Va.: E. Holt, 1949.

Hood, Henry G., Jr. *The Public Career of John Archdale (1642-1717)*. Greensboro: The North Carolina Friends Historical Society and the Quaker Collection of the Guilford College Library, 1976.

Hulton, Paul. *America, 1585: The Complete Drawings of John White*. Chapel Hill: University of North Carolina Press, 1984.

Hunter, Carey J. *Governor Kitchin: The Man and the Principles that Guide Him*. North Carolina: n.p., 1911.

Ivey, Alfred Guy. *Luther H. Hodges: Practical Idealist*. Minneapolis: Denison, 1968.

Johnson, Allen, and Dumas Malone, eds. *Dictionary of American Biography*. 20 vols. New York: Charles Scribner's Sons, 1928-1946.

Johnson, Guion G. *Ante-Bellum North Carolina: A Social History*. Chapel Hill: University of North Carolina Press, 1937.

Johnston, Frontis W. "Zebulon Baird Vance: A Personality Sketch." *North Carolina Historical Review* 30 (April 1953): 178-190.

Johnston, Frontis W., and Joe A. Mobley, eds. *The Papers of Zebulon Baird Vance*. 2 vols. to date. Raleigh: North Carolina Division of Archives and History, Department of Cultural Resources, 1963-.

Jones, H. G. *For History's Sake: The Preservation and Publication of North Carolina History, 1663-1903*. Chapel Hill: University of North Carolina Press, 1966.

Jones, May F., ed. *Memoirs and Speeches of Locke Craig, Governor of North Carolina, 1913-1917*. Asheville : Hackney & Moale, 1923.

_____. *Public Letters and Papers of Locke Craig, Governor of North Carolina, 1913-1917*. Raleigh: Edwards & Broughton Printing Co., 1916.

Jones, Rufus M. *The Quakers in the American Colonies*. Originally published in 1911; reprint, New York: Russell and Russell, 1962.

Konkle, Burton Alva. *John Motley Morehead and the Development of North Carolina, 1796-1866*. Spartanburg, S.C.: Reprint Co., 1971.

Kupperman, Karen O. *Roanoke: The Abandoned Colony*. Totowa, N.J.: Rowman & Allanheld, 1984.

Lawrence, Robert. *The State of Robeson*. Lumberton, N.C. [New York: Printed by J. J. Little and Ives Company], 1939.

Lawson, John. *A New Voyage to Carolina*. Edited by Hugh T. Lefler. Chapel Hill: University of North Carolina Press, 1967.

Lee, Enoch Lawrence. *The Lower Cape Fear in Colonial Days*. Chapel Hill: University of North Carolina Press, 1965.

Lee, Sidney, ed. *Dictionary of National Biography*. 63 vols. New York: MacMillian and Co., 1885-1900.

Lefler, Hugh, and Paul Wager, eds. *Orange County, 1752-1952*. Chapel Hill: University of North Carolina Press, 1953.

Lefler, Hugh T. "Anglican Church in North Carolina: The Proprietary Period." In *The Episcopal Church in North Carolina, 1701-1959*, ed. Lawrence F. London and Sarah M. Lemmon. Raleigh: Episcopal Diocese of North Carolina, 1987.

Lefler, Hugh T., and William S. Powell. *Colonial North Carolina: A History*. New York: Charles Scribner's Sons, 1973.

Lemmon, Sarah McCulloh. *Frustrated Patriots: North Carolina and the War of 1812*. Chapel Hill: University of North Carolina Press, 1973.

_____. *North Carolina's Role in World War II*. Raleigh: North Carolina Division of Archives and History, 1964.

Lounsbury, Carl. "The Development of Domestic Architecture in the Albemarle Region." *North Carolina Historical Review* 54 (January 1977): 17-48.

McKinney, Gordon B., Richard M. McMurray, and others, eds. *A Guide to the Microfilm Edition of the Papers of Zebulon Vance*. Frederick, Md.: University Publications of America, 1987.

McLean, Angus Wilton, et al. *Lumber River Scots and Their Descendants: the McLeans, the Torreys, the Purcells, the McIntyres, the Gilchrists*. Richmond: William Byrd Press, 1942.

Marley, Branson. "Minutes of the General Court of Albemarle, 1684." *North Carolina Historical Review* 19 (January 1942): 48-58.

Martin, Santford, comp., and R. B. House, ed. *Public Letters and Papers of Thomas Walter Bickett, Governor of North Carolina, 1917-1921*. Raleigh: Edwards & Broughton Printing Co., 1923.

Mitchell, Memory F., ed. *Addresses and Public Papers of James Baxter Hunt, Jr., Governor of North Carolina*, vol. I: *1977-1981*. Raleigh: North Carolina Division of Archives and History, Department of Cultural Resources, 1982.

_____. *Addresses and Public Papers of James Eubert Holshouser, Jr., Governor of North Carolina, 1973-1977*. Raleigh: North Carolina Division of Archives and History, Department of Cultural Resources, 1978.

_____. *Addresses and Public Papers of Robert Walter Scott, Governor of North Carolina, 1969-1973.* Raleigh: North Carolina Division of Archives and History, Department of Cultural Resources, 1974.

_____. *Messages, Addresses, and Public Papers of Daniel Killian Moore, Governor of North Carolina, 1965-1969.* Raleigh: State Department of Archives and History for the Council of State, 1971.

_____. *Messages, Addresses, and Public Papers of Terry Sanford, Governor of North Carolina, 1961-1965.* Raleigh: Council of State, 1966.

Monroe, Haskell. "Religious Toleration and Politics in Early North Carolina." *North Carolina Historical Review* 39 (July 1962): 267-283.

Montgomery, Lizzie Wilson. *Sketches of Old Warrenton, North Carolina, Traditions and Reminiscences of the Town and People Who Made It.* Raleigh: Edwards & Broughton, 1924.

Moore, Elizabeth. *Rice, Hasell, Hawks, and Carruthers Families of North Carolina.* Bladensburg, Md.: n.p., 1966.

Morrison, Joseph L. *Governor O. Max Gardner: A Power in North Carolina and New Deal Washington.* Chapel Hill: University of North Carolina Press, 1971.

Mullaney, Marie Marmo, ed. *Biographical Directory of the Governors of the United States, 1983-1988.* Westport, Conn.: Greenwood Press, 1989.

Murray, Elizabeth Reid. *Wake: Capital County of North Carolina.* Vol. 1. Raleigh: Capital County Publishing Co., 1983.

National Gallery of Art (U.S.) *The Watercolor Drawings of John White from the British Museum.* Washington: National Gallery of Art, 1965.

National Governors Association. *The Education of a New Governor.* N.p.: n.p., 1981.

Nelson, Paul David. *William Tryon and the Course of Empire: A Life in British Imperial Service.* Chapel Hill: University of North Carolina Press, 1990.

Neville, John D. *John White* (pamphlet). Raleigh: America's Four Hundredth Anniversary Committee, ca. 1985-1986.

*North Carolina Manual,* 1993-1994 (1993)

*North Carolina Manual,* 1997-1998 (1997)

Nugent, Nell M. *Cavaliers and Pioneers: Abstracts of Virginia Land Patents and Grants, 1623-1800.* Vol. 1. Richmond, Va.: Dietz Printing Co., 1934.

Oates, John A. *The Story of Fayetteville and the Upper Cape Fear.* Fayetteville: n.p., 1950.

Orr, Oliver H., Jr. *Charles Brantley Aycock.* Chapel Hill: University of North Carolina Press, 1961.

Osborn, Rachel and Ruth Selden-Sturgill. *The Architectural Heritage of Chatham County, North Carolina*. [Pittsboro]: Chatham County Historical Association, 1991.

Parker, Mattie Erma E. "Legal Aspects of Culpeper's Rebellion." *North Carolina Historical Review* 45 (April 1968): 111-127.

Parker, Mattie Erma Edwards, et al., eds. *The Colonial Records of North Carolina* [*Second Series*]. 10 vols. to date. Raleigh: Office of Archives and History, Department of Cultural Resources, 1963-.

Parramore, Thomas C. "The Tuscarora Ascendancy." *North Carolina Historical Review* 59 (autumn 1982): 307-326.

Patton, James W., ed. *Messages, Addresses, and Public Papers of Luther Hartwell Hodges, Governor of North Carolina, 1954-1961*. 3 vols. Raleigh: Council of State, 1960-1963.

Peele, W. J., comp. *Lives of Distinguished North Carolinians*. Raleigh: The N.C. Publishing Society, 1898.

Phifer, Edward William, Jr. *Burke: The History of a North Carolina County, 1777-1920, with a Glimpse Beyond*. Morganton: Edward William Phifer Jr., 1977.

Poff, Jan-Michael, ed. *Addresses and Public Papers of James Baxter Hunt, Jr., Governor of North Carolina*. Vol. 3, *1993-1997*. Raleigh: Division of Archives and History, Department of Cultural Resources, 2000.

_____. *Addresses and Public Papers of James Grubbs Martin, Governor of North Carolina*. 2 vols. Raleigh: Division of Archives and History, Department of Cultural Resources, 1992-1996.

Poff, Jan-Michael, and Jeffrey J. Crow, eds. *Addresses and Public Papers of James Baxter Hunt, Jr., Governor of North Carolina*. Vol. 2, *1981-1985*. Raleigh: North Carolina Division of Archives and History, Department of Cultural Resources, 1987.

Powell, William S., ed. *The Correspondence of William Tryon and Other Selected Papers*. Vol. 1, *1758-1767* and Vol. 2, *1768-1818*. Raleigh: North Carolina Division of Archives and History, Department of Cultural Resources, 1980-1981.

_____, ed. *Dictionary of North Carolina Biography*. 6 vols. Chapel Hill: University of North Carolina Press, 1979-1996.

_____. *North Carolina Lives: The Tar Heel Who's Who*. Hopkinsville, Ky: Historical Record Association, 1962.

_____. *The Proprietors of Carolina*. Raleigh: The Carolina Tercentenary Commission, 1963; reprint, Raleigh: North Carolina State Department of Archives and History, 1968.

_____. *Ye Countie of Albemarle in Carolina: A Collection of Documents, 1664-1675*. Raleigh: North Carolina State Department of Archives and History, 1958.

Powell, William S., James K. Huhta, and Thomas J. Farnham, eds. *The Regulators in North Carolina: A Documentary History 1759-1776*. Raleigh: State Department of Archives and History, 1971.

Price, William S. "'Men of Good Estates': Wealth among North Carolina's Royal Councillors." *North Carolina Historical Review* 49 (January 1972): 72-82.

_____. "A Strange Incident in George Burrington's Royal Governorship." *North Carolina Historical Review* 51 (April 1974): 149-158.

*Proceedings of the . . . Annual Session[s] of the North Carolina Bar Association*. N.p.: North Carolina Bar Association, 1912-.

*Prominent People of North Carolina: Brief Biographies of Leading People for Ready Reference Purposes*. Asheville: Evening News Publishing Co., 1906.

Puryear, Elmer L. *Democratic Party Dissension in North Carolina, 1928-1936*. Chapel Hill: University of North Carolina Press, 1962.

Quinn, David B., ed. *The Roanoke Voyages, 1584-1590: Documents to Illustrate the English Voyages to North America under the Patent Granted to Walter Raleigh in 1584*. 2 vols. New York: Dover Publications, 1991.

_____. *Set Fair for Roanoke: Voyages and Colonies, 1584-1606*. Chapel Hill: University of North Carolina Press, 1985.

Quinn, David B. and Alison M. Quinn, eds. *The First Colonists: Documents on the Planting of the First English Settlements in North America, 1584-1590*. Raleigh: North Carolina Department of Cultural Resources, 1982.

Ragan, Sam. *The New Day*. Zebulon, N.C.: Record Publishing Co., 1964.

Raimo, John W. *Biographical Directory of American Colonial and Revolutionary Governors, 1607-1789*. Westport, Conn.: Greenwood Press, 1980.

_____, ed. *Biographical Directory of the Governors of the United States, 1978-1983*. (Westport, Conn.: Greenwood Press, 1985.

Rankin, Hugh F. *Upheaval in Albemarle: The Story of Culpeper's Rebellion, 1675-1689*. Raleigh: The Carolina Charter Tercentenary Commission, 1962.

Raper, Horace W., ed. *The Papers of William Woods Holden*. Vol. 1, *1841-1868*. Raleigh: Division of Archives and History, Department of Cultural Resources, 2000.

_____. *William W. Holden, North Carolina's Political Enigma*. Chapel Hill: University of North Carolina Press, 1985.

Richardson, William H., comp., and D. L. Corbitt, ed. *Public Papers and Letters of Cameron Morrison: Governor of North Carolina, 1921-1925*. Raleigh: Council of State, 1927.

Riddell, William R. "Half-Told Story of Real White Slavery in the Seventeenth Century." *North Carolina Historical Review* 9 (July 1932): 299-303.

Roberts, Nancy, and Bruce Roberts. *The Governor*. Charlotte: McNally & Loftin, 1972.

Robinson, Blackwell P. *The Five Royal Governors of North Carolina 1729-1775*. Raleigh: Carolina Charter Tercentenary Commission, 1968.

_____. *A History of Moore County, North Carolina, 1747-1847*. Southern Pines: Moore County Historical Association, 1956.

_____. *William R. Davie*. Chapel Hill: University of North Carolina Press, 1957.

Rogozinski, Jan. *Pirates! Brigands, Buccaneers, and Privateers in Fact, Fiction, and Legend*. New York: Da Capo Press, 1996.

Sainsbury, W. Noel, J. W. Fortescue, and Cecil Headlam, eds. *Calendar of State Papers, Colonial Series, (America and West Indies), 1574-1739, Preserved in the Public Record Office*. 35 volumes. London: Her Majesty's Stationery Office and Public Record Office, 1860-1936.

Salley, Alexander S., Jr., ed. *Commissions and Instructions from the Lords Proprietors of Carolina to Public Officials of South Carolina, 1685-1715*. Columbia: Historical Commission of South Carolina, 1916.

_____, ed. *Narratives of Early Carolina, 1650-1708*. New York: Charles Scribner's Sons, 1911.

Saunders, William L., ed. *The Colonial Records of North Carolina*. 10 vols. Raleigh: State of North Carolina, 1886-1890.

Scott, William Kerr. "A Report to the People: The Administration of Governor W. Kerr Scott, 1949-53." N.p.: n.p., 1953.

Sirmans, M. Eugene. *Colonial North Carolina: A Political History, 1663-1763*. Chapel Hill: University of North Carolina Press, 1966.

Skaggs, Marvin L. "The First Boundary Survey between the Carolinas." *North Carolina Historical Review* 12 (July 1935): 213-232.

Snider, William D. *Helms and Hunt: The North Carolina Senate Race, 1984*. Chapel Hill: University of North Carolina Press, 1985.

Sobel, Robert and John Raimo, eds. *Biographical Directory of the Governors of the United States, 1789-1978*, 4 vols. Westport, Conn.: Meckler Books, 1978.

Spence, James R. *The Making of a Governor: The Moore-Preyer-Lake Primaries of 1964*. Winston-Salem: J. F. Blair, 1968.

Sprunt, James. *Chronicles of the Cape Fear River*. Spartanburg, S.C.: Reprint Co., 1973.

Steelman, Lala Carr. "Role of Elias Carr in the North Carolina Farmer's Alliance." *North Carolina Historical Review* 57 (April 1980): 134-158.

Stumpf, Vernon. *Josiah Martin: The Last Royal Governor of North Carolina*. Durham, N.C.: Carolina Academic Press for the Kellenberger Historical Foundation, 1986.

Swindell, M. Rebecca, and Norman H. Turner. *Edward Hyde: Governor of North Carolina, 1710-1712*. Fairfield, N.C.: Hyde History, 1977.

Tanzer, Lester, ed. *The Kennedy Circle*. Washington, D.C.: Luce, 1961.

Taylor, H. Braughn. "The Foreign Attachment Law and the Coming of the Revolution in North Carolina." *North Carolina Historical Review* 52 (January 1975): 20-36.

Todd, Vincent H., ed. *Christoph Von Graffenried's Account of the Founding of New Bern*. Raleigh: North Carolina Historical Commission, 1920.

Tolbert, Noble J., ed. *The Papers of John Willis Ellis*, 2 vols. Raleigh: North Carolina Division of Archives and History, 1964.

Turner, Herbert S., comp. *The Scott Family of Hawfields*. [Haw River]: n.p., 1971.

Turner, J. Kelly, and John L. Bridgers, Jr. *History of Edgecombe County, North Carolina*. Raleigh: Edwards & Broughton, 1920.

Wallace, Carolyn A. "David Lowry Swain: The First Whig Governor of North Carolina." *James Sprunt Studies in History and Political Science* (1957): 62-81.

Watson, Alan D. *Richard Dobbs Spaight*. New Bern: Griffin & Tilghman, 1987.

Watterson, John S. "The Ordeal of Governor Burke." *North Carolina Historical Review* 48 (July 1971): 95-117.

Weathers, Lee B. *The Living Past of Cleveland County: A History*. Shelby: Star Publishing Co., 1956.

Weeks, Stephen B. *Southern Quakers and Slavery: A Study in Institutional History*. Baltimore: The Johns Hopkins Press, 1896.

Whitener, Daniel Jay. *Prohibition in North Carolina, 1715-1946*. Chapel Hill: University of North Carolina Press, 1946.

*Who's Who in American Politics*. 29 vols. New York: Bowker, 1967-.

Wilcomb, Washburn E. "The Humble Petition of Sarah Drummond." *The William and Mary Quarterly* 13, 3d series (July 1956): 354-375.

Wright, Louis B. and Marion Tinling, eds. *The Secret Diary of William Byrd of Westover, 1709-1712*. Richmond, Va.: Dietz Press, 1941.

Wright, Stuart T. *Historical Sketch of Person County*. Danville: The Womack Press, 1974.

Yearns, Wilfred Buck. *The Papers of Thomas Jordan Jarvis.* Volume 1, *1869-1882.* Raleigh: State Department of Archives and History, 1969.

Zuber, Richard L. *Jonathan Worth: A Biography of a Southern Unionist.* Chapel Hill: University of North Carolina Press, 1965.

## Unpublished Works

Chapman, Margaret L. "The Administration of Governor Robert B. Glenn." Master's thesis, University of North Carolina at Chapel Hill, 1956.

Coon, John W. "Kerr Scott: The 'Go Forward' Governor: His Origins, His Program, and the North Carolina General Assembly." Master's thesis, University of North Carolina at Chapel Hill, 1968.

Hill, Michael, and Mark Wilde-Ramsing. "Historical Research Report and Underwater Reconnaissance of Salmon Creek in the Vicinity of the Batts-Duckenfield-Capehart Site, Bertie County." (Unpublished research report, North Carolina Division of Archives and History, 1987).

Horton, Sandra Sue. "The Political Career of Thomas Walter Bickett." Master's thesis, University of North Carolina at Chapel Hill, 1965.

Iobst, Richard W. "Personal Life of David Stone." (Unpublished research report, Department of Archives and History, 1967).

Magruder, Nathaniel F. "The Administration of Governor Cameron Morrison of North Carolina, 1921-1925." Ph.D. diss., University of North Carolina at Chapel Hill, 1968.

Paschal, Herbert R., Jr. "Proprietary North Carolina: A Study in Colonial Government." Ph.D. diss., University of North Carolina at Chapel Hill, 1961.

Smith, William S., Jr. "Culpeper's Rebellion: New Data and Old Problems." Master's thesis, North Carolina State University, 1990.

Underwood, Mary Evelyn. "Angus Wilton McLean: Governor of North Carolina, 1925-1929." Ph.D. diss., University of North Carolina at Chapel Hill, 1962.

## Newspapers

Each newspaper is listed with the appropriate date

*Asheville Citizen,* September 8-9, 1986.

*Bertie Ledger-Advance,* July 10, 1997.

*Charlotte Observer,* May 13, 1954; October 29, 1972; October 29, 2000.

*Durham Morning Herald,* November 8-9, 1954.

*Greensboro News and Record,* October 15, 2000; December 31, 2000-January 2, 2001.

*News and Observer* (Raleigh), May 1, 1920; December 29, 1921;
    June 10, November 10, 1924; June 22, 1935; April 22, 1936;
    February 1947; March 7, August 1, 1949; November 8, 1954;
    June 26, 1957; April 17-18, 1958; January 6, 1961; October 7, 1974;
    September 8-9, 1986; April 18, 1998; April 14, 2001.
*Winston-Salem Journal,* December 31, 2000.

## Archival Records and Private Manuscripts

Aycock, Charles Brantley. Collection. North Carolina State Archives,
    Office of Archives and History, Raleigh.

Bickett, Mrs. Thomas W. Papers. North Carolina State Archives, Office of
    Archives and History, Raleigh.

Bragg, Thomas. Papers. North Carolina State Archives, Office of Archives
    and History, Raleigh.

_____. Southern Historical Collection, Manuscripts Department, Wilson
    Library, University of North Carolina at Chapel Hill.

Branch Family Papers. Southern Historical Collection, Manuscripts
    Department, Wilson Library, University of North Carolina at Chapel
    Hill.

Branch Family Papers, 1778-1889. Rare Book and Manuscript
    Department, Perkins Library, Duke University, Durham.

Branch, John. Papers. North Carolina State Archives, Office of Archives
    and History, Raleigh.

Broughton, J. Melville. Papers. North Carolina State Archives, Office of
    Archives and History, Raleigh.

Burke, Thomas. Papers. North Carolina State Archives, Office of Archives
    and History, Raleigh.

_____. Southern Historical Collection, Manuscripts Department, Wilson
    Library, University of North Carolina at Chapel Hill.

Burton, Hutchins G. Papers. Southern Historical Collection, Manuscripts
    Department, Wilson Library, University of North Carolina at Chapel
    Hill.

Caldwell, Tod Robinson. Papers. Southern Historical Collection,
    Manuscripts Department, Wilson Library, University of North Carolina
    at Chapel Hill.

Carr, Elias. Papers. Special Collections Department, Joyner Library, East
    Carolina University, Greenville.

Caswell, Richard. Papers. North Carolina State Archives, Office of
    Archives and History, Raleigh.

_____. Southern Historical Collection, Manuscripts Department, Wilson Library, University of North Carolina at Chapel Hill.

Cherry, Robert Gregg. Papers. North Carolina State Archives, Office of Archives and History, Raleigh.

_____. Papers, 1914-1946. Rare Book and Manuscript Department, Perkins Library, Duke University, Durham.

Colonial Governors' Papers. North Carolina State Archives, Office of Archives and History, Raleigh.

Craig, Locke. Papers, 1865-1924. Rare Book and Manuscript Department, Perkins Library, Duke University, Durham.

Davie, William Richardson. Papers. North Carolina State Archives, Office of Archives and History, Raleigh.

_____. Southern Historical Collection, Manuscripts Department, Wilson Library, University of North Carolina at Chapel Hill.

Dudley, Edward B. Papers. North Carolina State Archives, Office of Archives and History, Raleigh.

Ehringhaus, John Christoph Blucher. Papers. North Carolina State Archives, Office of Archives and History, Raleigh.

Ellis, John W. Collection. Southern Historical Collection, University of North Carolina at Chapel Hill, Chapel Hill.

Fowle, Daniel Gould. Papers. North Carolina State Archives, Office of Archives and History, Raleigh.

Franklin, Jesse. Indian Treaty Papers. Southern Historical Collection, Manuscripts Department, Wilson Library, University of North Carolina at Chapel Hill.

Gardner, Oliver Max. Papers. Southern Historical Collection, Manuscripts Department, Wilson Library, University of North Carolina at Chapel Hill.

Governors' Letterbooks. North Carolina State Archives, Office of Archives and History, Raleigh.

Governors' Office Records. North Carolina State Archives, Office of Archives and History, Raleigh.

Governors' Papers. North Carolina State Archives, Office of Archives and History, Raleigh.

Graham, William A. Papers. North Carolina State Archives, Office of Archives and History, Raleigh.

_____. Southern Historical Collection, Manuscripts Department, Wilson Library, University of North Carolina at Chapel Hill.

Hawkins Family Papers. Southern Historical Collection, Manuscripts Department, Wilson Library, University of North Carolina at Chapel Hill.

Hayes Collection. North Carolina State Archives, Office of Archives and History, Raleigh.

_____. Southern Historical Collection, Manuscripts Department, Wilson Library, University of North Carolina at Chapel Hill.

Hodges, Luther Hartwell. Papers. Southern Historical Collection, Manuscripts Department, Wilson Library, University of North Carolina at Chapel Hill.

Hoey, Clyde Roark. Papers, 1944-1954. Rare Book and Manuscript Department, Perkins Library, Duke University, Durham.

Holden, William Woods. Papers. North Carolina State Archives, Office of Archives and History, Raleigh.

_____. Papers, 1841-1929. Rare Book and Manuscript Department, Perkins Library, Duke University, Durham.

Holt, E. M. Papers. Southern Historical Collection, Manuscripts Department, Wilson Library, University of North Carolina at Chapel Hill.

Iredell Family Papers. North Carolina State Archives, Office of Archives and History, Raleigh.

Iredell, Jr., James. Books. Southern Historical Collection, Manuscripts Department, Wilson Library, University of North Carolina at Chapel Hill.

Iredell, Sr., James, and James Iredell Jr. Papers, 1724-1890. Rare Book and Manuscript Department, Perkins Library, Duke University, Durham.

Jarvis, Thomas Jordan. Papers. North Carolina State Archives, Office of Archives and History, Raleigh.

_____. Papers, 1879-1891. Rare Book and Manuscript Department, Perkins Library, Duke University, Durham.

Johnson, Charles E. Collection. North Carolina State Archives, Office of Archives and History, Raleigh.

Kitchin, William W. Papers. Southern Historical Collection, Manuscripts Department, Wilson Library, University of North Carolina at Chapel Hill.

McLean, Angus Wilton. Papers. Southern Historical Collection, Manuscripts Department, Wilson Library, University of North Carolina at Chapel Hill.

Martin, James Grubbs. Papers. Southern Historical Collection, Manuscripts Department, Wilson Library, University of North Carolina at Chapel Hill.

Moore, Daniel K. Collection. North Carolina State Archives, Office of Archives and History, Raleigh.

Moore, Elizabeth. Papers. North Carolina State Archives, Office of Archives and History, Raleigh.

New Hanover County. Deeds. North Carolina State Archives, Office of Archives and History, Raleigh.

_____. Original Wills. North Carolina State Archives., Office of Archives and History, Raleigh.

Owen, John. Papers. North Carolina State Archives, Office of Archives and History, Raleigh.

Pollock, Thomas. Papers. North Carolina State Archives, Office of Archives and History, Raleigh.

Reid Family Papers. Eden, North Carolina.

Reid, David S. Papers. North Carolina State Archives, Office of Archives and History, Raleigh.

_____. Papers, 1837-1881. Rare Book and Manuscript Department, Perkins Library, Duke University, Durham.

Russell, Daniel L. Papers. North Carolina State Archives, Office of Archives and History, Raleigh.

_____. Southern Historical Collection, Manuscripts Department, Wilson Library, University of North Carolina at Chapel Hill.

Sanford, Terry. Papers. Rare Book and Manuscript Department, Perkins Library, Duke University, Durham.

_____. Southern Historical Collection, Manuscripts Department, Wilson Library, University of North Carolina at Chapel Hill.

Scales, Alfred Moore. Papers. North Carolina State Archives, Office of Archives and History, Raleigh.

_____. Special Collections Department, Joyner Library, East Carolina University, Greenville.

Scott, Robert W., II. Papers. North Carolina State Archives, Office of Archives and History, Raleigh.

Scott, William Kerr. Papers. North Carolina State Archives, Office of Archives and History, Raleigh.

Secretary of State. Council Minutes, Wills, and Inventories, 1677-1701. "A True Inventory of Estate of Thomas Jervis [_sic_] Esqr Late Deceased August 6, 1694." North Carolina State Archives. Office of Archives and History. Raleigh.

_____. Land Grants. North Carolina State Archives, Office of Archives and History, Raleigh.

_____. Records. North Carolina State Archives, Office of Archives and History, Raleigh.

_____. Wills, estates, and inventories. North Carolina State Archives, Office of Archives and History, Raleigh.

Smith, Benjamin. Papers. North Carolina State Archives, Office of Archives and History, Raleigh.

_____. Southern Historical Collection, Manuscripts Department, Wilson Library, University of North Carolina at Chapel Hill.

Stokes, Montfort. Papers. North Carolina State Archives, Office of Archives and History, Raleigh.

Stone, David. Papers. North Carolina State Archives, Office of Archives and History, Raleigh.

Swain, David L. Papers. North Carolina State Archives, Office of Archives and History, Raleigh.

Swain, David Lowry. Papers. Southern Historical Collection, Manuscripts Department, Wilson Library, University of North Carolina at Chapel Hill.

Van Noppen, Charles Leonard. Papers, 1881-1935. Rare Book and Manuscript Department, Perkins Library, Duke University, Durham.

Vance, Zebulon Baird. Papers. North Carolina State Archives, Office of Archives and History, Raleigh.

_____. Southern Historical Collection, Manuscripts Department, Wilson Library, University of North Carolina at Chapel Hill.

_____. Papers, 1857-1893. Rare Book and Manuscript Department, Perkins Library, Duke University, Durham.

Vance, Zebulon Baird-Harriette N. Espy Vance. Letters, 1851-1878. North Carolina State Archives, Office of Archives and History, Raleigh.

Williams, John Buxton. Papers. Special Collections Department, Joyner Library, East Carolina University, Greenville.

Worth, Jonathan. Papers. North Carolina State Archives, Office of Archives and History, Raleigh.

_____. Southern Historical Collection, Manuscripts Department, Wilson Library, University of North Carolina at Chapel Hill.

## Web Sites

www.governor.state.nc.us

# Index

## A

*Abigail* (ship), 153
Acting governor, 2, 22, 58, 63, 119
Ad valorem taxation, 47, 140
Adams, President John, 34
Adams, President John Quincy, 105
Adams, Spencer B., 5
Address, speech: delivered by Charles B.
  Aycock, 5, 6, Charles Manly, 97,
  J. C. B. Ehringhaus, 46, J. Melville
  Broughton, 13, John Owen, 113,
  Thomas Bickett, 7, W. Kerr Scott,
  129. *See also* Inaugural address
Adjutant general, 49, 130
Administration, Department of. *See*
  Department of Administration
Admiralty court, 149, 150
Adopt-a-Highway program, 102
Advancement School, 123
Advisory Budget Bureau, 95
African Americans. *See* Blacks
Agribusiness Council, 127
Agricultural Adjustment
  Administration, 45
Agriculture: commissioner of, 121,
  126, 128; decline in importance of,
  39; interests of, 21; new techniques
  for, 88; promoted by Benjamin
  Williams, 153, David Stone, 139,
  Gabriel Holmes, 73, James Iredell
  Jr., 82, Terry Sanford, 123, Zebu-
  lon B. Vance, 148; W. Kerr Scott
  completed degree in, 128. *See also*
  Department of Agriculture
Agriculture Committee, 129
Agriculture, State Commission of. *See*
  State Commission of Agriculture
Alamance County, 76, 125, 128
Alamance Creek, 76
Alamance, Battle of. *See* Battle of
  Alamance
"Alamance Plaid," 76
Albemarle: banishment from, 54, 132;
  boundary problem between Va. and,
  37; functioned briefly with two chief
  executives, 42; governors of,
  included Henderson Walker, 149,
  Henry Wilkinson, 152, Seth Sothel,

131, Thomas Eastchurch, 41,
Thomas Miller, 103; Lords
Proprietors sought to restore
legitimate government of, 60; as
part of the expanded colony, 93;
problems in, 60, 83, 86; residents
of, included John Jenkins, 85,
Thomas Jarvis, 83; return to, 61,
131; Samuel Stephens owned land
in, 136
Albemarle Council, 22, 54
Albemarle County: acting governor of,
  2; anti-proprietary leaders sent
  armed force to, 42; divided
  politically, 22; early settler of, 60;
  governors of, included Samuel
  Stephens, 135, William Drummond,
  36, 136; surveyor general of, 41
Albemarle Sound, 83, 150
Albright, R. Mayne, 128
Alcoholic Beverage Control, State
  Board of. *See* State Board of
  Alcoholic Beverage Control
Alexander, Margaret Polk, 1
Alexander, Moses, 1
Alexander, Nathaniel, 1-2
Alexander, Sarah Taylor, 1
Algiers, 61, 131
Alien and Sedition Acts, 134
*Almanac of American Politics* (book),
  79
Alum Springs, Va., 109
Alumni Association (UNC), 97
Amazon, 59
Ambassador to Great Britain, 53
Amelia County, Va., 111
American Party. *See* Know-Nothing
  Party
American Revolution, 1
"American System," 59
Anderson, Mary. *See* Turner, Mary
  Anderson
Anglican(s): appointments of, to
  government positions, 32-33;
  Edward Hyde unable to restrain, 80;
  experienced tension with non-
  Anglicans, 32; governors as,